White Men's Magic

White Men's Magic

Scripturalization as Slavery

VINCENT L. WIMBUSH

OXFORD
UNIVERSITY PRESS

Oxford University Press is a department of the University of Oxford.
It furthers the University's objective of excellence in research, scholarship,
and education by publishing worldwide.

Oxford New York
Auckland Cape Town Dar es Salaam Hong Kong Karachi
Kuala Lumpur Madrid Melbourne Mexico City Nairobi
New Delhi Shanghai Taipei Toronto

With offices in
Argentina Austria Brazil Chile Czech Republic France Greece
Guatemala Hungary Italy Japan Poland Portugal Singapore
South Korea Switzerland Thailand Turkey Ukraine Vietnam

Oxford is a registered trade mark of Oxford University Press
in the UK and certain other countries.

Published in the United States of America by
Oxford University Press
198 Madison Avenue, New York, NY 10016

First issued as an Oxford University Press paperback, 2014.

Library of Congress Cataloging-in-Publication Data
Wimbush, Vincent L.
White men's magic: scripturalization as slavery / Vincent L. Wimbush.
p. cm.
Includes bibliographic references (p.) and index.
ISBN 978-0-19-987357-9 (hardcover); 978-0-19-934439-0 (paperback)
1. Equiano, Olaudah, b. 1745. Interesting narrative of the life of Olaudah Equiano.
2. Race relations—United States. 3. Religion and culture—United States.
I. Title
E184.A1W516 2012
305.800973—dc23
2012000429

For Lauren
My
Only One
Who Like Her Ancestors
Has Learned to Read
Hearts

Contents

Acknowledgments

THANKS ARE DUE to many persons and institutions that supported me and this project along the way:

the Ford Foundation and the Henry W. Luce Foundation, for support of a research leave and of operations and programs of the Institute for Signifying Scriptures; foundation program officers Lynn Szwaja of the Henry W Luce Foundation; and Sheila Devaney and Constance Buchanan of the Ford Foundation, for their advice and support (especially Constance Buchanan, for her belief in and critical support of my work from the beginning, which proved critical to my being able to take transgressive steps in program and research orientation);

all of the Research Assistants of Institute for Signifying Scriptures over the years, especially current assistants Lalruatkima, Quynh Nguyen, Wendell Miller, Melissa Reid, and David Olali, for their able support in research, technical, and communications work; and all things in connection with this book project;

my daughter Lauren, for her preliminary work on the index;

students in the new Critical Comparative Scriptures program—and its previous iterations and figurations at Union Seminary, Columbia University, and Claremont Graduate University—for their challenge and inspiration;

educational institutions and scholarly organizations, for their invitations that allowed me to hold forth and get feedback about my work, and Quynh Nguyen and Lalruatkima for completion of work—Syracuse University (Iconic Book Symposium); Society for the Anthropology of Religion, Santa Fe, NM; California African American Museum; California State University, Dominguez

Hills (Liberal Arts Program); Pittsburgh Theological Seminary; Maryland Institute College of Art; University of California, Santa Barbara (Religious Studies); University of Oregon; Chapman College; Iliff School of Theology; Morehouse College (King Chapel), DePauw University; Mary Washington College; University of Washington (Simpson Center of the Humanities); University of Frankfurt am-Main (Dieter Georgi, deceased); Phillips Theological Seminary (Ministers' Conference); International Meetings, Society of Biblical Literature (Helsinki; Cape Town); Regional Meeting, Southeast Commission for the Study of Religion; and Rhodes College;

staff persons at the Honnold Library of the Claremont Colleges and at the Pasadena Public Library (Central), for their technical support;

reviewers for Oxford University Press, who gave the manuscript serious attention and provided constructive suggestions (much of which I accepted);

Cynthia Read and Sasha Grossman and the editorial staff at Oxford University Press for their professionalism and responsiveness in helping to make this project what I hoped for; and

colleagues and friends who over a period of several years and in recent times have sometimes knowingly, other times unknowingly, listened to me, encouraged and challenged me, and provided feedback to ideas and arguments that have helped shape the book—Leif Vaage, Barbara Holdrege, Grey Gundaker, Elisabeth Schuessler Fiorenza, Charles H. Long, Burton Mack, Kathleen Wicker, Lako Tongun, Wole Soyinka, Constance Buchanan, Mark Noll, Mustapha Marrouchi, Richard Rodriguez, Michelle Brown (British Library), Gauri Viswanathan, Sterling Stuckey, Leslie King-Hammond, Ronne Hartfield, G. Elmer Griffin, Thomas Scott, Norman Johnson, Sr., Santiago Slabodsky, James Watts; and my best friend, most honest and constructive critic, and ongoing conversation partner, who read and corrected and greatly improved early drafts of this project Rosamond C. Rodman.

White Men's Magic

Prologue

"... There's a whole heap of them kinda by-words... They all got a hidden meanin', jus' like de Bible. Everybody can't understand what they mean. Most people is thin-brained. They's born wid they feet under de moon. Some folks is born wid they feet on de sun and they kin seek out de inside meanin' of words."

—ZORA NEALE HURSTON, *Mules and Men*

You think your pain, and your heartbreak, are unprecedented in the history of the world. But then you read. It was books that taught me, the things that tormented me the most were the very things that connected me with all the people who were alive—who had ever been alive. I went into the 130th St. Library at least three or four times a week, and I read everything there, and every single book in that library. In some blind and instinctive way, I knew that what was happening in those books was also happening all around me, and I was trying to make a connection between the books and the life I saw, and the life I lived.... I knew I was Black, of course, and I also knew I was smart. I didn't know how I would use my mind or even if I could, but that was the only thing that I had to use. And I was going to get whatever I wanted that way, and I was going to get my revenge that way. So I watched school the way I watched the streets, because part of the answer was there.

—JAMES BALDWIN, *The Price of the Ticket*

MY INTERESTS AND involvement in the phenomenon touched on in the quotations above by Zora Neale Hurston and James Baldwin I now realize are longstanding, reaching back to my years as a somewhat odd, bookish, sometimes tortured, curious-minded boy. During those years I clearly did not understand what I was experiencing or what was at issue in the world that produced me. As I look back at my stumbling boyhood efforts, I think I was seeking to understand not simply knowledge about things but ways of knowing, how and why things—good things and bad things, hard to understand things—were as they were and how I and the folk around me fit into some larger scheme. Baldwin's statement expresses it exactly as I felt it—the elements and arrangements of my world seemed natural and singular, with all the pressures and anxieties and questions that such sentiment brought on. This I felt until my world began to explode through books and the writing, the communication, questing and questioning that books provoked. Others, including my peers and elders, will no doubt in some respects have different perspectives, but I do recall persistently raising questions of my elders, including ancestors and teachers. I recall even writing those who were some distances away and otherwise unknown to me—researchers, librarians, professors, ministers, college deans, and the like, held by many as authorities and knowing ones of some kind. Since my immediate elders could not answer my questions and since they assumed that the positions of authority these other persons held meant that they should know things, I pursued them with passion. Few satisfactory responses ever came my way.

Anxious about what it would mean for my profile in the neighborhood, I nevertheless sought to play with what Zora Neale Hurston had her folk characters in *Mules and Men* refer to as "by-words"—words with coded, freighted meanings—and through them approach the "inside meanin' of things."[1] So before relatives and community, including church circles, I learned somehow to "per-form"[2] as a young virtuoso—of words and texts. Relatives and circles of elders around me often said that I knew things beyond my peers, even beyond the elders. Of course, I did *not* know things, not even what they meant about my knowing things. But I seemed to (know how to) dazzle with words, with my ability to read and recite the Bible and any other texts I could get my hands on and to interpret and apply them to the world I shared with my peers and elders with what surely had to be feigned confidence. I became in my world boy-teacher/word shaman/information guru. These interests and performances were, I now know, ways of expressing my curiosity, my way, sensitive soul that I was, of handling the hard and ugly things around me. They reflected my thirst for ways of knowing, not merely things, but about why the world worked the way it did; they also demonstrated my faculty for mimetics.[3] These were the boyhood years.

Along the awkward way into maturity, I was fortunate to come to the attention of and apparently impressed some persons beyond home and relatives and neighborhood. A few strategically placed and sensitive persons[4]—in middle school, high school, at Morehouse College, and in graduate schools—took notice of me and encouraged and challenged me to continue on terms that I would partly determine for myself and partly stumble onto in an effort to figure things out. Ministry and academic pursuits became the twin default lines of pursuit: why would these pursuits not be the natural steps for a boy whom many in a late twentieth century U.S. southeastern urban black free church Protestant culture believed knew things and who seemed always to want to know more and certainly demonstrate that he knew more?

With two good internship experiences in church settings during divinity school years at Yale University, I experimented with ministry as far as I could. I nonetheless realized that it was not right for me: the continuing expectation of my possessing more answers than questions and the consistent narrowing of the questions and the terms of performance discouraged me and convinced me that I was not "called" thereto. I seemed less and less willing and able to perform in the way that ministry would demand of me. And I seemed more and more curious about issues that the academic world opened up to me. The quest to know became over time less and less about the facts—not even about my world or the texts at hand—and not at all about doctrine or piety, but more and more about how things came to be and how and why things in such arrangements persisted.

Although as far as I can recall I was neither prodded nor inspired by anyone in particular, I took up in the Ph.D. program at Harvard University the academic study of the Bible, with focus on Christian scriptures. As much as I try, I cannot recall any particular event or moment that determined the turn toward such a strange venture. The move in that direction may seem from a distance and in light of the black bible-reading Protestant culture that shaped me to have been natural. But this is to mistake the shared text with erasure of difference and with conflicts, in interest, agenda, and discourse from one world to another.

Yet as I slowly, warily embraced the academic study of the Bible, I found a touchstone: it seemed odd enough to be fascinating: it was somewhat like working on a puzzle or uncovering mysteries of some sort. To be sure, I was given what I think was the usual encouragement that fairly good students get from faculty in such circumstances. But now I cannot help thinking, with some embarrassment, that this move had to do not simply with my assumption that I already knew important things—don't all young aspiring scholars think so? So why not this field that seemed to wield the book that the world which I was still learning to negotiate deemed the key to knowledge? Perhaps my choice to commit to such studies had to do with my assumption (and hubris and naïvete, no doubt) that I was destined to deal with ways of knowing that were odd. And since in my immediate world it was understood, as it was in the folk culture that Hurston studied, that things really worth knowing were "hidden'...jus like de Bible,"[5] and since it was presumed that the double-sighted or most gifted within my tribe were enabled to "read" things, it now makes sense to me that—in spite of some fumbling about, feeling my way almost in the academic darkness, with a brief flirtation or two along the way with other professional and academic directions[6]—I chose the oddity that is the academic study of the Bible.[7] Beyond my hunches and hubris, I did not know at the time why I should take such a step or what I would make of it.

At any rate, without actually knowing what I was doing, I proved to myself that I had cultivated a highly developed mimetic faculty in another domain: I was able to apply such faculty in academic studies at the graduate level. Although I succeeded in one respect, having gotten through what was supposed to be a rigorous program in biblical studies that everyone around me said was the best, it may have been a somewhat Pyrrhic victory: What I encountered in such studies was so far removed from the interest and passion that I had developed over the years for learning and questioning, for excavation and examination of the things in the world that I really only muddled through to the end, including writing a fairly standard dissertation project. Some of the folk of my world would have said more honestly and directly about that project and the discourse it was intended to join that "they ain't talkin' 'bout nothing.'" Even though I have learned that the double negative in the discourse of the folk reflects not so much ignorance of "standard" rules of speech as emphatic judgment about the reality or truth of a situation, I am not sure I entirely agree even now with this sentiment. Yet I do recall that I wondered quite a bit about the import of the discourse. I was for most of those years unconnected, disoriented, reduced to intellectual stuttering: I could come to "proper" speech and offer good enough critical analysis in the classroom and the "program," dramatically contradicting Robert Penn Warren's clacking buzzard's assertion to Big Jim that his and my "breed"—"niggers"—"ain't hermeneutical."[8] But the truth is I was not making the connection with those issues I felt were important.[9]

Without mentors of the type who could understand much less sympathize with all that challenged me, I did what most insecure, frightened, human beings having already invested much in such situations do: I *soldiered* on, hoping it would soon begin to make sense. After having taken[10] the Ph.D. in 1983—having written a dissertation on a rhetorical expression in the New Testament as window onto early Christian and Greco-Roman world *askesis,* no less!—I had even commenced with the writing and the typical activities that were supposed to define the young scholar on the make. I was a long way from a situation in which I was something of a word-meaning wizard dazzling my grandmother's small Bible study group. The problem: I was no longer in pursuit of the ways of knowing and of hidden meanings; I was invested instead, sadly, like others I knew in my "field," in "drudgery divine,"[11] another kind of performance, of the worst kind—writing more and more about less and less of import. And why, I kept thinking and disorienting myself even more, must I prove anything to a buzzard?

Like the ancient and modern world ascetics whom I was now as scholar supposed to model, I continued with my first professorial appointment (at the Claremont School of Theology, just outside Los Angeles) to grind away. And after some years of stumbling through the usual professional advances, after years of fairly quiet but very serious self-reflection, and in response to the needs and provocations of some students with whom I worked—noting my own culpability in the facilitation of their socialization into a narrow professionalization that had in too many instances drained me of passion, socialpolitical engagement, and self-awareness—I was both inspired and forced to rediscover my early life quest. I picked up again my interest in ways of knowing, at a deeper level and in broader but also, quite paradoxically, more personal terms. I had slowly begun to grasp, as Rainer Maria Rilke put it, the need to try to catch that "ball" that had been "thrown" at me, at my "center," in one of those trajectories that only "God" can throw.[12] I then became convinced that I had nothing to prove to the buzzard; I had in fact some things to teach old buzzards. The effort to catch what was "thrown" to me is a quest for knowing, it is about getting at hidden meanings, riddles, puzzles;[13] this was, I learned, if not about me, certainly included me, included the self I had been, was at the moment, and wanted to be. I came to realize that this self was an unstable self, not at all a simple lone or essentialized self; it was a layered "self," overlapping with other selves that were complexly situated in worlds that feigned stability, even authority and finality. The quest to know was really the quest to know this self trying to negotiate worlds—the more immediate and intimate social discursive worlds (of black folk) and the larger social discursive (white and other) worlds beyond. I learned that negotiating these worlds required a certain faculty—for returning the "throw," for critical "reading." I also learned that such reading required in the world (in which nearly all of us are children of Gutenberg[14]) a facility for the reading of/performing "texts"—the signs, portents—of the overlapping worlds I experience, texts that held the key to the complexity and hidden meanings of these worlds. So as far back as I can remember I always worked hard to access in both worlds the texts as signs of special import. And I fashioned a "self" through performances in relationship to the texts.

Of course, this return to the earlier quest meant I needed to fathom to a more radical degree and in more creative and more intentionally (un-) disciplinary terms, not historical criticism but critical history,[15] a self construed in larger dynamic and layered historical terms. I would need to retrain or untrain myself: I would need to find a different discourse, a more radical orientation—or invent one for myself. In spite of conversations with a couple of colleagues at the Claremont School of Theology about how curricular changes might be made that would be consonant with my journeying (and those of others not invested in the German-inflected theological paradigm), nothing of substance was done. The strange mix of institutional, academic-guild politics and our own anxieties and lack of resolve insured such an outcome. But even as I feigned keeping myself disciplinarily "clean," I was already beginning to embrace for myself the conviction that anticipated the mantra from the domain of crude political discourse, "It's not 'the text,' but *texture*, not their past, but *this present*, not 'the ancient world,' but *this world* (in which I and my folk strive) that matters, stupid!"[16]

Physical transitions, crossing the mountains—first from west to east—and changing institutions (to Union Seminary in New York City), seemed to provide opportunity and more resolve on my part for explicitly modeling some academic-intellectual changes: the African Americans and the Bible research project, which I established in the mid-1990s, with its historical and social scientific focus on the conjuncture between the people and the text, was in terms of local and national curricular-institutional politics an important transgressive first step. This was not a project about finding blacks/Africans *in* the Bible; it was a project that made African Americans as a segment of the modern black Atlantic the focus of inquiry.[17] The copula "and" was intended to invite transdisciplinary investigations into the conjuncture of the two freighted categories. This was a shift in focus that for the time and given my institutional and "field" location—biblical studies in a theological seminary—was not particularly encouraged or embraced. Although the shift in my interest and orientation could not be stopped,[18] it could be and was circumscribed and negatively signified: it was considered a somewhat awkward fit for a school, notwithstanding its location at the mouth of Harlem and its claims regarding its social and political theological liberalism, whose curriculum structure was rather traditional, even anachronistic. My new transdisciplinary orientation was associated with "those no longer in the field;" it was considered by many to be "marginal," not reflective of what those doing traditional biblical scholarship did, with focus on (the theological and lexical meanings of) "the text"; yet some others seemed to overdetermine my initiative in terms of a *black* (biblical) studies, with interest in addressing only black peoples and in finding black peoples and black themes in the texts.

While some in the "the field" and in the school were mostly negative about or indifferent to the project—resisting my efforts to make the new project and practices a part of a more comprehensive change in the curriculum—intellectually promiscuous gatherings and conversations that I organized provided encouragement. I went forward: the next big step was to model on my own terms a change in orientation to scholarship in biblical studies altogether—from historical (and related types of) criticism to critical history, such that the time frame of my focus shifted: from an unproblematized "ancient" text or moment to the moments and dynamics and politics of the modern era, in which my own world would be found with its recognized voices and gestures. This shift then warranted other steps: reconceptualization of my teaching and research agenda and writing projects that might have the potential to model a way out of the (still largely non-self-reflexive historicist and theological) guild box in order to help provide safe and meaningful discursive space for others on a similar quest.

The momentum was great. But so also was the challenge and resistance. After more than ten years I had approached the moment for taking another step in my thinking and in initiatives. With much fear and anxiety over consequences I nevertheless realized that the time had come for another crossing of the mountain, this time from east to west (again); it also involved a change of type of work site, from seminary to graduate school, as well as work orientation. The move, to the graduate-only, nonsectarian Claremont Graduate University in California, an oddly shaped university in perpetual identity formation, led to the opportunity to establish in 2004 the Institute for Signifying Scriptures, with its risky agenda of institutional track-laying and the creation of safe space for odd transgressive discourse.[19] This was also the beginning not only of some painful personal domestic experiences but also psychosocial and intellectual work—deep-diving, brooding, care-taking, courage-building, self-examination, reconceptualization, reorientation work, including at first *refraining from* or *not* writing about less and less, then again taking up writing that (I would like to think) became slow-cooking, deeper and more expansive, more self-reflexive, poignant, intense, jazzlike. Such work has led to this book, the first volume of a proposed multivolume project.

The reconnection with and deepening of my youthful quest led me to an orientation to work that I think reflects my maturity and more expansive thinking about self and world. I understand this book project to be about my historicized and theorized self—an early twenty-first-century black Atlantic reading/writing self—looking inside, looking forward and backward, looking beyond and through the veil. It is a probing that entails placing that self in larger historical perspectives, digging into the conditions, limitations, possibilities, and determinants of self-cultivation. It is also a use of the self in order to think about thinking and knowing, creativity and power. It is now no longer enough for me to want to know the meaning of texts; I must know the meaning of the conditions—the challenges and possibilities and limitations—of my quest to know and my culturally inflected *mis*-readings.[20] I must know the meaning of Hurston's folks' and my childhood association of "hidden meanin'" with the Bible, as freighted site and fraught symbol-place-holder. I can no longer (merely) *exegete* (the text), I must now *excavate* (the historical self).

I now realize, for example, that contrary to official records and the testimonies of relatives, my beginnings are not in the mid-twentieth, but in fraught moments in the fifteenth through the nineteenth centuries, when the North Atlantic worlds came into contact with the people they then invented as Africans. Any effort to understand who I am and am still becoming must come to terms with this context and its complexities and perduring ramifications. I have for some time looked for a way *forward*, not backward, as in the simple past or the simplistic history, to my beginnings.

With the eighteenth-century ex-slave writer and activist Olaudah Equiano, also known as Gustavus Vassa, as an embodiment of the black subject as "stranger" and as complex and disturbing window-mirror; and with the Bible as example of the complex phenomenon of "scriptures" as analytical wedge, I have found a way forward. This book is an excavation of such beginnings. It is about my beginnings as part of the beginnings of the modern era. It is about the historical development of such beginnings into the occluding metadiscursive regime, structural arrangements, and relations of knowledge and power—what I term "scripturalization"—that obtain, notwithstanding some permutations in representations, in the modern West, now complexly inclusive of, determinative of, and redefined by the world of the black Atlantic.

As all critical readers of his narrative have come to recognize, Equiano can be made to represent and speak to many things. I am interested in what it may mean to press the matter of his uses of scriptures into service for criticism. As I read my story in relationship to Equiano's, I can understand my story as a type of "scriptural" story. This is so precisely because Equiano's "interesting" story can be said to be for the modern black Atlantic world a paradigmatic story. It is a "scriptural" story in the most fundamental terms, not only because it is *about* a particular set of "scriptures," a reading of parts of the English Bible as scriptures; it is, as I hope to make clear, a reading of readings/uses of scriptures, including how they are made to function in a complex social-political and discursive regime. Most interesting and fundamental for my purposes, Equiano's story is a scriptural story because it is an epic story, a story about a great journey, a great struggle, a story about trauma and survival, about the "fall" into "sin," about "salvation" and transformation, about knowing things and accessing and wielding power.[21]

Equiano's story as scripture is not simply about the fate of one person or one people. It surely is about the one person poignantly and doubly named Gustavus Vassa and Olaudah Equiano. And insofar as it is about this complex person—both highly unique in some respects, and in other respects highly representative—it is also about the situation of black peoples, who were made to undergo the North Atlantic slave-trading worlds long before and long after this now famous figure of the mid- to late eighteenth century. But the story is most basically an articulation of some of the timeless challenges and problems that are arguably universal: facing the trauma of being an abject outsider and, through enormous determination and ingenuity and "fortune," transforming such a situation into survival and some success. The hero of this adventure is a black person, but being black is not the chief issue. In plainer terms, the story is about how a formerly enslaved black person comes to call himself "African," "Christian," and "almost an Englishman"; about what such transformation of identity means, what it entailed, what it assumed, what it required; and about how what is called "the scriptures" or "the Bible"—as a fraught catchphrase or abbreviation for historical and ongoing nearly taken-for-granted psycho-social-cultural phenomena and dynamics—is made to work in the world he experienced and how such working facilitated his survival and success. So Equiano's story is not *simply* a story about any one people or tribe or individual. With the complexity and politics of even the author's name registered in its title,[22] the story seems to be a pointed status-sensitive reflection—on the part of one who was a "stranger" made to be a slave and who is black—about identity formation, status-movement, if not transcendence, and about the quest for integration, agency, and power.

That such fraught issues are registered by a formerly enslaved black person of the eighteenth century is not to be taken lightly: for obvious reasons, few black peoples in the eighteenth-century worlds of the North Atlantic were expected to be capable of coming to speech and writing in English (or any other of the languages of the dominant peoples of the North Atlantic) about anything, much less about themselves, to the extent and on the discursive-political terms represented by Equiano's book. Equiano may not have been unique, but he was, as the British were given to saying, a rare bird indeed.[23] Yet Equiano's story is most "interesting" for my purposes here not because of those unique aspects of his life, but because of his story's rather sensitive articulations of some of the fundamental challenges, pains and traumas, and survival strategies that characterize the history of almost all black persons in the North Atlantic worlds. Although it is clear that the larger political circumstances placed different types of psychological constraints upon him as writer,[24] and although he seems to be sensitive about whether he was registering sentiments of all black peoples of his time, Equiano's registering of his experiences with identity formation and social integration has for a long time, from the mid- to late eighteenth century and far beyond, been a controversial, painful, and unsettling site for black persons in the North Atlantic worlds.

I contend that Equiano's story is *my* story insofar as his story names issues and problems that define the journeying, the quest for salvation and knowing and transformation that define black existence in North Atlantic worlds. I thought it not only appropriate but also potentially revealing of the complexity of power relations and structures of North Atlantic worlds, and black Atlantic contributions to and participation in them, to name both my story and Equiano's story as scriptural stories. I hope to establish in this book how excavation of his story may help me re(dis)cover my own. Even more important, I hope that with such interfacing a more complex framing of black and subaltern history in the North Atlantic worlds will be constructed, and in relationship to such construction there will be wider resonances with other peoples and their journeyings and quests. A different view of the larger shared world is also thereby made possible.

Equiano's story is illuminating and compelling for me in my quest to know my self and its beginnings, the beginnings of the black Atlantic, precisely because it is a story about "beginnings," about "first contact," and about how that contact was experienced, rationalized, conceptualized, and survived. Historian of religion Charles H. Long has set forth the issues most pointedly:

> [T]hrough conquest, trade, and colonialism, [the West] made contact with every part of the globe... religion and cultures and peoples throughout the world were created anew through academic disciplinary orientations—they were signified...
>
> names [were] given to realities and peoples...; this naming is at the same time an objectification through categories and concepts of those realities which appear as novel and "other" to the cultures of conquest. There is of course the element of power in this process of naming and objectification... the power is obscured and the political, economic, and military situation that forms the context of the confrontation is masked by the intellectual desire for knowledge of the other. The actual situation of cultural contact is never brought to the fore within the context of intellectual formulations.[25]

Anthropologist Michael Taussig makes much the same point but also stresses the possibilities that the initial forced contact subsequently opens up—for critical signifying agency on the part of those signified upon, for one thing. Such a development is not a necessary result, but in the context of volatility and instability it is one among many possibilities:

> [F]rom First Contact time... to Reverse Contact now-time... the Western study of the Third and Fourth World Other gives way to the unsettling confrontation of the West with itself as portrayed in

> the eyes and handiwork of its Others. Such an encounter disorients the earlier occidental sympathies which kept the magical economy of mimesis and alterity in some sort of imperial balance.[26]

Insofar as I am concerned here with a radical exploration—how and why and with what consequences I came to use the Bible as scriptures—I must also be interested in a larger, more rounded and layered history of scriptures, not the history of the lexical content meanings or the historical backgrounds of those characters and events referenced in the texts, but the psychology, the phenomenology, the sociology, the anthropology, the invention and uses, and the political consequences of the uses of the texts. Following Long and Taussig, I am convinced that an important and necessary, even if not the only appropriate, framework and starting point for such a history is the beginning of the modern era. This is after all the era that has "signified" me and my tribe as the "savage," "black," "Negro," "colored," "African American," and so forth, and in conjunction with such signification, that is, as an instrument for the advancement of the political work that is signification in general, invented a collection of texts, as "scriptures," "the Bible," "the Word of God," and so forth. Although some of the names of these two categories may actually go back much further in time than the onset of modernity, there is no avoiding the reality that the determinant significations and spins that mark us and our contemporary practices and dynamics and politics and psychologies have their origins in the era of the first and ensuing contact, and so the latter must be confronted, addressed, engaged. There can be no serious self-reflexive critical work apart from consideration of the meaning and consequences of such contact.

Far beyond the easy and flat assumptions and explanations—the general penchant for or obsession with the "spirit" world, their history in the southern U.S. "Bible Belt," or even the larger American Protestant evangelical tradition as matrix—for the black Atlantic's engagement of things religious, the complexities of the experience of first contact for all concerned, both dominant and dominated, enslaved and enslaver, would need to be probed. The matter regarding what conditioned, provoked, and inspired Equiano's and the black Atlantic engagement with the European-translated Bible and the behaviors that have defined such engagement need to be understood in light of the terms of the first contact. There is no doubting many influences in the black Atlantic translation of the world in general, but if the behaviors-and-practices-in-relationship-to-the world in my story, the black Atlantic stories, are to be accounted for, as Taussig would have it, in terms of the "mimetic faculty"—shockingly and poignantly made clear in the Kafkan ape's dissertation about the universality of the experience of feeling the "tickling at the heels" by those located differently on the chain of being, those confronting "the nature that culture uses to create second nature, the faculty to imitate, make models, explore difference, yield into and become the Other"[27]—how might we proceed to reconstruct a history of the exercise of this faculty? The transdisciplinary reading of Equiano's story as a story about first contact and the resultant construction of the modern world is what I offer in this book.

The effort to bring into conversation the making of modernity in the confrontation of the dominant West with the Other who is race-d and a history of (the invention and uses of) scriptures that includes my scriptural story can hardly avoid a consideration of the concept of the fetish (from the Portuguese, *fetico*). The discussion about the latter in the critical literature of many different fields and disciplines is voluminous and wide-ranging and layered and fascinating, if not always clarifying.[28] Fetishism has more recently and generally been understood by critics to revolve around a state of critical consciousness, "the imputation to others of a false understanding of the divisions between human and nonhuman, subject and object, an error that threatens human agency."[29] It is easy in wading into this discursive thicket to be pulled in many different directions. Given my focus on my story in relationship to Equiano's story, I have found helpful an argument made by literary critic Srinivas Aravamudan. As he addressed the issue of the function of the fetish in the context of the initial contact between the dominant West and the Other, Aravamudan made it clear where and how intellectual energies should be focused: "Rather than worry about its epistemology we ought to acknowledge the role of fetish as pragmatic application... Modernity... is a perspective that distinguished fact from fetish and truth from error."[30] Summarizing and following the theory of Bruno Latour, Aravamudan suggested that scholars instead orient themselves "in favor of a perspective from *a* modernity... [that] tracks the subject's capacity to make do (*fait faire*) with the fetish, a process that dispenses with questions concerning belief and instead concentrates on those oriented around practice."[31]

Practices, uses—not the truth-claims about or within any collection of texts, not the lexical meanings of any text-part—are my interests in this book. I seek to understand the practices and uses of the Bible as scriptures that were part of my story, with an honest effort at some sensitive modulation of both critical engagement and critical distancing for the sake of theorizing. What I require is some sort of interpretive framework that will facilitate the deep historical and interpretive excavation that will help me see more clearly what conditioned the practices and orientations and forms of consciousness that are part of my story as a black Atlantic story. Of course, I aim to follow Kafka's ape's challenge by making an effort to help readers understand that the tickling-fetishizing-mimetic faculty in my story is, if not universal, certainly closer to them than they appear (as the side mirror on cars still remind us). Yet rather than begin with an argument about the universal or even the general and widespread phenomenon, I think it more interesting and appropriate to begin at home, in one's own circle, with the self, and then move outward in thinking and argumentation. The framework within which I want to interpret more fully and deeply my story is an-*other's* story. By placing my story within or seeing it as part of a story with a larger (historical-cultural-comparative) arc, I aim to gain deeper perspective on my own.

But of course it matters what that other story is all about. For me that story is Equiano's story as wedge story as window-opening, mirroring story. Equiano's story originates in the period of first contact; it reflects an attempt to *make sense of* and *make do with* the modern world of the North Atlantic as the latter was built upon and, in economic and social-psychological-ideological-political terms, turned around the capture, enslavement, bartering, and humiliation of black peoples. It is a story told by a black person about such a world and about his own (decidedly male) experiences in it. It is a story about one who knows himself to be a "stranger," on the margins of this world, one who positions himself to take a sensitive critical look at this world. It is a story that seeks to *make sense of* and *make do with* the fundamental ideological elements of this world, especially the elements of "make-believe" that undergird and structure this world and constitute its reality. Among the most important of the elements of "make-believe"—the "magic"—that are addressed in this older framing story are the invention and uses of the Bible as scriptures.

The Interesting Narrative of the Life of Olaudah Equiano or Gustavus Vassa, the African. Written by Himself[32] has since its initial publication in England in 1789 been read and interpreted on both sides of the Atlantic for many different purposes—in literary and cultural criticism; in eighteenth-century English social-cultural history; in the history of abolitionism; and in black studies and African diaspora and slavery studies.

It has been noted again and again by critics that Equiano's story has been read to advance many different interests and agendas: academic-, ideological-, cultural-, social-political.[33] As one of the earliest and most successful and widely known black Atlantic writers in the English-speaking world, Equiano was for the English-speaking black Atlantic world a powerful freighted symbol and heroic figure. Differences in spin and interpretive approaches on the part of the different types of readers notwithstanding, it has always mattered that Equiano's story be viewed as significant and that Equiano be viewed as heroic. Among black peoples on both sides of the Atlantic, as well as in (west) Africa, there has long been a need for Equiano's story to be a story about black survival and heroism. There is no doubt that his story came to be seen as desperately needed, for a lot of reasons, by his black Atlantic successors. I count myself among them.

It is partly because I was aware of how strongly Equiano's story registers in political and ideological terms across academic fields in the history of interpretation that I made the decision to make use of his story in this book. But I find him to be important not so much in terms of having all the right answers to our questions or the strategy for the correct political-economic-ideological course for black survival and thriving; I find him significant because in his story is one of the earliest efforts to identify and face with creative and artful sensitivity and passion the major questions, challenges, and problems involved in being a black "stranger," a black and enslaved person, in the North Atlantic worlds. This is done through the telling of his life story that is also a powerful interpretation of the social-cultural situation which he as black stranger and "white men" (as dominant parties) and others share. Insofar as that world that Equiano negotiated, read, and commented on is structured—in terms of power—still pretty much along the same lines, it makes compelling sense to put my story in relationship to Equiano's as a foundation-story about black survival and meaning-seeking in the modern world dominated by "white men" and their ways ("magic").

Although there have been many efforts within many disciplines to interpret Equiano's story, there have been no extensive efforts to interpret it in terms of the history of religions, much less in terms of the problematics of (the uses of) scriptures. To be sure, there has been recognition of Equiano's strong religious conviction, sentiments, and language, but the recognition tends to lead either to explaining away the depth and sincerity of his (Christian) religious-ness altogether—arguing it to be only a ruse, a mask for the more authentic sentiment of resistance—or to advancing a rather flat understanding of his religious conviction as that which renders him simple and naive.[34] Insofar as all critics agree that Equiano's story is a religious story of some sort, that is, a story that registers and makes religious conviction a serious matter, if only for narratological effect, and because he has not yet been interpreted in extended terms in this discursive key, I think it very important for a scholar of religion—not the tribal theologian interested in the registration of tribal doctrines, but a historian of religion interested in how and why the language of religious sentiment is registered or made to work—to weigh in on Equiano.

Equiano's narrative is particularly interesting for the historian of religion for a couple of reasons. First, the story rather dramatically opens a window onto the thinking that has come to be known as the history and comparative study of religion in the modern world: Equiano depicts himself as the missionary-ethnographer, sometimes the insider, at other times the outsider, chronicling and criticizing different cultural and religious traditions, their sentiments, practices, and special sacred objects, all as a part of his artful telling of his life story. He showed himself to be a student of religion and culture, specially positioned to convey his critical but also rather creative tendentious British-inflected Protestant observations and intentions. It is precisely the manner in which Equiano throughout his story differently positions himself as here and now the insider devotee, and then and there the outside critic looking in that makes his story so interesting for the scholar of religion. Some religious practices and sentiments are seen as dramatic examples of fetishization, the unself-conscious practices and sentiments of primitives ("my countrymen," "Eboes," "Indians"); at other times he takes note of the rational faith of a mature and sophisticated people (the English; Europeans). But his words about such matters drip with irony. It is precisely Equiano's reflections on his positionality, especially regarding things religious, that have to be investigated with care and that may prove to be one of the most important keys to understanding him and the issues he addresses.

Second, because of the manner in which Equiano figures himself as focal point of contemporary moral and political-economic crises brought on by violent conquest, disruption, and enslavement, he makes himself a compelling figure in any attempt to understand modern existence and self-consciousness, including, obviously, black existence and self-consciousness, about which for the times in which he lived we know precious little. He figures himself in his story—as mature narrator—as qualified insider ("almost an Englishman"), having been outsider

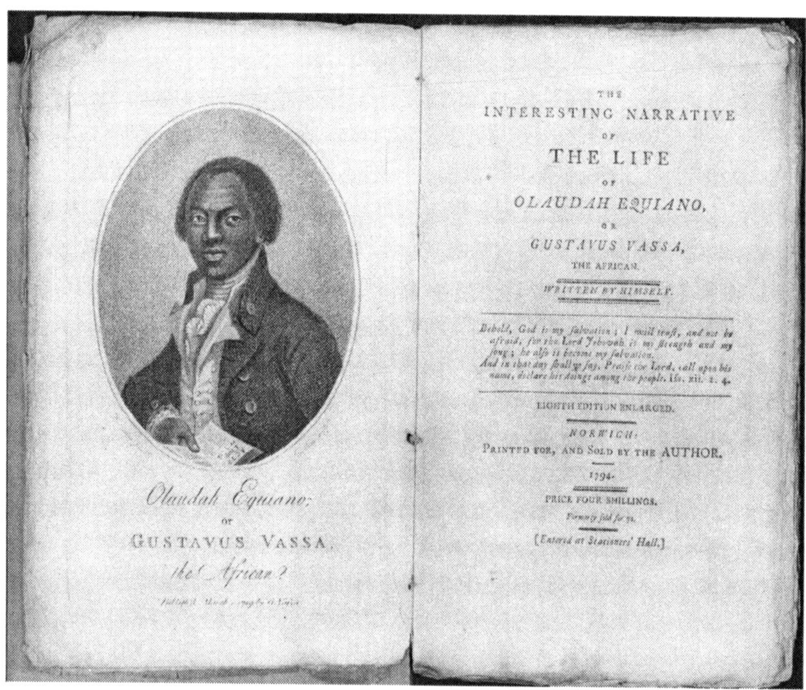

FIGURE 0.1 Frontispiece from Olaudah Equiano, *The Interesting Narrative of the Life of Olaudah Equiano* (1794). Library of Congress, Prints & Photographs Division, LC-USZ62–54026.

("stranger" = slave) looking in, the one to whom initially the English books did not "speak," yet one who, as the frontispiece (see Figure 0.1) of his published story shows, is, at the point of the telling of the story, complexly in possession of, and self-possessed in complex relationship to, the supreme (English) Book, the Bible. This image of Equiano signifies pointedly about what Equiano intended to communicate and about what must be the focus of this book about him (and about my story and the story of so many other black peoples of the modern Atlantic worlds). Notwithstanding decades of dazzling critical attention given to Equiano's story, much of it ignoring or stumbling over his Bible-wielding image and the consistent attention given to it throughout his story, Equiano virtually shouts out his attention to the Bible as a key to his story-telling. With this book I challenge other critics to remove their earplugs.

Equiano does not merely quote the Bible; he is not an unthinking mimic of British evangelicalism; he makes his story about the phenomenon of the Bible as part of the construction of the world of the dominants, with the focus on the British. In order to make sense of Equiano's story, the reader has to come to understand that he came to understand the Bible as the fetishized center-object around which British society was structured. Through his initial involuntary but later strategic, voluntary travels by ship and his associations with other "strangers" ("Indians") and ex-centrics (white religious dissenters, thinkers, and politicians), Equiano was able to make the English Book (and by logical extension, all other books, of course) "speak" to him and, through his own writing, "speak" back to the structure that I term "scripturalization." His story can be understood as an (English-inflected) "epic"—a *script-ur[e]-alizing*—of life in the Black Atlantic diaspora in order, it seems, to advance an agenda of a more radically (= racially) inclusive social order. He does this by signifying on (more broadly European but English-inflected) scripturalization and implicitly and haltingly and preliminarily offering an alternate scriptural text or construal and model of scripturalizing, one that calls for an end to slave-trafficking. More was at stake than one man's survival—or his providing proof of his cleverness. And there was more at issue than the laying of tracks for a literary tradition.[35] What compelled such track-laying? What did it mean? Even as it is clearly literary and rhetorical production and performance, Equiano's scripturalizing represented sharp and deep social criticism that teaches much beyond the domain of the literary and rhetorical. I contend that that something more can and must be probed. It is the focus of this book.

Although Equiano was in many respects somewhat unusual in some of his experiences, his "making do" with the Bible (understood by him as nationalist-cultural fetish) remains fairly typical of black folks' "making do" with the North Atlantic worlds they had been made to undergo, whether slave or "free" (the latter always and everywhere in the eighteenth century throughout the Atlantic worlds understood in highly qualified terms on account of widely and contradictory codes and laws). Metonymic of the black-inflected vernacularization of scriptures, Equiano's story provides the outline for a layered history of black North Atlantic representations, gestures, and mimetic practices as a history of scriptures.

Equiano's life story is a dramatic window onto the North Atlantic worlds' humiliation of the black self. But with the talking book story more is signified: scriptures are signified upon, insofar as Equiano understands that the dominant social and political structures in place are built around the Bible, drawing justification and power therefrom; so he proceeds to construct his life story in signifying/mimetic relationship to such arrangements. The black struggle for survival, freedom, and acquisition of power are understood by Equiano to turn around awareness of and response to the dominant culture's festishizing of the book, the Bible.

This awareness inspired Equiano to structure his story as a scriptural/biblical story that signifies on the very use of scriptures—what I here call *scripturalization, a social-psychological-political structure establishing its own reality.* His signifying practice is at the same time an example or model of the vernacular, for the sake of resistance, survival, freedom, and independent thriving, in complex response to scripturalization as a type of fetishization, "white men's magic"—practices, arrangements, behaviors, and rhetorics that were astonishing and befuddling—as Equiano himself experiences it and in qualified terms participates in it. Equiano's story does not represent a fully explicit theory about scripturalization; it is really only a naming of the problem and the modeling of the beginning of a strategic psycho-cultural response to it. His story can be taken up not with a view to addressing the entire story or addressing all issues, it is only a window onto the phenomenon and dynamics of scripturalization, as well as the laying of tracks for creative responses among North Atlantic blacks.

Using Equiano's story as analytical wedge, I theorize scriptures in terms of scripturalization and have isolated four stages in or aspects of the phenomenon: (1) scripturalization as social-cultural matrix, within which ideological and discursive rules and practices are made evident and common; (2) scripturalization as framework for nationalist polity and the politics of nationalization, in which the evident and common ideological and discursive practices are legitimized, encoded, and regulated; (3) scripturalization as socio-psycho-logical carapace/overcoat, by which the evident, common, encoded, and regulated discursive practices are naturalized for the sake of social regulation, self-regulation in the social-cultural matrix and the nation; and (4) scripturalization as the translocal/transcendent field on which or regime in which power dynamics and strategies are played out or advanced as discursive coercion and sometimes negotiated and resisted on these terms.

These aspects are not explicitly named and isolated as such in Equiano's story, but as my chapter titles indicate, they are handles or expressions in Equiano's own language that I judge to be correlative of the stages and aspects I have isolated. I suggest that the different stages in and aspects of scripturalization can be reasonably inferred from episodes of Equiano's story and that they provide a useful and sharp wedge for understanding not only the design and aims of his story, but also the larger set of historical, psycho-social-cultural, and political dynamics within which Equiano and his readers, and in which I and my readers, in different complex ways, fit.

The different aspects of the scripturalization correspond to the core chapters of the book (3 to 7). These core chapters are framed by other chapters that introduce Equiano (1) and scripturalization as phenomena (2), and by a summary chapter (Epilogue) that draws out larger theoretical implications and psycho-social ramifications. Each chapter title reflects Equiano's language. Each will have an epigraph that captures a narrative moment and feature of a scriptualization as white men's magic in the story. There is no intention in this book to cover all problems and issues; the aim is simply to make the case for scripturaliztion as white men's magic as a major running theme throughout Equiano's work and to explain the importance of such.

Chapter One, "'...unbounded influence over the credulity and superstition of the people...': Magic as Slavery, Slavery as Magic," is a framing analytical chapter. It establishes Equiano's general self-reflexive critical perspective that different worlds represent different epistemologies or different ways of knowing. He makes the point by focusing first on his homeland as a way of knowing, a kind of "magic," that has enormous influence over the people. Through focus on Equiano's comparative culture and religions discussion, making his invented homeland the baseline for initial consideration, this chapter establishes how different episodes and arguments fit together, how the entire narrative is woven together as a riff on "white men's magic" (in the form of "scripturalization" as the framework that enslaves all).

Chapter Two, "'...the white men had some spell or magic...': A Black Stranger's First Contact with White Men's Magic," is the chapter that begins to show how Equiano began to establish the argument about white men and their magic. It focuses on Equiano's beginning effort to figure himself as "stranger" or outsider who looks at the white dominant world and offers his readers startling new critical insights into it, including magic as its foundation and framing logic.

Chapter Three, "'...every person there read the Bible...': Scripturalization as Matrix of White Men's Magic," identifies Equiano's identification of white men's magic as scripturalization, an ideological formation that includes but goes beyond the Bible as scriptures.

Chapter Four, "'to the Britons first...the Gospel is preached': Scripturalization in the Nationalizations of White Men's Magic," draws attention to Equiano's awareness of and strategic narratological play with the use of scriptures in the formation of the nation.

Chapter Five "'...in the Bible, I saw things new...': Scripturalization and White Men's Magic as Orientation," focuses on Equiano's narration of his conversion experience as full entry into the discursive regime of scripturalization as magical arts.

Chapter Six, "'...take the book...and *tell* God to make them dead...': Scripturalization as White Men's Hegemony," opens a window onto Equiano's understanding and practice of the power that scripturalization represents.

Chapter Seven, "'I could read it for myself': Scripturalization, Slavery, and Agency," focuses on Equiano's arrogation of his right to read scriptures and the world on his own terms, and the implications and ramifications of such in the story.

The Epilogue revisits the implications of tying together in critical analysis Equiano's story and my own, including our mutual interest in knowing white men's magic.

1

"... unbounded influence over the credulity and superstition of the people ...": Magic as Slavery, Slavery as Magic

> *[W]e had priests and magicians, or wise men.... They calculated our time and foretold events.... They had ... some extraordinary method of discovering jealousy, theft, and poisoning; the success of which no doubt they derived from their unbounded influence over the credulity and superstition of the people.*
>
> —OLAUDAH EQUIANO, *Interesting Narrative*, chapter 1

THE WAY EQUIANO begins his story is fascinating and puzzling. The story begins with Equiano reflecting the consciousness of his mature self, an African Christian who is "almost Englishman," looking back on what his native ("Eboe") peoples and their ways and traditions mean to him and should mean to his (assumed to be mostly sympathetic and mostly white British Christian) readers. In this looking back at the ways of his native world he attempts to communicate to readers ultimately not so much what is in the mind of the youthful Equiano looking back at the world of the Igbo people, but the sentiments and narratological agenda of the mature story-telling, book-writing, talking-back-outside-of-the-narrative Equiano. The youthful Equiano does not really emerge in the first chapter; he is assumed to be the source of perspectives on the past. Beyond the felicitous expressions in the dedicatory section of the book, it is in this first chapter that Equiano creatively defines himself and orients the reader: he sums up who he as writer understands himself to be and signals what for him is the point of his story-telling. He takes stock of and analyzes those worlds that now define him—on the one hand, that "world" (as goes the story) into which he was born and that initially shaped him, the world that was his own tribe, located in a part of what is today Nigeria and (per the argument of Vincent Carretta), perhaps, Nigeria via South Carolina; and the strange new world of the white men, on the other. This first chapter sets up Equiano's "re-memory"[1] of that first world, of his beginnings, the world before or certainly different from the one in which he was made a slave and stranger, into which he would later, with some limited degree of success, be integrated.

The look back upon the world of his "origins" ironically serves both as Equiano's most forthright and most elusive message: the entire story is at one level a look back—for the sake of eliciting certain emotions and responses from his readers. With the European-defined early modern-inflected comparative religious and sociological description and analysis—of the different ways of the two worlds he puts in relationship with his look back upon his origins—his first chapter frames the entire story, sets its tone, sets forth its major themes and structure; everything that follows is meant to be interpreted in light of this first chapter. In this chapter he does not merely register the first phase in the unfolding of a life, he communicates what his story is fundamentally about. The subsequent chapters represent the episodic unfolding of the message of this first chapter.

What is communicated in this first chapter is the message that notwithstanding some fairly superficial differences—such as in languages and speech and certain customs—between the world of the British and the world of the "Oye-Eboe," the two peoples are similar in matters that are for Equiano fundamental and profound. That is, far beyond minor cultural differences, in dress, in matters more fundamental, having to do with how these worlds are structured, how they are made to work, how knowledge and power are mediated in them, and so forth, the two worlds are assumed to be, for the most part, very much alike, considering differences in some domains of advancement along the way. To be sure, the British had been able to develop in terms of complexity and volume of commerce, but the larger point for Equiano was that both societies were established and fundamentally defined around some basic and perduring social principles. Such an assumption can be seen as part of Equiano's agenda to bring his readers to a point of (re-)provincializing[2] Britain and the rest of Europe, defamiliarizing their own cultural practices, and challenging them to come to terms with the violence associated with radical essentialisms and binaries produced by their crafted univeralisms.[3]

Equiano the African Christian narrator thought that the differences between the British people (and by logical extension all Europeans and North Atlantic peoples) and the black peoples now being called Africans (whether in England and in other North Atlantic worlds or in Africa itself) were not beyond bridging. And along with a few others in his time, he saw some advantages—social-cultural, but especially commercial and economic—for both groups in the transgressing of differences and in the move toward real and sustained conversation and cooperation.

At the end of Equiano's first chapter is an exhortation that is a quotation of a collation of radical-utopianist sentiments found in the New Testament. The first part of the quotation, Acts 17:26, appears quite frequently throughout Equiano's story and serves, along with Acts 4:12, as the window onto Equiano's story-telling mind, interests, and agenda. The intentional, tendentious decontextualizations of the passages quoted are fascinating: as they are pressed into service, they articulate the logic of the arguments made throughout the chapter. The force of the quotation is almost startling in the unqualified stance it represents regarding not merely the unity of all peoples, but, as he decontextualizes and applies to his own world situation, the utopianist ideology that argues for the delusion and obsolescence of racial differentiation:

> God... hath made of one blood all nations of men for to dwell on all the face of the earth; [God's] wisdom is not our wisdom, neither are our ways his ways. (45)

This utopianist sentiment rhetorically positions Equiano to shift to the issue he considered most fundamental and pertinent—"wisdom," in this context, about how the world was begun, how it works, about the structure of power and knowledge, especially knowledge about the divine or the ultimate mysteries of life, and the media by which such power and knowledge are accessed and the institutions and figures through which they are interpreted and controlled.

Equiano's story and his letter-writing and engagement in public debates[4] make it clear that he was quite aware of the importance of responding to the structure and center or holders of power and their authorized representatives in British society.[5] He seems to have figured his character, from the period of precocious youth to that of the aggressive and persistent adult, as one who is almost obsessed with if not inordinately curious about how things—from small objects to the social and political domains—are made to work. Equiano clearly tried, in solidarity with the "Black poor," to have an impact on the political structures and politics of the British people. Through his associations with abolitionist organizations, he had direct or indirect communication with a few members of Parliament. He also understood the power of communicating by letter with royalty and other powerful figures. His narrative and his letters suggest that he knew who and what was powerful and how to negotiate with, apply pressure to, and affect channels of power.

Equiano seemed most adept and intelligent in his recognition of how much powerful officials—political, financial, ecclesiastical—in British society were affected by what now may be termed the politics of the structure and media of knowledge and opinion. This would include the power of the press, which depended on the power of literacy. He figured out that British society, with its genuflections toward and experimentation with types of freedoms, including a certain limited amount of religious freedom, depended on an informed public. With the invention of the printing press and the thriving (Protestant) religious market that had become Britain, it was literacy (and printing), not any single institution or person, that was all-powerful.[6] This recognition helps explain Equiano's obsessive quest to learn to read and to communicate in writing.

Somewhat in the tradition of an ethnologist (eighteenth-century style), Equiano figured out that one of the most important aspects of the structuring of authority and power in the Protestant British world was the facility for reading the book, *the* Book, the (English) Bible. Equiano has his character note the fetishistic status of the Book that was the Bible in Protestant England. What an ironic twist: the black person, the one who in the minds of the British belonged to one of the many recently "discovered" and exploitable "exotic," "savage" "tribes" traditionally signified by Europeans as fetishistic and primitive in mindset and practices, such a person notes and writes sardonically about the British people as one among the exotic "white" tribes with *their* fetishizing mindset and practices. The book, the book, the book, indeed! Robinson Crusoe, indeed.[7]

Yet the twist is not a complete reversal of a Robinson Crusoe story, in which the white protagonist explorer or missionary or merchant discovers the nonwhite other: even as Equiano sees himself as the character who as "stranger" with double vision is able to see the inside and outside and who at times appears to be the curious and knowing ethnologist, his character is nevertheless also clearly circumscribed in many respects; and he is to a great extent made to desire and imitate the ways of the whites. In some cases that imitation seems disturbingly simple. The overall situation that the reader was allowed to see determining the mimetics, the desire to be "almost an Englishman," was complicated and disturbing. Ultimately, Equiano was to be neither simply Crusoe nor Friday, at least in sustained terms: he was never really empowered enough and was for the most part too estranged, from himself and his origins, to play Crusoe in any sustained manner. But is not his situation—that is, not ever really being empowered enough in the world of the whites to sustain playing Crusoe—one of the major points he wanted to bring to his readers? Precisely because he could eventually come into (standard English) speech for himself—"read [English books] for myself" (191)—he made himself more powerful and potentially more embraceable, but also, paradoxically, he seems to be even more estranged from himself than the Fridays of the world.[8]

What was at stake for Equiano was agency, finding and drawing on such agency in negotiating the world that made him a stranger. Neither the Robinson Crusoe story nor any other paradigm of transformation could be applied very far as direct influences on or parallels to Equiano's story; with its sometimes disturbing imitations, sometimes subtle, sometimes radical differences from some literary sources, Equiano's story is not *simply* the mirror or the exact opposite of any other story. Although clearly drawing on many different rhetorical and narrative strategies and constructions that were at hand[9]—travel narrative; explorer's epic; conversion story—Equiano seemed to realize that the situation that defined him as black stranger was new and required the invention of a different heretofore unconstructed and untold story, one that could unify those black peoples of different tribes who had been dispersed across the Atlantic including the Equiano of his first chapter. Such folk now needed a story to live by, to fall emotionally into, to process and think with. Such people now living under rather strange and stressful circumstances would require an epic, scriptures, something akin to what the white men seemed to have.

Whether Equiano thought himself writing such a story, not to mention an epic or scriptures, is not clear and need not be pushed here. But I think he was conscious of writing to a great degree the sentiments and experiences of other black persons in the North Atlantic worlds about such needs and desires and even in some respects performing what he thought was needed. This awareness is evident in the abundance of collaborative writing projects with which he was involved and, perhaps, initiated.[10]

Equiano's writing—the very *(f)act* of his writing!—must be seen as the profound response to the British world.[11] Whatever the sources of inspiration or influences on his decision to write his story—evangelical-abolitionist group interests and strategies; economic interests, and so forth—Equiano's story-telling is a reflection of awareness of and response to the assumptions of the early modern British and the larger Atlantic world about the capabilities of black peoples, especially as regards the engagement of North Atlantic world scripts and books, expressions of ideas and sentiments. Beyond the disturbing fact (in the minds of many whites[12]) of his kind's learning the master/learning to "master," that is, to read and write, English, his learning to "hear" the English book "talk" (68) and his learning to "talk back" to it and to the world of the book, Equiano made his story-telling a critical-analytical and political "reading" of the British world (and by extension the North Atlantic worlds). His primary agenda seems to have been to fathom and critique this world, not for the sake of general inquiry or the mere curiosity of the explorer or the ethnologist, or even, in the tradition of the "signifyin(g) monkey,"[13] merely to upbraid and pun on it, but, perhaps—all of the above in tow—with the goal of carefully integrating himself into a differently defined and oriented English world.[14]

Equiano's chapter 1 sets up a salient and poignant comparison between the British world and the world of his homeland in Western Africa. This comparison has to do with the underlying systems in each world. Again, writing like the "stranger" who was also an early modern explorer or ethnographer/ethnologist who had traveled and observed quite a bit, Equiano notes first what was the basis of operation of the world of his birth and earliest years. He states that that world was run through the offices of those figures he seems to recall were called "Ah-affoe-way-cah"—priests/magicians/wise men:

> Though we had no places of public worship, we had priests and magicians, or wise men. I do not remember whether they had different offices, or whether they were united in the same persons but they were held in great reverence by the people. They calculated our time, and foretold events, as their name imported, for we called them Ah-affoe-way-cah, which signifies calculators, or yearly men, one year being called Ah-affoe. (42)

Equiano's source(s) for the figures and the phenomena referenced may never be settled with any certainty. Did he remember being told, as part of a chain of rich oral traditions, about the/a homeland by others, some elders, in his midst? Did he read about the situation in a book here and there, picking up snippets of "facts"? Or might he have picked up bits of information from reports and stories communicated by white travelers, explorers? Some of the details may have been a reflection of the exercise of his somewhat tutored imagination. He comes close to registering fairly authentic even if also tendentious images.[15]

Equiano's "re-memory" of what went on in his homeland, in particular, what offices were associated with those he remembers as "Ah-affoe-way-cah," may with some profit for analysis be compared to divination systems, especially African divination systems. Elaborate structures and operations, divination systems represent "ways of knowing," the fathoming of complex problems and situations that would otherwise be left unacceptably mysterious and unaddressed by individuals and groups. Given this general functioning, divination systems have the potential to help seekers to transform, overcome, or sustain a given situation. That is, what divination ultimately represents is human effort to assume some control over vicissitudes, problematic situations, challenges, deficits, and so forth.[16]

The "wise men" described as being part of Equiano's childhood world should be seen in this light—as diviners. They were remembered as those who knew things—things "hidden," mysterious, and unknowable through conventional means. They represent Equiano's assumptions about how this earlier other world operated or was structured. The Ah-affoe-way-cah were understood to be those who through their knowing had control over the operations within, behind, and beyond the quotidian and surface activities that made the Igbo world what it was. What Equiano's short description of these men seemed to suggest was that over time and through various means, ludics, and strategies, the Ah-affoe-way-cah secured for the inquirers knowledge about the way things were and what things were to happen in the future.

Because he did not feel the need to elaborate, and given its placement in his narrative, Equiano's discussion about the Ah-affoe-way-cah would seem to suggest that he understood what they represented in cross-cultural terms: a type of knowledge and power structure. Such a structure was assumed to be a necessary part of all worlds. The names of the operators and operations may be different from one world to another, but that there must be operators and operations for each world, that there must be an orienting center of each world—large or small, simple and complex—seemed to be taken for granted. Equiano no doubt thought it important to recognize who or what was the center, responsible for securing the center and the center-ing, stabilizing work in each world. One might even assume that Equiano assumed, like most people in most worlds, that without such operators and operations only chaos would ensue, that being without such forces and operations was unthinkable. And in the course of his narrative, Equiano betrays strong personal sentiments about what it means to be in a world without understanding such operations—*he* would remain alienated and powerless, without orientation, doomed to being outsider, a "stranger," unable to negotiate the world. That such an assumption was, of course, a reflection of his actual socialization and conditioning is clear.

The reason for the descriptive comparison of the two worlds in this first chapter of Equiano's story was, then, not simply to relate the details about the world of his origins. Not only was such a project not really feasible for Equiano, it did not square with his (narratological/political) agenda. His agenda was to comment on that world only insofar as it provided a narratological setup for his more extended commentary on his "new" world, the world in which he was made a "stranger" and a slave, the world in which and for which he writes—for the most part.[17] With its sketchy comparative discussion, his chapter 1 sets up his life story as a story that was meant to inform the reader, not only that he had overcome tremendous odds to become something other than "stranger," but also *how* he had done so. It also established his having become an African "Christian" and "almost an Englishman," who could now read and write and in fact contribute to the spreading of the English-inflected Protestant Christian faith and culture. It analyzes and critiques and challenges the slave-trading and slave-holding British society. It provides a vivid first-hand account of the brutality of the black slave's experiences. It addresses the plight of the "poor Africans" spread throughout England and her colonies and the Africans in his homeland. So the matter of *how* he overcame the odds to become an English-evangelical-abolitionist-activist-writer is especially important for Equiano's story.

But we must go back to the point about the comparative social descriptions and analyses in Equiano's chapter 1. The "descriptive" comments regarding Equiano's homeland set up the episodes in later chapters; they are seen more clearly in light of the full story. The descriptions must not be seen as primarily apologetic, that is, as an attempt to convince the reader to see the world of Equiano's birth as being similar to and somehow thereby acceptable to the British world. There is no doubt that there is an element of this agenda in chapter 1, as Equiano's language regarding "strong analogy" suggests. But if this were all that was at stake for Equiano, his story would have been and would continue to be rather differently received: it would have been read as *mere* mimetics, without the "surplus" or "excess" that I think, following Taussig, is so important to a critical stance.[18]

The "strong analogy" in Equiano's chapter 1 offers something beyond simple mimetics. The focus from the beginning—but perhaps not made clear until later—is not really on the world of Equiano's origins; it is on the British world, the world about which he writes, the world that he had learned to survive and to negotiate. The full story is commentary on the British world through the eyes of a "stranger." It is trenchant, poignant commentary by one who was a "stranger" on account of his having been enslaved and having been, on account of his blackness, persistently threatened with re-enslavement. It is commentary by one who became ex-slave only by dint of his persistence, wiles, strength, and on account of his understanding that he had been made "a particular favourite of Heaven" (31).[19] It is commentary written by one who learned to "read" the British world, especially the terms on which it understands and mediates power. It is a strategy advanced by one who intends to convince his readers that although he writes with obvious intelligence and wit and charm and conviction and shared with them a background of fundamental sentiment and sensibilities,[20] he had paradoxically been made a slave and stranger. The readers facing such paradoxical truth would be moved to act appropriately. They would at the very least be disposed to reading on, in order to determine the larger meaning of the comparisons made.

So in his chapter 1 Equiano used some arrangements of the world of his origins in order to relate them to what he as historical figure had already experienced, what he as narrative figure would in the unfolding story experience—as "stranger" in the North Atlantic worlds. Of course, Equiano understood that in the British and all other North Atlantic worlds there were no "Ah-affoe-way-cah" to speak of.[21] And he got the point that "Eboe" rituals were neither known nor respected in Britain. But he also recognized the strategic political-narratological importance of setting up the descriptions of the ways of the "Eboe": he made discussion about the latter into categories or points of reference that he set up for his (white Christian) British readers. This arrangement allowed him to describe and comment on the British (and larger white Christian) world; it was part of his interest in pointing out the compelling moral logic and cultural appropriateness of his integration into this world.

The world of the "Eboe," according to Equiano, was not like the world of the British in that the former was, as an example of a somewhat superficial matter, without "places of public worship" (42). Yet in an important respect, in "Eboe" world there were nonetheless "priests"—"Ah-affoe-way-cah"—who, the reader is meant to assume, could be usefully compared to those "priests" (and perhaps also the learned or university men) of the British world. He argued that the "Eboe" priests possessed knowledge about how things came to be and, by logical extension if not also translation of some still unidentified sources, the meaning of things in the present and the way of things in the future. There was also the assumption that the British counterparts—"priests"/learned men—possess that same sort of knowledge and power. This was a reflection of seriously playful,[22] that is, self-reflexive, cultural practices, as well as nuanced comparative theorizing about cultural practices and culture-making.[23]

Most important was what Equiano indicated were the powers of his tribal priests and the operations they represented. He did not seem to know details, but he surmised, or had been told, that they "were held in reverence by the people," that they were successful in "healing wounds and expelling poisons," and that they possessed powers of insight and knowledge that were intimidating and disturbing, beyond the ken of ordinary folks: they had "some extraordinary method of discovering jealousy, theft, and poisoning." (42). These powers, according to Equiano, made that world work. In the priests/magicians/physicians was power, having to do with knowledge, about how things began and how things continued to operate. Most important, these figures seemed always to know what "time" it was: they could "calculate" or figure out the import of things that took place. They could untie knots, figure out the enigmatic.[24]

Although the unsuspecting reader is not given all the clues in Equiano's chapter 1, his story eventually comes to a point of making clear that what the British had instead of the powers of the "Ah-affoe-way-cah" were books and the capacity to "hear" the books speak to them and in turn make them "talk." It is this observation of the British people's engagements with books that helped the historical Equiano over time to come to associate books, especially the Good Book, the Bible, with knowledge of the origins of things, with the ability to know or "calculate" the times in the British world. Those Britons who could read—even those, in Equiano's time, who were *not* priests in the narrow sense of the term—were seen to be knowledgeable and powerful. Those who could not read were seen to be severely disadvantaged. Indeed, those who could read were understood to be more authentically British! And the closer one was positioned to books the more powerful one was thought to be. Priests in the British world were certainly considered powerful, but also powerful were scholars, journalists, pamphleteers, exhorters, jurists—in short, any handlers and wielders of books, all of whom were with few exceptions, elite (= "white") males.[25]

For the phenomenon of the social structuring and centering around scripts, books, reading, around the Book that was the Bible, Equiano had no one particular name or category per se. But this does not mean he did not recognize the phenomenon as such. Beyond his chapter 1 there are repeated references to books, to reading, to the Bible, and how important they were in British society. The reading of books was shown to be important to him as he sought to be integrated into a book-centered, book-reading society. His persistence, even obsession, in learning to read books in general, the Bible in particular, was one of the most important signs of his having become "almost an Englishman." This lack of explicit naming of the phenomenon seems to me to be critical; actually, its absence seems very much by narratological design—part of the narrative-dramatic buildup that shows how Equiano became a mature reader-writer-Christian-almost-Englishman. Certainly, as the story of his life unfolds, the reader can see much evidence of the view of British society as a book-, even more so, a Bible-reading, society. But in Equiano's chapter 1 is only a brief description of the writer's world of origins and perspective on an aspect of its traditions. With some audacity, if not also a bit of playfulness, Equiano here establishes the origins and orientation of his journey toward becoming the type of reader-writer who should be integrated into, even model, modern-day British-ness. The focus on the "Ah-affoe-way-cah" makes a statement not about the facts but about what Equiano wants the reader to understand about Igbo society, and through such, about him and other displaced black peoples.

What clues the reader about Equiano's agenda is the commentary he adds to his description of the work of the Igbo "priests" that serves to explain their power:

> They likewise had some extraordinary method of discovering jealousy, theft, and poisoning; the success of which no doubt

> they derived from their *unbounded influence over the credulity and superstition of the people.* (42; italics mine)

The description/commentary here is very significant. It reveals Equiano's fundamental understanding of what the priestly-magician-shaman-diviner figures mean in terms of the structuring of the society he claims as his world of origins. What does it mean that that society was structured around the "unbounded influence" that the "priests" had "over the credulity and superstition of the people"? What does Equiano want it to mean?

Note again that the statement occurs in a chapter in which the express point was to highlight "the strong analogy" between the Igbos and the ancient Jews, "which... induce[s] me to think that the one people had sprung from the other" (43–44). Two peoples are here imagined and compared: the Igbo and the ancient world (= biblical) Jews: the "one people" is thought to have originated from the other, although this sort of hermeneutical play that involved identification with biblical-world Jews was on Equiano's part a bold argument and mimetic gesture. It identified the people from whom Equiano claims to have sprung: the ancient-world Jews depicted in the Bible. This mimetic gesture made powerful and perhaps disturbing sense precisely because European Christians, both before and in the wake of the development of modern nationalizations,[26] including the British Protestant world that Equiano at that time called home, had come to identify themselves explicitly with such people.[27] Was such a rhetorical move by the Europeans appropriate or compelling? Was Equiano's interpretive play here less appropriate or any more outrageous? Quite obviously, as actual historical tropings of and actual relationships with Jews in early modern Europe indicate, "such people" were only an idealized self-reflection or wedge for modern nation-building. It was because of European Christians' rather long and even taken-for-granted appropriation of—one might even say, expropriation of—biblical-world Jews, on the one hand, and his interest in being integrated into their world, on the other hand, that Equiano thought it logical to analogize in this peculiar way. Imitation, indeed. Equiano was showing himself to be a good Christian (as defined by Europeans).

That the work of the "priests" who made the world of the "Eboes" a "success" is said to be structured on the basis of "unbounded influence over the credulity and superstition of the people" is a rather astounding registration of critical psycho-social analysis, self-consciousness, and positionality: on the one hand, only a person who had already been psychically and socio-politically socialized into or who was at least invested in ingratiating him- or her-self into one of the early modern worlds of the North Atlantic would likely so sharply overdetermine non-Europeans, especially blacks/Africans, by referring to their orientations and sensibilities with freighted terms such as "credulity" and "superstition." One must be socialized into, be taught, such language, such arrogance and prejudice, by a discursive and political system or regime.[28] Equiano's language is a very small step away from Defoe's Crusoe and his language of "my savage," or the "primitives," and so forth, reflecting the sensibilities of European provincials, ironically claiming all the while to represent universals. Such language is a reflection of positionalities and forms of consciousness and power dynamics from the history of first contact between the West and the rest and the beginning of the fateful consequences from such an orientation. It is also clearly status-specific, reflecting the prejudices of dominants within European tribes.[29] Put more specifically, it is language that is reflective of the sensibilities and prejudices of elite Western Europeans. And Equiano's imitation must have greatly disturbed the peace that is in denial about the freighted and contradictory situation.

On the other hand, a person in a profoundly liminal position, on the psycho-social border, not totally integrated into the Western world but also not untouched by it, would likely analyze the work and power of the Igbo priests in terms of "influence." The latter term was not the obvious one for an (uncritical) insider to use to refer to the work or power of these homegrown priests. It is not that an insider would disagree that the Igbo priests had influence; it is simply that the term would hardly seem appropriate for capturing the offices and power of the priests. "Influence" seems to reflect too much the critical, dismissive mindset of the outsider. And an insider would have learned to take for granted, not questioning, the registration of knowledge and power of such persons.

As for "unbounded," few persons in Equiano's homeland would have disagreed that the power of their priests was so. When inspired or challenged to think about the situation, Britons would likely have indicated that the term was not the most apt description of the power or authority that the priests in the British world held: but they were, to be sure, deemed authoritative. They controlled the rituals, including that ritual having to do with interpreting scriptures. But here, again, few unalienated, nondissenting insiders likely raised questions about the extent of the power with which the priests were associated. Only a rather alienated insider or an outsider close enough to notice would likely think about the extent of that power.

Simply raising the issue of "influence," ostensibly in relation to the world of the "Eboes," was a reflection of Equiano's heightened social criticism. Since it was very unlikely, as I have already argued, that Equiano was drawing on first-hand experience or knowledge regarding such a world, but was likely drawing on perspectives from some written sources or an amalgamation of oral sources, what Equiano reveals with such commentary is, to say the least, a rather complex positionality and consciousness. The description of and commentary on the world of the "Eboe," on the one hand, and the rather careful nuanced spare references to the ways of the British world, on the other, are a reflection of Equiano's agenda and the identity of his readers and his intention to move them in a particular way. He sought to move his white evangelical and traditional Christian British readers to see in him one who has become a (qualified) reflection of what they were or said they were. He was commending himself as a model carrier and translator of British orientations and sensibilities. He aimed to make his readers respond to him as one who thinks and writes as one of them. This is the reason there is little need in his chapter 1 to describe and offer commentary about the British world; that world, at least up to this point, is to be taken for granted, to be seen as natural, the center of consciousness, the cultural canon, the lens through which other worlds were to be viewed and judged. What needs description and commentary is that other world, in relationship to which Equiano positioned himself in complex and sensitive terms. Was he really one of the "Eboes"? He claimed to be. He seemed to know some things about them, but not a great deal. What he did seem to know a great deal about—paradoxically evidenced through his depiction of the "Eboes"—were the ways of the British. The description and analysis of the Igbo priests were more reflective of British sensibilities and scope of knowledge than about actual Igbo sensibilities and knowledge.

Equiano writes to and for an imagined British audience with some qualifications, anxiety, and doubt in his own mind about being one of them—he is "almost an Englishman." Notwithstanding some references within the story that make a point about Equiano's origins—in some exotic place that is very far away—in terms of an understanding of the way the world is organized and works and in terms of types of basic sensibilities, the readers are made to understand Equiano as one of them—sort of. What accounts for the qualification? It goes unnamed—Equiano never indicates that the problem he faces in Britain in spite of his good cultivated British ways and sensibilities is that he is black. But how could readers not connect Equiano's narratological dots? How could they not get it—that the problem is antiblack prejudice? Readers are made to know, even if it is not made explicit, that this is the haunting problem throughout the story.

To be sure, the discussion regarding the Igbo priests in chapter 1 notwithstanding, the one who writes—in English—does *not* present himself as reflecting the consciousness and sensibilities of the people in the world of the Igbos, at least not in consistent and unqualified terms. No, the person who writes understands himself as a black "stranger," and the white readers must come to terms with the profoundly odd situation that this writer who engages them—in *their* language, indeed—moves about in their discursive house with ease and grace and wit and passion, but is constantly subjected to physical violence, humiliation, and the threat of re-enslavement. What "almost" as in "almost an Englishman" represents, then, is very much to the main point of the story: to be explained in the story is how Equiano has the consciousness and sensibilities of one who is somewhat inside the British world. This dual positionality then provides the agenda for the rest of the story: beyond his chapter 1 Equiano goes on to explain how he became an English reader/writer; and this means he has the opportunity and burden to offer some commentary on the inconsistent ways and the complex structure of the British world as he experiences it.

This means that the characterization of the work of the Igbo priests in terms of "unbounded" influence" over the people needs to be looked at more carefully. This characterization could easily be understood as the type of license for hyperbole associated with story-telling. But I think more is at issue here: "influence" here can be understood as a chilling and freighted euphemism, a British understatement, that begs the reader to see Equiano's creative critical sensibility and the complexity of his self-identity. What identity among the realistic options presented in the worlds of the story must be assumed in order to think of the work of priests/magicians/shamans in any culture in terms of "influence"? How many clues did Equiano need to put in place for the reader to get the point? Already I have indicated that the terms "credulity" and "superstition" locate Equiano, vis-à-vis the "Eboe" world, as an outsider, a critic reeking of that slight condescension, if not contempt, that marked elite Britons if not most Britons, and elite Europeans if not most Europeans.

Even those Europeans who were not able to travel the seas and make contact with non-Europeans were socialized to regard others as provincial and defective in relation to their grasp of universals and mastery of the known world.

Yet I should like to argue further here that these terms—"credulity," "superstition"—suggest that Equiano is commenting not so much on the gullibility and lack of critical skills of the Igbos; he was really focused on the structure, associated with the work of the priests and magicians, that he understands to have enveloped and overdetermined the thinking and actions, that which served as "unbounded influence" over the Igbo.

In order to gain more perspective on what may be at work in Equiano's use of the term "influence" in discussing the knowledge and power system associated with his homeland, it may be helpful to consider by comparison terminology employed in another domain—cyberspace. Historian of science, philosopher, and social theorist Pierre Levy challenges us to consider the now ironically more easily understood notion of cyberspace in which the "collective intellect" can aid our understanding of what may really be at work in the formation of human culture as a space for the transmission of information and knowledge and sentiment:

> The collective intellect is its own formal cause. Its appearance is not conferred upon it by some external entity. It emerges continuously from the multitude of free relations that are formed within it. Far from being represented by some discrete entity that oversees and structures it, collective intellect expresses itself within an immanent space. Freed of transcendent unity, it will continue to produce and reproduce the folds of its envelope, to redetermine that which will populate its world. It does not need to elect representatives or destroy idols for it to change shape or transform itself, since it is by means of a single continuous movement that creates itself, knows itself and produces its own image. The ability of the collective intellect to become its own formal cause is its greatest achievement, the touchstone of its immanence.... And the more its members are involved in its permanent re-creation, the more the immanent dynamic of expression will favor the proliferation of ways of being.... In this way collective intellect creates a new space.[30]

We are also provided a more widely opened window onto the nature of the "influence" about which Equiano writes from the perspective of what Levy calls cyberspace's "unbroken plane, the *continuum indivis*, the living and changing bath that united signs with living beings, as it did signs with signs."[31] A society can work as a culture—a "new space"—only insofar as there is recognition of some sort of collective intellect or perceived system by which or within which "influence"—reality, knowing, power—is translated. The actual terms on which any society comes to such recognition may differ greatly.

Equiano's language regarding "influence" is even more suggestive and evocative of some of the concepts of semiotics, more specifically, the concept of the "reality" that is the "semiosphere." Semiotician Yuri M. Lotman has taught us to think about the functions of language in terms of the "semiosphere," the "synchronic semiotic space" in which one finds the invention, placement, and valences of separate signs as well as the work of signification, that space which "fills the borders of culture, without which separate semiotic systems cannot function or come into being."[32] Lotman has made an elaborate and convincing summary argument for the study of the semiotics of culture as the study of human "intelligence." The latter, he argues, can be thought about in terms of the three important functions—the transmission of available information (that is, of texts); the creation of new information (that is, of texts . . . which are to some degree unpredictable); and memory (that is, the capacity to preserve and reproduce information).[33]

Lotman's elaborations are especially helpful in provoking questions regarding Equiano's and others' uses of language insofar as he argues that the functions of semiotic systems as he isolated them are also characteristic of semiotic objects. So he argues that the first function—communication—is found in texts; the second function—creation of new information or perspective—is found in artistic "texts"; and so forth.

> [A] minimally functioning semiotic structure consists of not one artificially isolated language or text in that language but of a parallel pair of mutually untranslatable languages which are, however, connected by a "pulley," which is translation. A dual structure like this is the minimal semiotic object such as culture. Thus culture is (as a minimum) a binary semiotic structure, and one which at the same time functions as an indissoluble unit. Thinking along these lines has led us to the concept of the semiosphere and convinced us of the importance of studying the semiotics of culture.[34]

We may with the concept of the semiosphere gain another helpful perspective on Equiano's assumptions about and use of "influence." The latter is now even more suggestive of a type of power structure, turning around signs or discourse.[35] Equiano's thinking of such a system in terms of a semiosphere is illuminating: his story clearly aims to describe the construction of power in the British world. How could he, a sensitive, creative, and articulate person involuntarily pushed onto the peripheries of a dominant society, not be interested in fathoming how that larger dominant world worked, how it was structured? But *how* to think about "it," what to call "it," and how to hold forth about "it"—these were the challenges. Using the obviously self-interested imagined "culture" of the "Eboes" to think with, an inflection of the English term "influence" came to mind. This term served as conceptual place-holder, as poignant abbreviation, code; it stood for that semiotic space, that bubble, that "world" within which the separate discourses, signs, events, and actions (of the imagined world of the Igbos and of Britain and of all worlds beyond) are made to mean. "Influence" conveyed "world"—not merely space or environment, but a discursive space, meaningful space, space in which certain assumptions were made, in which languages and their constitutive units were structured in certain ways.

"Unbounded" refers to the extent or degree of something or to which something obtains. In the context of Equiano's story the term modifies "influence." So he aimed at describing the structural arrangement or system that is in several different respects rather powerful, beyond the ken of ordinary folks to counter. Modifying "influence," "unbounded" here adds up to a structure that can hardly be recognized for what it is much less be easily resisted or overturned.

This description of what the general populace faced in his homeland ultimately reflects less knowledge about and commentary on the Igbos than on Equiano's structure-sensitive and crafty thinking about the British world. He hardly lingers in describing the "Eboes." He applied his early modern somewhat protostructuralist and semiotic thinking in fairly superficial terms to this world; he did not perfectly balance discussion in this immediate context in chapter 1 with the same kind of focus—with description and commentary—on the British world that would follow in narrative line. Yet the discussion about the Igbo did set up the British world for an extended complicated comparison. Equiano discussed how the "Eboe" world was structured and ordered and what and where were the most powerful "unbounded" "influences" on the people. He figured out where he needed to position himself in relation to this sort of arrangement: he registered the Igbo culture and knowledge system as fascinating, noble, and steeped in "superstition." So although he does not in this immediate context elaborate on his thinking about the structure of the British world in direct terms, given the interest in setting up happy comparisons in the chapter, he does imply that the British, and all other tribes of the world, must also have some structure or system of "unbounded influence." And in the story he shows us how his character discovered the British tribal version of the structure, how he came to recognize it, and how with great ingenuity and strength of character he managed to negotiate it with success. He thereby figured himself a savvy translator, reader, and negotiator of cultures; and he challenged his readers to be likewise.

Given this perspective on what Equiano seemed to be doing in terms of the perspective on the two different worlds that his story brings into view, the language of "unbounded influence" takes on special significance. The terminology seems odd, anachronistic, as though Equiano were reaching back—or perhaps upward, in terms of class-specific sentiments. Who thinks and talks this way?[36] The learned (university) men? The British priests? Explorers? Merchants? The language about "unbounded influence" along with the term "superstition" suggests a sneering attitude, even contempt. Whose attitude was this? And why would Equiano want to associate himself with it? Did he believe there was only one legitimate belief system? One legitimate language or discourse system? Language and sentiment here are clearly those of white British elites. Notwithstanding some romanticizing, even idealizing, of the ways of the Igbo peoples, Equiano in the end conveyed the sentiment of white British elites in his comments. The comment that the otherwise noble and powerful "Ah-affoe-way-cah" had "...unbounded influence over the credulity and superstition" of the Igbo people represented the carrying of elite British (or even pan-European) ideological water. Given Equiano's history of enslavement and humiliation at the hands of the British, this was a rather astounding development. Here was represented, for European readers, the contemptuous attitudes of the Europeans about the noble but quite savage other.

But like so much in Equiano's story, things are more complicated. There was likely much more at issue for Equiano than sneering at Igbo culture as "superstition" with "unbounded influence" over the people. As readers, we are addressed by a self-described "stranger" in the British world who sees that empire through a particular set of eyes.[37] So then there is the double irony: not only is Equiano, in terms of both space and time, separated from the world of the "Eboes," he is also psychically separated from it. Yet that very separation afforded him a particular perspective on the British world and gave him a language and conceptual categories with which to comment on and negotiate it. Further, his marginal status far from the center, as well as his activities in and around London in association with elements of its elites and its subalterns, afforded him opportunity to see that world differently, to inhabit it differently.

The notion of "influence" has implications far beyond the world of the "Eboes." In addition to directly registering class-specific sneering, it may also reflect Equiano's boldness and playfulness—with deadly serious implications, of course. It may suggest that Equiano was willing to name and confront and possibly undermine dominant cultural sentiments and stereotypes. The very broaching of the subject, after all, suggests that he had learned to think about worlds in complex hypercritical terms: his thinking went below and beyond the surfaces.

"Influence," then, may be taken, especially in light of what follows in the story, as irony: the picture of the Igbo is a picture of all "tribes" of the world. And the extent to which Equiano sneers a bit at Igbo, he positions himself to be able to sneer at other kinds of "tribes," white tribes, most notably the British. The use of the freighted terms would then seem to indicate his critical positionality, even regarding his homeland. The system that he describes in connection with the Igbo is not accepted by him as natural or legitimate. Indeed, "superstition" and influence" betray just a hint of a suspicion that the system that controls the world is to an extent smoke and mirrors, make believe. That such terms are used in a discussion about the operations of those understood to be "priests"/"magicians"/ "physicians" is most telling: since these individuals were the ones who by "some extraordinary method" knew things—including how to "calculate" the times, read hidden emotions (42), and know "how all things had a beginning" (68),[38] they had insight into things that others could not possess. They controlled the substance and media of knowledge.

What Equiano was arguing about in regard to such individuals was that they had enormous power. But the "success" they had was not something that should be associated with breaking rocks or manipulating the weather, and so forth. No, the "extraordinary method" that resulted in their "success" should be associated with their capacity to convince the people, to manipulate their minds and sentiments in ways and to degrees that established and sustained—that is, make people accept or naturalize, "make do with"—the larger order, structure, and arrangements. It was in this respect that what they represented was "unbounded influence." What Equiano seemed to have discovered, and aptly applied first (in narrative order) to the "Eboe" world, was the ability on the part of the priestly figures to "make-believe," to practice "magic."[39] His larger interest had to do with registering the complex establishment of a system of knowledge that represents a certain "reality" within which people are oriented.

As disturbing as the terminology regarding "unbounded influence" and the analysis of it in terms of "semiosphere" and "reality" may seem, it is important to understand that Equiano does not express displeasure with the situation he describes. On the contrary, he views the situation with some detachment.[40] The "Eboan" priests are not characterized as being duplicitous hyprocrites or shady swindlers who have duped the people; they are understood as creative powerful individuals filling roles mapped out for them and expected of them. Equiano's perspective on these figures opens a different critical-analytical window onto these roles in society and culture in general. Through his "sketch," a "strong analogy" between (biblical not early modern or contemporary) "Jews" (43–44) and (romanticized narratologically invented not contemporary) "Eboan Africans" (44), the reader is deliberately led to wonder to whom these figures, their operations, and the consequences of such may be compared among contemporaries. His interest was not historicist. That Equiano was indeed thinking and arguing about the contemporary situation and its challenges, about how the "Eboe" priests may be identified and understood in the contemporary British world, is made clear enough in the discussion in which he quickly pivots his "sketch" away from ancient-biblical "Jews" ("Israelites") and ancient-biblical-world-like Igbo (= "Africans") to "modern Jews" and "Eboan Africans"/"natives of Africa":

> Like the Israelites in their primitive state, our government was conducted by our chiefs, our judges, our wise men, and elders; and the head of a family with us enjoyed a similar authority over his household with that which is ascribed to Abraham and the other patriarchs. The law of retaliation obtained almost universally with us as with them;... we had our circumcision... we also had our sacrifices and burnt-offerings, our washings and purifications, on the same occasions as they had....

> As to the difference of colour between the Eboan Africans and the modern Jews, I shall not presume to account for it. It is a subject which has engaged the pens of men of both genius and learning, and is far above my strength.... [The many attempts to address the issue] it is hoped may... remove the prejudice that some conceive against the natives of Africa on account of their colour. (44–45)

It could not be made clearer to the reader that here Equiano's bottom line interest has to do with *contemporary* Africans in the North Atlantic and the challenges they face—including enslavement. That he at some points puts the matter in more delicate and indirect terms—"difference of colour," "the prejudice that some conceive against the natives of Africa"—(ironically) reflects his sensitivity to his (primarily white) readers. But he cannot sustain his delicateness of expression: he picks up a bit of sarcasm in order to begin to reveal one of the major issues behind the writing of his story:

> The Spaniards, who have inhabited America, under the torrid zone... are become as dark coloured as our native Indians of Virginia, of which I myself have been a witness. There is also another instance of a Portuguese settlement at Mitomba, a river in Sierra Leone, where the inhabitants are bred from a mixture of the first Portuguese discoverers with the natives, and are now become, in their complexion, and in the woolly quality of their hair, perfect negroes.... Surely the minds of the Spaniards did not change with their complexions! (44–45)

In this same context he ratchets up the rhetorical heat as he addresses even more pointedly the European Christian-cultural irrationality of antiblack prejudice and the subjugation and enslavement of black peoples:

> Are there not causes enough to which the apparent inferiority of the African may be ascribed, without limiting the goodness of God, and supposing he forebore to stamp understanding on certainly his own image, because "carved in ebony"? Might it not naturally be ascribed to their situation? When they come among Europeans, they are ignorant of their language, religion, manners, and customs. Are any pains taken to teach them these? Are they treated as men? Does not slavery itself depress the mind, and extinguish

> all its fire, and every noble sentiment? . . . what advantages do not a refined people possess over those who are rude and uncultivated? Let the polished and haughty European recollect that his ancestors were once, like the Africans, uncivilized, and even barbarous. Did nature make them inferior to their sons? And should they too have been made slaves? Every rational mind answers, No. (45)

At the very end of this chapter Equiano includes what becomes a rhetorical pattern—he appends at the end of many of the chapters that follow what may be labeled something approaching scriptural exposition, almost homiletical in style, complete with quotations of passages. Chapter 10, which includes Equiano's conversion episode, not surprisingly, has in it the most extensive focus on scriptural passages, but it is nonetheless an exception in terms of the end-of-chapter scriptural exposition; that exception that makes the point here: chapter 10 and the blocks of scriptural passages within it seem to be the lynchpin of Equiano's story. When the frontispiece—a portrait of Equiano depicted in English gentleman's clothing holding a Bible open to a particular passage (included above in the Prologue)—is added to the chapter endings, an agenda is made even clearer: Christian scriptures, normally assumed to be confused with being British, normally assumed to be authoritatively traduced and translated and interpreted by the British authorities (more specifically, the British priests), are now understood to be used in particular ways for the sake of the re-construction and maintenance of society as Equiano's story envisions. This is the situation about which Equaino's rhetorics regarding the "unbounded influence" of the "Eboan" priests hinted. This is the chief point of his "analogy" between the two worlds. It is a hard truth to fathom: there is in it a "hidden meanin'." In Equiano's story scriptures are understood to function in ways that comport with the Igbo structure of divination. They are understood to unveil the most sensitive, controversial, painful, and troubling truths. They are used to communicate in other terms—terms that are indirect and deflecting yet pointed because they communicate what matters most that are supposed to matter most.

Most important for Equiano, scriptures were "used" because he came to understand them to be fully implicated, perhaps, as the most important underlying factor, in the structuring of the British world. The establishment clerics and the evangelical exhorters in the one world, and the "Eboe" priests in the other, were seen by Equiano as inhabiting the same roles. So the reason to conclude every chapter with references to the Bible, to have oneself visually depicted on the frontispiece of his book as a rather earnest teacher of the Bible, is not so much because of a flat and amorphous apolitical assumption or argument about biblical authority, but in order to register a sensitive and sharp awareness of the way things were ordered in the British world.

The "unbounded influence over the credulity and superstition of the people" that in Equiano's chapter 1 is identified with the "Eboe" priests leads Equiano to implicitly compare to the phenomenon of the reading of scriptures in the British world. Equiano schematizes his story so that it makes plain the significance of scriptures, to every British citizen, and to himself. In spite of the enormous challenges and setbacks he experienced, the Equiano of the story seeks to learn to read the scriptures every chance he gets. Only when he has learned to read and to understand books, particularly the Bible, on certain terms (first Anglican, but then a construal of Protestant evangelical), does he become "almost an Englishman," or an "African Christian."[41] In fact, the quest to learn to read the scriptures could be said to be the theme of the story. At any rate, in his quest to learn, Equiano betrays his understanding that the key to knowing the structure and terms of negotiation of the British world are in direct relationship to the scriptures. The latter may in his mind represent many things, but among them is his view that they are the key to the semiosphere that was the British world.

Equiano has no explicit term that he uses throughout his story to refer to what scriptures meant in the British world. If appropriate comparison is made between scriptures and (his description of) the operations of the priests of the Igbo world, then Equiano's interest in the story-telling that follows his chapter 1 had to do with the connection between scriptures and the "make-believe" that accounts for the structures and arrangements of the British world. The term "make-believe" is particularly apt, but not because it has to do with un- or sur-reality. It is both constructed and real: it is real-ity precisely because it is layered and complex, operating above and below the usual levels of "reality" and appearances. It is reality insofar as it is a reflection of some aspects of both coercion and assent, a reflection of different types and degrees of violence as well as different forms of the giving of credence. I prefer here to call this structure of "make-believe" that Equiano does not really name but nonetheless dramatizes and problematizes, that is, uses as a basis for the advancement of his story of his life, "scripturalization."

This term is my reference to much more than text—including the one text that is the Bible. Although there is no doubting that the Bible holds the greatest social-cultural symbolic significance in terms of constellating the phenomenon of scripturalization, this phenomenon needs to be distinguished from any one text that may be abstracted from it. Scripturalization is also not to be collapsed into textuality; the latter represents only the historically persistent and dramatic surfacing and pinpointing of the phenomenon of scripturalization. What I argue in this book—as an elaboration and rationalization of Equiano's narratization of his life—is that scripturalization should be conceived as a *semiosphere, within which a structure of reality is created that produces and legitimates and maintains media of knowing and discourse and the corresponding power relations.* Although this structure is not to be collapsed into texts, in the modern period of history—on this side of Gutenberg—it revolves mainly around issues having to do with texts. It is sustained in complex relationship to texts and so begs to be complexly analyzed, viz., viewed through the creative application of the ethnography and ethnology, the sociology, social history, politics/power dynamics, and social psychology of reading texts, reflecting social textures that are ideological-discursive, social-political, social psychological in nature.

But these are simply fancy categories for the raising of basic issues about Equiano's life. His story raises basic but utterly disturbing and even threatening questions and issues—about many things, many phenomena, many situations, having to do with scriptures. Approached through the critical lenses named and their questions and issues, scripturalization as semiosphere will be seen to be not simply *about* literacy or the capacity to read in general or even to read a canon or classic text of the society. Recognizing that this phenomenon is not the same as but revolves around texts, and acknowledging the need to raise a complex of basic questions and issues, it becomes clearer that the created structure that we must seek to understand is a "reading formation"[42]—a particular orientation, a way of seeing and engaging the world, a make-believe, that is most apparent through the engagement of texts. Such a formation can obtain only within a structure. Equiano turns the reader's attention to this phenomenon of scripturalization through his experiences as being both inside and outside the structure, outside the world he faced and negotiated. He raises the issue of scripturalization as the arrangement of that world; he does not make it less complex; he does not explain all that is to be explained about its origins; and he does not chart the course of its history. He makes compelling the fathoming of the phenomenon as he shows us how he managed to identify, engage, and negotiate it as a complex world.

Finally, the "unbounded influence" that Equiano calls "magic," and that I call "scripturalization," refers to a type of structure of power and can be otherwise understood in terms of slavery. Of course, given what Equiano had been forced to be and do, slavery would be another reference that would be poignant and illuminating. Insofar as the magic of the priests is held to be without limits, its operations and calculations held to be dazzling, mystifying, and left unquestioned—to this extent it is lord and master. The silence of the book in relationship to the young Equiano in Equiano's story (his chapter 3) who was as a slave a nonreader made sense, especially since the reader of the narrative is made to understand "reading" in broad terms. Those who cannot read letters and read worlds are deemed slavish. The incredulity and superstition of a people already means enslavement—"someone or something with 'unbounded influence' over another" (his chapter 1). Notwithstanding some differences in customs, the two worlds—Igbo and white men—have in common systems of magic that are systems of enslavement that need to be critically analyzed and negotiated.

In the following chapters I allow Equiano's story to raise different aspects of scripturalization as the system of magic that defines the world of the white men. These aspects are discussed as different stages in and aspects of the evolution and complexity of the phenomenon. In chapter 2 I attempt to explain scripturalization as social-cultural matrix, within which ideological and discursive rules and practices are evident.

2

"...*the white men had some spell or magic*...": *A Black Stranger's First Contact with White Men's Magic*

I was now more persuaded than ever that I was in another world, and that everything about me was magic.... I was very much affrighted at some things I saw...any object I saw filled me with new surprise.... I...asked...the use of it, and who made it.

—OLAUDAH EQUIANO, *Interesting Narrative*, chapter 2

IN THE PROLOGUE I indicated that I had come to recognize my beginnings in relationship to the phenomenon of the fraught moments, from the fifteenth through the nineteenth centuries, having to do with the "first contact" between the West and the worlds of the Other. The historical situation and the dynamics and phenomena that ensued from these moments—most notably transatlantic slave-trafficking systems and their correlative economies, politics, and practices—must be confronted in order for us to understand what we as differently positioned moderns have become. Those moments and the deeds done in them lead us to some of the issues that Equiano's story opens up for critical thinking. Among many such issues, inspired by the anxieties felt by the dominant Europeans in their interactions with the dominated nonwhites in Africa and elsewhere, was that of the making (or at least fateful shaping) of what we now all too casually call "religion."[1] The latter was not so much created in this situation as it was re-created, re-activated, and re-intensified, made meaningful on the different terms that the new situation of contact made pressing. "Religion" came to be experienced and understood as a "site" or domain of enormous complexity. The European "discovery" of the Other led to the construction of a wedge, a mark of difference, between dominants and nondominants—the "savage" and the "civilized." The intense interest in drawing lines of distinction and hierarchies provoked the question about "religion"—what it was, to what it pertained, to whom it belonged, where it was to be located, what forms and gestures and practices were to be associated with it, and so forth. In this new situation and its discursive-political climate, dominated peoples—savages/primitives—could now be seen as being either hyperreligious or not religious at all, or not religious on the right terms. Such peoples were thereby defined in terms of their geographical and linguistic-discursive distance from the center defined by the dominants. Dominants came to associate themselves with certain formations and practices that they named "religion," the most important of which was related to various European vernacularizations of ancient (Near Eastern and Mediterranean) traditions, including what they coopted as their "classical" or canonical or "sacred" languages and texts.[2]

What was set in motion was a history of rigid classifications and hierarchializations that in effect codified the characteristics that were invented on the basis of the first contact. This effect probably obtained on both sides, at least in the earliest period of contact, the period in which Europeans found themselves on African soil without control.[3] (That this situation would not long obtain is of course the history that everyone in the Atlantic world knows and now must respond to.) The classifications and hierarchializations that set in for the long, violently discursive haul not only determined the fate of those who were signified as "other," they also sadly (mis-)shaped European discursivity and self-awareness and made toxic its relations with the differences that it now confronted.

Consider, for example, the development of early modern European forms of nationalization. Along with, if not in fact nurtured by, oligarchic capitalist economic interests, the sense of adventure, curiosity, and daring, the spirit of risk-taking, and modernist sensibilities, clearly one of the most important factors that led to the domination of the peoples of the newly "discovered" worlds, was the development of a supratribal spatial-extensive nationalist consciousness. Given impetus from the violent and all too costly multigenerational European wars and conflicts of the sixteenth and seventeenth centuries, modern European nationalizations both reflected and generated changed views about many issues and arrangements long taken for granted.[4]

Among the many changes that took place in this volatile situation was "religion." Conflicting dynamics emerged and required negotiation. For different reasons—war-weariness, social and religious conflicts, emerging ethnographic studies, and the orientations and sensibilities of "enlightenment" figures—there emerged the broadly shared if not pan-European view that what had been taken for granted as "religion" should be reconsidered, paradoxically, to be both relegated more strictly and consistently to a particular domain (the "spiritual"/"private," as opposed to the "secular"/ "political"/"public") in society and culture and at the same time made more influential in its relations with the newly discovered peoples in their newly "discovered" behaviors. Even as "religion" became more restricted and less pervasive in traditional or superficial terms, it became more powerful in terms of providing, for example, the ideological and discursive framework for the modern nations.

A most interesting example of how religion was made to work in this period can be seen in the phenomenon that social historians of the period have called "confessionalization."[5] On one level, this phenomenon may seem to reflect only the narrow religious-doctrinal schisms that had defined the period. But it may also be seen in terms of the dynamics of sociocultural and political differentiation, that is, the explosion or breakup of what had been the reigning traditional ecclesiastical monoculture of the European-defined "medieval" period. What confessionalization represented was a vehicle for the establishment of ideological-political definition and delimitation. It contributed to the ideological and political shaping of the emergent civilizational movements (otherwise known as Protestant and Catholic nations). Thus, Catholic countries could recognize and ally with their own kind and Protestant countries, their internal differentiation and infrapolitics notwithstanding, could recognize each other and collaborate. Differences over dogma were only the surface issue; it was not that doctrinal differences were not real, but broader issues—social-cultural, economic, political—were at times so difficult, if not impossible to address for what they were, never mind negotiate; and of course, the heritage of the Holy Roman Empire with its cooptation of the texts and discourses and other traditions of the ancient Mediterrranean and Near Eastern worlds easily lent itself to the explosion of doctrinal disputes.

What was fundamentally at issue in or behind the confessionalization movement was a kind of discursive logic built upon literacy—the reading and sometimes excruciatingly detailed exegesis of the pan-European culturally shared authoritative texts. Belonging to the newly defined "nation" also meant understanding or at least formally acceding to the creedal formulations by which each had distinguished itself. Because they represented the relatively new formations, the Protestant nations were prolix in their registrations and more aggressive in their intonations. Catholic nations were not without their responses to such practices. Acceding to certain creedal statements signified social-cultural and (emergent) national affiliation. What obtained was a situation that was defined by the offensive and defensive practices of the politics of exegesis translated into the politics and persistent violence of modern nation-building.

This was at least an important aspect of the situation that obtained in Britain when Equiano wrote his story. Britain had come to understand itself as a particular confessional society insofar as it arrogated to itself authority as a scripture-reading nation. As I will argue in more detail in chapters 2 through 4, precisely because of his status as the "stranger," around which he built his story, Equiano saw more clearly the nature of the ideological structure of British society, especially its fetishistic uses of scriptures.

The power dynamics that are part of the contact between the West and the rest of the world, and the European infrapolitics that also obtained in the beginning of the modern era, make genuinely outsider perspective hard to come by; outsiders have historically been rendered silent or their sentiments ignored. Therefore, it is rather important that we have in Equiano's story one of the few layered and complex registrations of sentiments about the larger situation. His story reflects the discursive forms (novelistic life story), conceptualizations (British scripture-reading), and the language of the dominants; yet no reader can avoid learning that his story is written by one who was made to be a "stranger" by the violent dynamics of first contact. There are enough ironies and paradoxes in this fraught situation to be quite "interesting."

Equiano's narrative is particularly "interesting" for the window it opens onto the power situation inherent in the dynamics of fetishization[6] and vernacularization.[7] Equiano sees himself as focal point of moral and political-economic crises that were brought on by violent conquest, disruption, and enslavement. He sees himself as qualified insider ("almost an Englishman"), having been made outsider ("stranger") through expropriation of his labors. Given his enslavement and the persistent humiliation that followed his "freedom," given his worldwide travel and work experiences, his highly developed sensibilities (developed and communicated mostly through religious conversion),[8] and given his reading and writing skills, he understands himself to offer in his story a (singular or unique) picture (also, window-mirror?) of one looking in on the society that thinks itself a unique part if not the center of the world.[9]

Equiano's story reflects awareness of and a creative response to the mid-to-late eighteenth-century situation that was itself a legacy of the previous centuries of European internal religious-inflected conflict. This was also the century when more extensive and complex commerce and trade developed among European nations, including slave-trafficking as a significant part of its underpinning, which had as collateral toxicity increasing anti-black racialist rhetorics as rationalization and legitimation. As reflected in the letters and petitions to which he was signatory, if not also instigator and author, Equiano's activism was a response to the increase in volume—and shrillness—of "scientific," literary, and "religious" discourses about race. Few persons of the period, certainly few non-Europeans finding themselves involuntarily in Europe and European colonies, would be unaware of such rhetorics and their effects. "Strangers"—non-Europeans recently "discovered"—were directly affected in all sorts of negative ways. They could not fail to notice that in social locations ranging from the universities to palaces and parliaments to churches and taverns and debating halls they were the focus of discussions and scholarly inquiry. They were very much aware that they were overdetermined, were made to be in such discourses, for the sake of nationalist politics and commercial interests, what Europeans wanted and needed them to be.

The blacks-made-slaves were aware of the contempt in which they were held among Europeans. They were aware of how they ranked in the regime of the new racial hierarchializations of that period. In the Europeans' new ideological schema, inspired by the "discovery" of the Others, captured most vividly in the notion of the "Great chain of being," blacks were clearly at the bottom, both reflecting and legitimizing their humiliation as "hewers of wood and drawers of water."[10]

The historical backdrop of this humiliation as Equiano and his black contemporaries experienced it in England is in the early- to mid-seventeenth century. This was a period of social and political upheaval in North Atlantic worlds—England in particular—in which, as Peter Linebaugh and Marcus Rediker put it, "variously designated dispossessed commoners, transported felons, indentured servants, religious radicals, pirates, urban labourers, soldiers, sailors, and African slaves," along with some women who crossed many of these categories, made common cause to a degree and for a limited time, as a monstrous and threatening "many-headed hydra."[11] Note should be taken of some aspects of this period in order to gain perspective on what Equiano experienced.[12]

Since the beginnings of English colonial expansion in the seventeenth century the powerful had been given to referring to the myth involving Hercules and the hydra as a way to describe the challenges of imposing "order" on the new mixed global rabble of laborers. The colonizers were cast as Hercules, the rabble as the hydra. The use of the myth in this period expressed the fear in the new situation that the volatility might bring chaos and disaster.

While the socioculturally and economically powerful, for some obvious reasons, tended to lump together all the nonpowerful as constant potential threats to their position—Edmund Burke's "swinish multitude"[13]—it is both fascinating and chilling to note that among the nonelites, those who imagined themselves radical transformers of the already transformed world, blacks were singled out as outcasts, as signs of evil, the all too convenient discursive code to reflect the antithesis of their identity and aspirations in the new context.[14]

An especially unnerving and uncomfortable example is found in John Bunyan, then and even now in many circles the famous icon of European religious radicalism. Known among the "roarers," "ranters," "bell-ringers," and "soldiers" in opposition to establishment government, church, and society, converted by a woman who led him to membership into one of those radical female-directed religious formations (congregationalists of all sorts), Bunyan became the heralded hero of a far-flung and complex movement. Yet on the other side of the revolutionary period, his somewhat nostalgic millenarian writings also carried a rather virulent strain of antiblack rhetoric. In his famous heavily allegorical work *Pilgrim's Progress* (1678) blacks were all too easily made to figure sin and evil, the antagonist of the Christian. The protagonist Christian encountered "a man black of flesh," who "flattereth his Neighbour [and] spreadeth a Net for his feet."[15] Christiana, wife of Christian, met "the vile person" who, like the Ethiopian referred to in the Bible, "can never be washed clean."[16] In a poem for children Bunyan contrasted Moses as "fair and comely" to his wife, "a swarthy Ethiopian."[17] In his war memoirs (*The Holy War* [1682]), Bunyan begins with the following allegorical backdrop that poignantly reverses and undermines the historical truth about colonial violence:

> Well, upon a time there was one Diabolus, a mighty Gyant, made an assault upon this famous Town of Mansoul, to take it, make it

> his habitation. This Gyant was King of the Blacks or Negroes, and most raving Prince he was.[18]

What might we make of Bunyan, this hero of (British) radical Protestant evangelicalism? What of his rhetorical moves? What of his consciousness and politics of an allegorical-symbolization system that makes use of a racialized, specifically antiblack, ideology to advance a radically absolutist and polarized piety?, Even as it seems to be focused on purely spiritual conflicts and strivings, does not such a system contribute to an unacknowledged and unnamed ideology of dominance of whiteness? Why otherwise were black peoples figured as evil at the expense of solidarity with them as co-dissenters, as being among those who were ex-centrics and critics of the center? What was the chief motivation for the antiblack figuration? Where was the fault line, if it was not at the point of faith or outsider status? Was it simply a matter of lazily falling back upon centuries-old tropes for the sake of advancing and sharpening a polarity? If not, what should we make of throwing real black peoples under the rhetorical bus for the sake of sharpening the religious-ideological polarity?[19] Whatever the motive, was not the result a more explicit whitening of Christianity? Did such rhetorical practices not lead to the easy but fateful confusion of evangelical piety and existence with being white, sin with being black?

Lest the example of Bunyan's rhetorics be understood as too convenient a critical target, somehow atypical of European sentiments about black peoples and about race and race-ism during the period—merely a matter of rhetoric run wild, of allegorizing run amok—I turn to another example, from the same historical period, also included in Linebaugh and Rediker's volume—the story of a black woman named Francis. A religious radical ("Anabaptist"), an independent and outspoken woman, and a black ("West Indian")—in one person, she was a triple threat in the minds of those threatened by hydrarchy. Her story, or the part of her story that can be stitched together from the one fraught and tendentious source left about her, makes the powerful case about how strong and pervasive, how basic and sedimented, just how complexly real was the structure of what I term scripturalization, how powerfully ramifying it was in the confusion of Christian faith and whiteness. That this was the case within the dynamism that was the radical evangelical subculture of the seventeenth century should be noted as our current situation in the world in terms of racial hierarchializations and religious fundamentalisms is inventoried and analyzed.

Linebaugh and Rediker draw to our attention precious little but rather freighted information available about "a Blackymore Maide Named Francis" of mid-seventeenth-century England. We know about this woman only through the writing of Edward Terrill, an elder of one of those female-inspired "radical religious congregations" that had emerged from the revolutionary period. As part of his apologetic and nostalgic history of the church—*The Records of a Church of Christ in Broadmead, Bristol, 1640–1678*[20] (later formed and called a Baptist church)—Terrill, drawing upon his various written sources and oral histories, including interviews with founder Dorothy Hazzard, made reference to Francis. It is poignant that no other name is given her, only the demeaning overdetermining "blackymore." It is likely that "Francis" was referred to by the (fictive) "family" of congregants as "sister," possibly even as "mother." That Terrill, writing as member of the "family" himself, did not bring himself to describe her in this way speaks loudly, in anticipation of a problem to which the critical reader-interpreter must be alert. To whom was he writing? For what cause, that sister Francis should be referred to in such a manner? Sister Francis was obviously an important member of the congregation—"pillar" is a word often used to refer to such persons. In the telling of the story of the congregation this "one Memmorable member" very likely could not possibly have been overlooked if Terrill wanted his "history" to be considered in some sense honest and accurate. At any rate, as will be made clear, in the end Terrill made Francis serve his writing agenda.

Also referred to by Terrill as a "servant," as an "Ethyopian," as "this poor Aethiopian" (in bold), sister Francis was certainly nonetheless in the "record,"[21] if not in intimate memories, kept in her place, very much overdetermined as an inferior (even as she was, according to Terrill, much beloved, of course). Part of what was at issue was the handling of the truth about sister Francis's conversion experience and powerful charismatic and spiritual leadership, including her office of "exhortation." This truth could not be altogether denied or erased from the record; but for certain reasons it had to be nuanced, spun, carefully scripted.

> [S]he gave greate ground for Charity to believe she was truly brought over to Christ...and she walked very humble and blamelesse in her Conversation, to her end; and when she was upon her death bed: She sent a Remarkable Exhortation unto ye whole Church with whom she walked, as her last request unto them: which argued

> her holy, childlike fear of ye Lord; and how precious the Lord was to her Soule; as was observed by the manner of her Expressing it. Which was this, one of the Sisters of ye congregation coming to visit her, in her Sicknesse, She solemnly took her leave of her, as o this world; and pray'd ye sister, to remember her to ye whole congregation, and to tell them, that she did Begg every soule, To take heed that they did lett **The glory of God to be dear unto them** a word meet for ye Church ever to remember; and for every member to observe, that they doe not loose ye glory of God in their families, neighbourhoods or places where God casts them: it being ye dyeing words of a Blackmoore, fir for a White heart to store. After which this Aethiopian yielded up ye Spirit to Jesus that redeemed her and was Honourably Interred being carried by ye Elders & ye chiefest of note of ye Brethren un ye Congregation (Devout men bearing her) to ye grave.[22]

It was not enough for Terrill simply to describe sister Francis's power and the congregation's esteem and love for her. He included what are likely some of her words, as remembered by parishioners.[23] The emphasis that he placed (bold in his text) on "The glory of God to be dear unto them" as among the likely final words of sister Francis (communicated to another sister) reflects his recognition of her prophetic offices and powers, probably including her co-founding of the congregation. But again, he needed to put his spin on this situation. That spin drew upon the Bible in an effort, at the very end of the focus on Francis, to make certain that "this poor Aethiopian" would nonetheless be put into proper perspective for the (later) reader "in our days"[23]:

> By this in our days, we may see, Experimentally, that Scripture made good, *oux est proso poleptes ho theos. Alla en panti ethnei*, that God is no respecter of faces: But among all nations, &. Acts 10:34:35.

The normal English translation of the Greek *poleptes*, is "persons," not "faces," as Terrill has it. This translation is quite fascinating, incredible even: "faces" as the translation draws attention to physical features, to sister Francis's *black* face, a sign of the status of her humiliation in the larger dominant *white* world.[24] Terrill seemed to need to remind the reader that sister Francis was after all a "blackamoor," with no real status, no rights, no privileges appertaining therewith. The point surely was to readjust the focus—from the radical view of Francis as "sister," as equal, with differences that have come to be associated with color and race greatly relativized as part of what was understood to be the biblical-spiritual ideal, to a view (his own, but surely also representing others in his circle in time) in which her difference is highlighted and made to serve the infracultural apologetic interests of a congregation defined by and centered around whites and whiteness while feigning only otherworldly interests. Francis (and her kind) came to be troped (away); her membership in the circle of believers was deemed a dramatic fulfillment of scriptures, insofar as she was black-faced: "God is no respecter of" difference. Never mind that sister Francis was actually very likely one of the dynamic and defining forces if not also one of the founders of the congregation. She was a pillar, not a commercial for evangelical growth and establishment. That the congregation, as part of the story it told about itself, originally experienced tensions with the larger world around these very issues, having defined itself as part of the promiscuous rabble constituting the monstrous hydra, makes Terrill's scripture-inflected revisionism all the more poignant—and violent. In the slightly later period in which Terrill writes, the church defines its constituency and its ideology as white and, as such, at the expense of, albeit in loving memory of, Francis the "Ethyopian." We should wonder how Francis used scriptures and what *she* would have made of the verses Terrill played with.[25]

So Bunyan's runaway allegorical games do not seem so innocent or merely spiritual. One can, with Edward Terrill's inscriptions,declaring interest only in the "facts," see more clearly what games and gestures and politics they reflect and what realities they create. His writings were, like most writings, viewed as dazzling, mystifying, somewhat "magical" in their power. Blacks in the Europe of the seventeenth and eighteenth centuries were very heavily signified as different and inferior beings whose humiliation and subjugation could be understood within a developing racial classification schema and ideology such that the cultivation of "whiteness"—associated with being the most fortunate, the strongest, most robust, most intelligent, most adventurous, and so forth—could be contrasted to the blackness of the "negroes."

This development led to rather difficult and challenging circumstances for blacks in Britain.[26] The eighteenth century ushered in even more virulent racialisms in "scientific" and "philosophical" discourses from the pens of those who were and still are held to be the best minds of humankind. So David Hume in his "Of National Characters":

> I am apt to suspect the negroes and in general all other species of men (for there are four or five different kinds) to be naturally inferior to the *whites*. There never was a civilized nation of any other complexion than white, nor even any individual eminent either in action or speculation. No ingenious manufactures amongst them, no arts, no sciences.... Such a uniform and constant difference could not happen, in so many countries and ages if nature had not made an original distinction between these breeds of men. Not to mention our colonies, there are negroe slaves dispersed all over Europe, of whom none ever discovered any symptoms of ingenuity; though low people without education will start up amongst us and distinguish themselves in every profession. In Jamaica, indeed, they talk of one negroe as a man of arts and learning; but it is likely he is admired for slender accomplishments, like a parrot who speaks a few words plainly.[27]

The cultivation of modern world white-ness in relationship to blackness—recently "discovered," up close and chained—led to ever more phenomenal jaw-dropping blanket assertions, descriptions, and explanations that have nonetheless long been accepted by many as truth. So Immanuel Kant in his "On the Different Races of Man":

> [A]ll humans in the whole world belong to the same natural genus.... Among the deviations—i.e., the hereditary differences of animals belonging to a single stock—those which, when transplanted... maintain themselves over protracted generation, and which also generate hybrid young whenever they interbreed with other deviations of the same stock, are called *races*. [his emphasis].... In this way Negroes and Whites are different species of humans (for they presumably belong to one stock), but they are different races, for each perpetuates itself in every area and generate between them children that are necessarily hybrid, or blendings (mulattoes).... I believe it is necessary to assume four races of man in order to derive from them all the differences which are ascertainable on first sight and which perpetuate themselves: They are (1) the race of Whites, (2) the Negro race, (3) the Hunnic

> (Mongolian)or Kalmuck race, (4) the Hindu or Hindustanic race.... The reason for assuming the Negroes and *Whites* [my emphasis] to be fundamental races is self-evident.... To be sure we cannot hope any more to come upon the unaltered original human form anywhere in the world. Precisely because of Nature's propensity to adapt to the soil everywhere over long generations, the human form must now everywhere be supplied with local modifications. But that portion of the earth between the 31st and the 52nd parallels in the Old World (which seems to earn the name of Old World even from the standpoint of peopling) is rightly held to be that in which the most happy mixture of influences of the colder and hotter regions and also the greatest wealth of earthly creatures is encountered; where man too must have departed the least from his original formation because from here he is equally well prepared for all transplantations.[28]

These sentiments reflected and constructed the larger dominant discursive world in which Equiano found himself. It was a world full of people, in dominant and nondominant circles, who had come to think of themselves as white, grounding their superiority on the basis of their whiteness, in sharp contrast to all other colored peoples, especially the black peoples of the world.

In the wake of the discoveries of the "savages" and the possibilities for their subjugation and exploitation in the sixteenth and seventeenth centuries, every sector of European life by the eighteenth century had come to register the dominance of the European world. And it was skin color, such an easy and obvious point of difference, that was made to signify the dominance. Yet what was needed for the trick—dominance based on whiteness—to continue to work, to represent the surety of the dominance, was some rather dramatic focal point. That focal point turned out to be something mysterious (of course!), variously referred to as beauty, sentiment or sensibility, imagination or reason. In all categories and in all respects that said to matter, blacks are found wanting. So Thomas Jefferson:

> Comparing [blacks] by their faculties of memory, reason, and imagination, it appears to me that they are equal in memory to the whites; in reason much inferior, as I think one could scarcely be found capable of tracing and comprehending the investigations of Euclid; and that in imagination they are dull, tasteless and anomalous... never

> yet could I find that a black uttered a thought above the level of plain narration; never seen even an elementary trait of painting or sculpture. In music they are more generally gifted than the whites with accurate ears for tune and time.... Misery is often the parent of the most affecting touches in poetry.—Among the blacks is misery enough, God knows, but no poetry. Love is peculiar oestrum of the poet. Their love is ardent, but it kindles the senses only, not the imagination. Religion indeed has produced a Phyllis Whately [*sic*!]; but it could not produce a poet.... I advance it therefore as a suspicion only, that the blacks... are inferior to the whites in the endowments both of body and mind.[29]

Terrill was unwilling to record the truth about Sister Francis's spiritual virtuosity; Jefferson considered such interest and adeptness hardly worth mentioning. There was in this situation very little opportunity left for the development of black humanity and agency.

Back to Equiano: surely one of the reasons the episode about the "talking book" has resonated so powerfully with Equiano and other black Atlantic writers from the eighteenth century to the present has to do with the need to pinpoint the problematics around and ultimately enhance black agency. With the episode one could name the focal point of difference and claims about dominance and the needed response to such. In light of the developing European traditions of mystifications and obfuscations of racial superiority as historical backdrop, how Equiano made use of the talking book story, with its obvious focus on the relationship of a black character to a signal object of the white world, assumes importance. Discussion turned on this matter will in turn help with a sharper analysis of the "white men's magic" that Equiano addressed.

The "talking book" episode is particularly important for my purposes in this chapter—to focus on Equiano's discovery of the nature of "white men's magic:"

> I had often seen my master and Dick employed in reading; and I had a great curiosity to talk to the books, as I thought they did; and so to learn how all things had a beginning; for that purpose I have often taken up a book, and have talked to it; and then put my ears to it, when alone, in hopes it would answer me; and I have been very much concerned when I found it remained silent. (68)

This story, or some version of it, was made quite significant as motif and trope for some of the earliest North Atlantic black writers. It was made to serve some slightly different even if also shared overlapping functions having to do with observations about black life in the eighteenth and early nineteen centuries of the North Atlantic worlds. In addition to Equiano, the trope appears in the life stories of Albert Gronniosaw, John Marrant, Cugoano, and John Jea, among the earliest black Atlantic writers. It is also picked up and used throughout the history of black writing.[30]

The origins of this story lie in the West's fearful and arrogant thinking about itself, its perceived differences from, and relations with, the (non-European) others it claims to have "discovered" at the outset of the early modern era. Europeans' writings about the Others were at the same time writings about themselves as those somewhat insecurely positioned atop the chain of beings. The early modern racial hierarchialization seemed to turn around many factors, especially (Western conventional forms and traditions around) literacy, the uses of the book, and writing. Cugoano was a close friend of Equiano; like Equiano, and unlike Gronnisoaw, Marrant, and Jea, he authored his own text.[31] It is Cugoano's employment of the story as a trope or figure that opens the clearest and widest window onto the likely original source and also provides the most helpful perspective on how Equiano revised the story.

Cugoano introduces the story of the talking book as part of his criticism of the Spanish for their treachery in dealing with the native peoples in Africa and the Americas. With attention to the violent exploits of Pizarro to put in place in what was the ancient Peruvian empire (the Incas) a new regime under the banner of the Spaniards as backdrop, Cugoano focused on a story, handed down in colonial Spanish Catholic oral and literary traditions, with complex and conflicting tendentious glosses, but which he likely accessed in book form. The story involved a Catholic priest, his missionary zeal and rigidity and treachery in dealings with local leader Atahualpa. What took place on this occasion Cugoano understood to represent the plight of all the Others with whom the European came in to contact during this period:

> As [Atahualpa] approached near the Spanish quarters the arch fanatic Father Vincente Valverde, chaplain to the expedition, advanced with a crucifix in one hand and a breviary in the other, and began with a long discourse, pretending to explain some of the general doctrines of Christianity...; and that the... Pope, Alexander,

> by donation, had invested their master as the sole Monarch of all the New World...[Atahualpa] observed that he was Lord of the dominions over which he reigned by hereditary succession; and said, that he could not conceive how a foreign priest should pretend to dispose of territories which did not belong to him, and that if such a preposterous grant had been made, he, who was rightful possessor, refused to confirm it; that he had no inclination to renounce the religious institutions established by his ancestors; nor would he forsake the service of the Sun, the immortal divinity whom he and his people revered, in order to worship the God of the Spaniards,...And he desired to know where Valverde had learned things so extraordinary. In this book, replied the fanatic Monk, reaching out his breviary. The Inca opened it eagerly, and turning over the leaves, lifted it to his ear: This, says he, is silent; it tells me nothing; and threw it with disdain to the ground. The enraged father of ruffians, turning toward his countrymen...cried out, to arms, Christians, to arms; the word of God is insulted; avenge this profanation on these impious dogs.[32]

Cugoano was following Sir Paul Rycaut's 1688 English translation of Gracilasso de la Verga's 1617 *Historia General del Peru, Part II*, of his *Commentarios reales del Peru.*[33] This story as it has been handed on is about nothing if not about the differences and dramatic confrontation and power play between two worlds. In the one world, represented by Atahualpa, Christian doctrines and presumptions regarding Christian superiority make little or no sense: because they were conveyed without any acknowledgement of the serious differences (and similarities) in basic assumptions about reality, because they were communicated only with bluster and without humility or sensitivity and a patient effort to erect conceptual bridges, they were considered babble and were rejected. And the book? It was viewed by Atahualpa and the world he spoke for as an object, an interesting and potentially special object, but an object nonetheless; but insofar as it did not represent the discourse or media of communication that marked his world, it was considered worthless and treated so. In the other world, that of the priest, Father Vincente, the rejection of his arrogant communication of presumptions—of scripturalization—provoked great anxiety and this led to outrage and an irrational fit of violence.

Whether the scene described ever actually happened with the principals as de la Verga or Rycaut indicated is not clear. But there are no reasons to doubt the big picture—regarding conflict of worlds—that is presented, even if some of the details are questioned. And Cugoano, understandably, for the sake of advancing his interests, may have taken some liberties, for example, in making the Catholic priest seem more impetuous than some memories hold or evidence might suggest. What Cugoano takes from the story is a moral about the difference in the ways of the two worlds. As Gates makes clear, in the way Cugoano manipulates and employs the story—"as a fiction of a fiction, as a story about a story"—in stark difference from the other slave narratives written by Gronniosaw and Marrant and Jea, he removes it from narrative flow and thereby makes of it a specially highlighted and noticeable trope. He intensifies the conflict by making the story work for him as an "allegory of storytelling," about the discourses and ways of the West, of the white men, including their irrational violence in defense of their "magic" associated with their books.[34]

Equiano's revision of the story shows conversation with, if not influence of, Cugoano. Far from being a forgettable minor incident in the recording of the "facts" about his life, the trope is significant as part of Equiano's construction of an "interesting" life: it is part of his attempt to write what may be called a "fiction" of "self-creation."[35] This little story within Equiano's life story is made into a trope signifying (the young) Equiano's situation as "stranger"—as one who is ignorant of and outside the ways of the dominant white world.[36] The ironically named "talking book" scene occurs within the larger narrative in which the young Equiano is seen to be fascinated by and confused about the world in which he finds himself: having been taken away from "my own nation," he found himself a "stranger," as slave and freedman, in a strange world: from his experience aboard ship he was "persuaded that I had gotten into a world of bad spirits" (55) and that in that situation "the white men had some spell of magic they put in the water when they liked in order to stop the vessel" (57). He was often astonished by what he saw and heard: "everything about me was magic" (59). The new, the strange, the frightening—these could only be thought to be about magic.

As he continued to chronicle his youthful self's education in the strange world, Equiano the writer includes a poignant description of that self's encounter with names, functions, and imports of different objects—basic, taken-for-granted things, among them a clock hanging above the chimney, a portrait, snow, and, finally, a book. The clock the boy Equiano thinks of as a machine that records all he does and reports all he does to (white) authorities. The eyes on the face of the hanging portrait he assumes to watch his every move. Seeing snow for the first time, he assumes it to be salt (63–64).

And the book? It was the last of the list of strange objects and phenomena associated with the world of the whites; its inclusion here puts it in the line of traditioning/revisioning of the talking-book story. It was the uses of the thing that was the book that the young boy of the narrative had to ponder. Like Atahualpa and so many other Others, the youthful Equiano thought the book to be a special object—one with which he thought he could communicate, as whites did. He observed that a person could speak to, be spoken to, and be acknowledged by the thing that the whites call "the book." The clock and the portrait seemed to represent the severest of gazes. They afforded little or no opportunity for interaction, serious or playful. They did not acknowledge his humanity. They were only recorders of his presence as interloper, as though he were dangerous. But they were to him quite threatening, fear-inducing, oppressive. With such objects what could he do? It seemed that he could only be seen and reported by, or try not to be seen and reported by, such objects.

But the thing that was called the book seemed to mean more, require more, and promise more. The whites engaged it as though it were special. Not only did the book require engagement on the part of the one holding it, it also held the promise of providing valuable information and perspective—about "how all things had a beginning" (68), in the tradition of the Igbo magicians, who were understood to have "calculated our time" (42). This promise of the book reveals the baseline interest of the mature story-telling Equiano: such interest lies not in literacy for its own sake, but that which literacy opened up. Here is definitely not to be found the still ignorant and somewhat romantic widely held notion about the black/African/primitive/savage who is placed in intellectual-cognitive and emotional oppositional stance against scripts, against reading and writing.[37] But here is also not to be found Cugoano's and others' sentiment, registered in the construal of the Atahualpa story, that the two worlds are so diametrically opposed to each other that conflict, following utterly frustrating communication, inevitably ensues, with the one destroying the other in fits of rage. Indeed, in Equiano's mind something rather different is represented: we find in the book-reading, book-writing, book-selling Equiano a heightened curiosity about the "magic"—the depths, the mysteries, the secrets, the social and political power—that books may represent or communicate. The young Equiano senses dimly but pointedly the iconic, fetishizing status of the book and the corresponding operations and politics in the dominant culture. He points to the mature Equiano's eventual successful handle on and practice of the magic. This is the basis of the movement of Equiano's story.

Given the way it figures in the frontispiece and throughout his story, and given the societies and cultures that Equiano was forced to negotiate, the book that was of interest to Equiano, even if other books are in mind, was most likely the Bible.[38] That this book did not speak to him, did not acknowledge him, but "remained silent" is clearly very disturbing to Equiano, rendering him at first silent, seemingly distraught, vulnerable, powerless, paralyzed. Unlike Gronniosaw's use of the talking book story (to reflect his ardent frustrated desire to be accepted into white dominant culture) or Marrant's use of it (to provide evidence of his inside and superior status relative to the Indian) or Cugoano's use (to castigate modern world slavery, racism, and colonialism based upon twisted exegetical treatments) or Jea's use (to indicate the spiritual power involved in the reading of the book that is the Bible, and how relative to such he assumed freedom), Equiano preferred to say little more than that he was (within narrative time), and remained at the time of the writing of the narrative, "very much concerned."[39]

This reaction, however, is something of a clever understatement; and it is reflective of a rather different narratological interest and strategy in relationship to the other writers. Even if Equiano as narrator does not say much about the situation in the immediate context, the "silence" of the book within the narrative speaks rather loudly. The silence of the book in the hands of the young Equiano is not comic relief: it is meant to point out a serious problem and challenge: it is an indication of the basic difference between the world that shaped Equiano and the dominant world of the peoples of the book. Basic because the young Equiano within the narrative seems to represent for the mature narrative-writing Equiano the epitome of that part of Africa that he claims as his homeland.[40] But in Equiano's retelling of the story, the silence of the book symbolizes, in contrast to others' uses of the trope, not as sharply and definitively the opposition of worlds. Equiano's lack of knowledge of English letters; his incapacity to reason; his status as primitive or savage—these are factors that divide the worlds but they are not considered to be the wide chasm that can never be crossed in Equiano's narrative. The reader of Equiano's narrative is made to understand that who the young Equiano is, what he represents in regard to the silence of the book is not consonant with the larger world defined by the book, including book-talking or book-reading. But Equiano's larger story is not left there.

The silence is met with silence. The latter must cover up for the young and the mature Equiano a mix of strong emotions—awe, fear, suspicion, bemusement, humiliation, hesitation, reservation, resistance. Only such a mix of responses can explain what the mature Equiano was doing with the story he writes: he writes/talks back, against his youthful self's experience of the silence of the book. The writing of the narrative on the part of the mature Equiano belies the paralysis and silence of the young Equiano. Through the (actually *non*-)talking book scene a fundamental instance of cultural clashing "contact" between worlds is set up: more than any other object-symbol, the book is made to represent the dominant white world into which Equiano has been thrust. Like (mis-)identifying and (mis-)understanding the import of snow or a clock or a portrait, being engaged by and knowing how to engage a book signifies deeply: being able to "talk" to it and being addressed by it is the mark of belonging to, participating in, the worlds of the whites, the type of worlds defined by the dominants Equiano was made to serve. Here the book is the door, the window, the mirror, the key—the fetish, if ever there was such. Not being able to "talk" to the book and not being addressed by it are signs of being a "stranger" in the worlds of the "white men."

Since the onset of the modern world, with its attendant cultural contacts and discoveries (otherwise known as invasions and conquests), relationships to the book have figured prominently in self-definitions and the contours and dynamics of power.[41] Although the discourses about such matters have taken place largely on the terms set by white dominants, Equiano, as one among the newly "discovered" made a slave, provides some rare and valuable perspectives on the issue. Although he was likely encouraged by religious dissenters to write his life story,[42] there should be little doubt, as I have already argued, that he was under considerable psychological pressure if not also sociopolitical and physical restraints at the time of the writing of his narrative. Yet Equiano does manage to articulate sentiments about the book that are reflective of the major sensibilities and orientations of the peoples of the black Atlantic. This articulation of sentiments about the book, sometimes directed to the black Atlantic, sometimes veiled or heavily coded, is what makes Equiano's story so compelling. And it is precisely the need to address the "hidden meanin'" of things having to do with his existence (as a black stranger) that makes the engagement of scriptures so important. Such existence could hardly be brought into language except through scriptures, that is, through some sort of veiling or coding.

On the surface these sentiments appear simply to represent in relationship to the book and to literacy the negative or absence.[43] There is no doubt that the (non-)talking book story in general aims to establish a rejection or conflict in relationship to the dominant culture. But we should not assume that the "very much concerned" young Equiano in the older Equiano's rendering of the trope in the story thinks only about his deficit in relationship to the book, his inferiority in relationship to the culture of the book. I think something rather different is registered here.

It needs to be remembered that neither the young nor the maturing Equiano is characterized as a pathetic figure. To be sure, through the course of his life Equiano goes through many heartbreaking experiences and losses. He acknowledges these experiences and seems often to sigh in discouragement, loneliness, and near resignation; but he does he not allow such experiences to paralyze him and render him hopeless. He is nothing if not remarkably resilient and strong and even somewhat wily. In his chapter 3 Equiano makes his character a young naïve boy experiencing the white world.[44] As the narrative unfolds and as the character develops into maturity he is depicted as negotiating worlds without the sense of fixed naturalized inferiority vis-à-vis white men.

What is striking is that the young Equiano seems, in response to the non-talking book, to be relatively silent. Although clearly not happy about the book's snub, he is not thrown back upon himself in shock and dejection. He does not view himself as pathetic in not being talked to by the book. He does not become angry at the refusal of the book to acknowledge him, does not hold forth about it as a reflection of the antiblack racism and colonialism. He does not even seem to personalize the matter. He does not appear to react as though the situation had anything to do with who he was, where he came from. His silence in the face of the (book's) silence is profound: it is one of those rare moments in which Equiano the writer has little to say. Or does he?

Another way of reading Equiano's seemingly muted immediate responses to the book's repeated failure to acknowledge him is to look at how he looks at his own story as published book, that is, his development into a reading and writing figure of some renown. In this story of his development into a famous writer he not only "talks back" to the book, he makes the book "talk" to him with a vengeance. Because he makes the subtle but powerful connection between his writing and the silence of the books of his youth, he does not feel the need to hold forth through his youthful self at any length about the meaning of the incident. This suggests that there was interest on the part of the mature story-telling Equiano—in the construal of the story about the (non-)talking book—in signifying on the book and on (conventional = European forms of) literacy. That it was a youthful Equiano who has the experiences with the book is most important. This suggests that the mature–story-telling Equiano had in mind the construction of his life story in relationship to this phenomenon of the (non-)talking book that for obvious reasons has to prefigure the development of Equiano into a famous writer and citizen-activist. In other words, everything in Equiano's story turns around the (non-)talking book, without making much of the trope in immediate narrative context. Surely, something poignant or ironic must be at work here. How could the youthful Equiano who is rejected by the book be associated with the mature Equiano who is the well-known, well-received writer? The incident must have been intended to force the reader to see that the silence of the book was not only not the end of the matter, it was a particular type of beginning—the beginning of Equiano's negotiation with the dominant white world and warrant for Equiano's telling of his life story.

This beginning of the negotiation of the dominant white world was carried out around a specific issue. The (non-)talking book incident is a prefiguring—it hints that the major divide between the world that Equiano constructs as his original formative world and the dominant white world into which he has been thrust is literacy, represented by the book; it is assumed that no one can successfully participate in the dominant white world without the ability to handle books, viz. to read them if not also write them. That there were illiterate whites was always evident. Yet the marker that seemed most dramatically to set apart blacks (and other nonwhites) from whites and to justify the continued subjugation of the former to the latter was literacy—at least literacy in relation to the scripts and related practices of European cultures.[45] Not specified, at least in the context of the story about the talking book, are the structures and arrangements and practices and traditions that defined, and facilitated communication within, that world that Equiano defined as his homeland.

Equiano makes the major difference between the two different worlds as he understands/remembers and experiences them revolve chiefly around the issue of European-styled literacy. The identification of such an issue is also acknowledgement that the two worlds represent two different sets of sensibilities, different epistemologies and world orientations.

There is significance in having the youthful Equiano be the one who experiences the repeated snub on the part of the book: in terms of the narrative timelines, he is the one who is closer to (the memory of) African tribal customs and sensibilities. The mature story-telling Equiano seems to want to make the interaction between his literarily fabricated youthful self and English books a matter of pointed conflict. This conflict is important to the story-telling Equiano not so much in order to inveigh against the evils of the dominant white world, and certainly not so that he might establish his and his kindreds' inferiority; it was important in order to make his story "interesting." And the story was made to be "interesting," viz. poignant, ironic—in this immediate narrative context, to be sure, but also throughout the story—through the communication of the repeated silence of the book.[46] This repeated act in turn became the basis of conveying Equiano's remarkable development. The silence and snub on the part of the book was made to represent for Equiano the point of radical conflict between who he was in relationship to his African homeland and who he was becoming in relationship to the world he eventually successfully negotiated. It was in Equiano's narratological-political interests to include the story about the non-talking book because his placement of the story makes the point of the little story and the big story less about (white world) evil deeds, hypocrisy, and moral corruption, on the one hand, and (black world) weaknesses, shortcomings, and deficits, on the other, than about the stark difference between the two worlds that the book reveals and what heroics it took for him to overcome that difference. Finding himself unable to negotiate English letters, how could Equiano be seen as or see himself as other than "stranger," as a someone standing on foreign cultural-ideological grounds? How could the youthful Equiano, made to be so ignorant about the major issues involved, respond except in terms of "concern"?

The youthful Equiano's ultimate concern was not the same as that of the mature writer by the same name. The concern on the part of the latter was about how to register in the story of his life how he had obviously *already* negotiated the world to which he had been considered a stranger, that world in which he had generally been regarded as an inferior and was met with contempt and disdain, that world which assumed him to be incapable of participation in the public square. The challenge for Equiano the writer was to make clear to readers the terms on which such negotiation could be and had been represented in him. The talking-book story provided Equiano the writer the baseline or wedge-story by which he could make the point that successful negotiation of the dominant white world by a black person was and should be a "concern"; it is made extremely difficult, but it was not impossible. The story also pinpointed the issue around which Equiano (along with some others, to be sure) thought the issue of black integration and negotiation revolved—literacy, engagement of Western (in this case, English) letters. Equiano needed to establish that the axis, the intrepid problem and the ongoing possibility, around which black participation in and negotiation of the white world turned was making the book talk, that is, strategic, self-reflexive, self-empowering use of that language used in the dominant world.

The issue of literacy here masks the issue behind the issue—power. But it is important to be more specific about how and what kind of power is at issue. In Equiano's story, power is at issue in the use of literacy as marker that erects and maintains cultural boundaries, that identifies and keeps in place insiders and outsiders. This was, to put it in other words, in Equiano's words, the "white men's magic" that represented "unbounded influence" on the "credulity and superstition" of the people—in this case, of course, white peoples.

It was the "white men's magic" that the young Equiano in the story was confronted with. The boy was depicted as outsider, stranger, not first strictly on account of his origins, his "countrymen," his "race," but on account of his lack of facility with the book, the special instrument of white men's magic. The racialization of his status as stranger was not named as explanatory factor. Equiano's racial-ethnic identity was in the story sometimes seen as part of a belated rationalization or grudging explanation for his being the stranger. But by refusing to name explicitly white racism as the decisive factor for the exclusion, Equiano allowed himself the opportunity to develop his story as his "interesting" story, that is, as his struggle to acquire the skills of literacy, the white men's magic.

Understanding the social psychology of Equiano's "use" of literacy—what kind of work he made it do for him—can shed light on the larger dominant social-cultural, including political, construal of reading. Equiano's construal of the talking-book story did not concern itself with revelation of the great evil or recalcitrance of individual whites. With some notable exceptions, the individuals who fell into this category in Equiano's life story are characterized as fair-minded, or ignorant; but they were not ultimately at issue. What was at issue for Equiano was the unmasking and accounting of the chief differences in the orientation to the world between the world he constructed as his homeland and the world of the whites as he experienced it. Of course, he had also to address the stated assumptions about the superiority of the orientation associated with the world of the whites. It is the orientation of the dominant white world and its registrations of a certain kind of power in association with literacy that Equiano's construal of the talking book story identifies and problematizes.

Equiano puts before readers the challenge of coming to terms with his coming to terms with the North Atlantic worlds. What he does with the story of the talking book is to point to the basis for his successful negotiation of the North Atlantic worlds: it was his recognition that such worlds were built around a certain kind of magic, the fetishization of the book and correlative assumptions; that humanity is recognized and certified through the engagement of (Western) letters in the book; that black peoples on account of what they must be made to represent insofar as they are made to be slaves could not/should not engage such letters; and that, because of the proscriptions associated with them and their incapacities in relationship to the letters of the book, black peoples were not to be considered high on the "great chain of being."[47] The most important point Equiano seemed to want to make in his story-telling, especially the talking-book story as its core, is that notwithstanding the befuddlement of the youthful Equiano—unlike the treachery experienced by sister Francis in an earlier England or the violence experienced by Atahualpa and his people in another era and another world, unlike the bitterness and painful rejection experienced and articulated by fellow writers Gronniosaw, Marrant and Cugoano—he was not undone by the book's silence but went on to live and thrive, to take up and use white men's magic, that is to say, to learn to read, to experience talking to the book and making the book talk back to him. Indeed, this silence on the part of Equiano makes clear the make-believe work of the book in the dominant culture. He is essentially made to communicate to the readers the (most profound) meaning of the book before he as character in the narrative is shown mastering it (in conventional terms).

Coming to a point of taking up, using, and even exploiting the white men's magic was not for Equiano capitulation or assent or defeat. Engagement and even imitation of a sort were understood to be in order. It represented a realistic view and realistic strategy for survival and thriving born of his extensive if sometimes turbulent times at sea and in the many societies that seafaring afforded him opportunities to experience. These experiences led him to the view that in spite of some minor differences in arrangements and styles, black existence was everywhere in the North Atlantic worlds a matter of struggle, opposition, humiliation, challenge[48] that also warranted critical engagement and mimetics. Negotiation was thought possible only insofar as the Western structure of dominance was viewed realistically and honestly. In order for this to happen, a critical balance of perspective about the orientation of whites to their (book/script) "magic," on the one hand, and blacks and their orientation to their "magic" (in association with the Igbo elders and priests), on the other, would be required.

That Equiano's recognition of and negotiation of the complex white tribal phenomenon of scripturalization as a type of magic requires unpacking is obvious: he was a stranger in the white world; and the white world had in fact given him the language and concept of the category of "magic" as critical handle by which he could analyze the politics, psychology, and operations of that world. As part of the unpacking of the world of the whites through the phenomenon of scripturalization, I have isolated what I consider some of the historical implications and social-cultural-political ramifications of some of the major problems, questions, challenges, and opportunities that the phenomenon of scripturalization, with its mystification of white access to knowledge, represents. Some of these issues and problems are only hinted at and are not explicitly named by Equiano. This book uses Equiano's story not only to name the phenomenon, but also to fathom implications and ramifications flowing from it, how they travel and what they mean.

Having made the case for Equiano's story as reflecting among other things his character's first-contact recognition and negotiation of the worlds of the Europeans as a semiosphere of whiteness that makes use of scriptures as ideological bulwark, a further unpacking of this complex phenomenon should follow. This unpacking in the next few chapters focuses on different aspects of the phenomenon by using scripturalization as analytical wedge or window onto what Equiano's character develops, as he experiences more about how scripturalization operates and how scriptures in broad and narrow terms are made to work. Yet it is important for the reader to note that notwithstanding the significance of using Equiano's story as a springboard for the discussion of the phenomenon, the implications and ramifications are taken beyond Equiano's character and beyond Equiano the writer. Scripturalization is bigger than either the historical or the literary Equiano. Scripturalization was not invented by Equiano; but it is after Equiano never again to be overlooked, unnamed, or unanalyzed.

So having taken note of Equiano's (narration of his) first encounter with white men's magic as scripturalization, there is a basis for the analysis of some of the different aspects of the phenomenon. In the chapter that immediately follows is discussion of the magic of scripturalization as it is made evident in the larger social-cultural matrix.

3

"...*every person there read the Bible...*": *Scripturalization as Matrix of White Men's Magic*

I had frequent contests about religion with the reverend father, in which he took great pains to make a proselyte of me to his church; and I no less to convert him to mine. On these occasions I used to produce my bible, and shewed him in what points his church erred. He then said he had been in England, and that every person there read the Bible, which was very wrong; but I answered him, that Christ desired us to search the scriptures.

—OLAUDAH EQUIANO, *Interesting Narrative*, chapter 11

The encounter between Europe and the Americas juxtaposed a vast number of inconvenient facts with the elegant theories embodied in previously authoritative books. The discoveries gradually stripped the books of their aura of completeness as repositories of information and their appearance of utility as tools of interpretation. The encounter with naked inhabitants of the world, in short, enabled intellectuals to make naked experience take the place of written authority.

[T]his account has been questioned and even contradicted...[some] have argued that in fact the discoveries had little impact on European thought. They left European notions of history and civilization intact. They did not shake but confirmed European prejudices about the superiority of white Christians to those of other breeds and creeds. The New World proved easy to reconcile with

the biblical account of human history and the classical accounts of the physical world.

The [authoritative] texts provided European[s] not with a single grid that imposed a uniform order on all new information, but with a complex set of overlapping stencils, a rich and delicate set of patterns and contrivances. These produced diverse, provocative, ultimately revolutionary assemblies of new facts and images.

—ANTHONY GRAFTON, *New Worlds, Ancient Texts: The Power of Tradition and the Shock of Discovery*[1]

IN HIS FASCINATING book, from which the second quotation above is taken, historian Anthony Grafton elegantly, but in my view also somewhat fretfully and nervously, sums up the mixed views among historians about the complex situation that obtained in the century and a half that followed the European "discovery," beginning in the fifteenth century, of the rest of the world and what this meant for European identity. Although the concept of the semiosphere does not appear in the quotation above or in the title or in any single pointed sentence or argument of the book, the term "bound" appears in the title of his first chapter ("A Bound World: The Scholar's Cosmos") and the concept of being "bounded" is addressed indirectly throughout the book.[2] "Being bound," "bounded," "binding"—these terms were taken up by Grafton as he followed his sources in order to understand aspects of and issues having to do with "tradition." The latter referred among others things to that which was the focus of the reading formations of elite males. Except for very recent situations in some parts of the world, such individuals were the only ones with access to and facility for engaging the texts that defined and carried tradition. The authoritative cultural texts are the means by which the sociocultural binding is accomplished and sustained. At a point early on in his argument, Grafton makes explicit the connection between the binding and books. He does so through focus on the mentalities and sensibilities and practices and orientations of high-born male "intellectuals":

> Their mental world was bounded by the knowledge contained on their library shelves: knowledge produced in and largely limited to

> the ancient Mediterranean and Near East and medieval and modern Europe, though occasionally penetrated by a trickle of information from more distant realms to the east or north.[3]

Most of Grafton's book is an attempt to explain the historical ramifications of the bounded-ness of a world through the varied assumptions and arguments about and engagements of canonical texts. The binding that obtained among Europeans was partly in spite of, partly on account of, the "shock" of the discovery of the "new" and "different"—naked dark peoples, lands, languages, smells, plants, gods. The binding has survived instability and even the threat of extinction, and it has experienced intensifications and revivals.

Of course, Grafton also makes it clear—in an odd half-apologetic, half-defiant mode, made to seem to be the establishment of clarity of purpose and delimitation—that his treatment of this history of the binding is about, and most definitely from the perspective of, the Europeans:

> This is a story of Europeans, told from a European point of view. We[!] seek to understand the experiences and visions of European intellectuals and explorers, not to recover the ways in which the peoples they conquered understood the West—much less what sufferings those peoples certainly endured or what benefits they possibly drew from the encounter. Though a limited tale, this one seems eminently worth telling now.[4]

How strange that it could be considered acceptable, even excellent, scholarship to address the dynamics of the contact between Europeans and the Others only "from a European point of view." Odder still to resolve "not to recover the ways in which the peoples [whom the Europeans] conquered understood the West," even if, for some strange reason, one wanted only to get at the European perspective. How can one understand one side of a contact experience without taking the other side into account? And why would one ever *want* only *one* side, *one* perspective, from such experience? The seeming comfort level with a forging ahead to account for the European response to contact without allowing the interruptions of the others is troubling and shocking. It is a reminder of just how powerful and intoxicating and obfuscating is the center—for all, including venerable scholars.

What for me is most telling about Grafton's decision to probe only from a "European point of view" is his acknowledgment that the Europeans who are the focus of his book "did not see the New World 'as it really was.'"[5] I take it that he understood that their views had been constructed for specific purposes—political-ideological-discursive strategic?—within the "bound world" that his book attempts to open up for the reader. The construction and maintenance of that "bound world" rested mainly on the basis of "authoritative texts" that were also used as "tools" for "understanding the thoughts and values of alien societies."[6]

The bounded state of medieval and early modern European societies as a "narrow, orderly place," revolving around a certain "standard" library of, and (reading) orientation to, books, is illustrated, according to Grafton, most tellingly in the publication of encyclopedias. Originating in the wealthy cities of Upper Germany at the beginning of the sixteenth century, encyclopedias were a response to the interests and needs of patrician merchants. Many of them were well educated—in the European-defined and coopted "classics"—and well traveled. They became the driving force behind the production and printing of the texts. Notwithstanding their training in the "authoritative texts" of their world, they were not "university men"; they felt they needed among their libraries handy tools, such as a "small-scale reference work," to help them retain a handle on the knowledge that had been identified for the time as that which every literate man should know.

Gregor Reisch's *Margarita philosophica*, published in 1503 (see Figure 3.1), was one of those works that filled the need: a cultural proto-encyclopedia, it handily presented everything that was "fit" to be known: in it everything was

> [I]n order, neat and tidy. Grammar, the art of reading, gives entry to a world of knowledge entirely bounded by authors, one per subject: Euclid for geometry, Ptolemy for astronomy, Peter Lombard for theology. The traditional arts and sciences appear as finished, perfect entities that invite study rather than improvement. And the body of the text presents, between two covers and in a modest format, everything one could possibly wish to know. Grammar, the arts of argument, the natural sciences, theology, Creation and Damnation jostle here, none treated at great length. "Sermons in books, stones in the running brooks"—so one might summarize this all-too-simple authoritative message.[7]

FIGURE 3.1. Title page from Gregor Reisch, *Margarita philosophica* (Frieburg, 1503). This item is reproduced by permission of The Huntington Library, San Marino, California.

Reisch's publication reflected what Grafton awkwardly called the "not idiosyncratic" class-specific tastes and interests of the times. This did not mean, however, that the engagement of the publications was simple or without controversy. With the sensibilities and practices of the new *studia humanitatis*, "humanities" men—such as Lorenzo Valla and Erasmus—as well as the new aggressive and creative explorers and experimenters, such as Francis Bacon, whose name is now synonymous with discovery of and openness to new things and peoples and ways of the world, disputes about how to read the texts and textures of societies became very much evident.[8] These differences reflected the expansiveness of European cultures, but they did not undermine the reality and power of such cultures as a bounded world of discourse, a semiosphere. Even the most adventurous and transgressive explorers, scientists, and humanists of the time tended to find their way back to and orient themselves by the culture's authoritative texts. The latter provided for cultural engagement and negotiation "a complex set of overlapping stencils, a rich and delicate set of patterns and contrivances."[9]

In an article about the "new worlds" "discovered" by Europeans in the sixteenth and seventeenth centuries, historian Michael T. Ryan seems to be in agreement with Grafton on matters set forth here, but he makes the further point that the strangeness and newness that contemporary "exotics" and "savages" represented were expropriated by Europeans and assimilated into their "houses of discourses" and made to explain and further legitimize Europeans' traditions and worldviews. And, incredibly, this was the case notwithstanding the dramatic interruptions of the greatly enlarged world that "savages" represented. Although I think Ryan and Grafton as well as the early modern-era European elites themselves may have protested too much in being nonplussed or unthreatened by the ("discovery" of) "savages"—what else should we make of the rhetorical, social-psychological, physical, and institutional violence and preoccupations in relationship to such populations that immediately ensued and remain to this day?—I take their most important argument to be that there was, according to Ryan, certainly no genuine interest in them, no respect for them as complex human beings. The interest "was clearly and openly self-validating, like so much erudition in premodern Europe."[10]

Even more illuminating, however, is Ryan's conclusion that such myopia and self-interestedness on the part of Europeans was expected, even inevitable; it was not as if "an alternative stance was possible."

> There is nothing in travel literature, in works describing the aims and goals of travel, or in the situation of observers, the best of whom were missionaries interested in the ultimate elimination of difference, that demanded or valued a type of description which had as its object the representation of difference on its own terms. The world, after all, was discovered by Europeans, not vice versa.

> And that fact implied a certain ownership, if not legal then at least intellectual and psychological.... The world was given to them, and it was taken by them.[11]

Such sentiments are so strongly articulated and so easily registered that one should be forgiven for questioning whether they reflect the views of (in this case, early modern) historical actors alone or whether the late modern ones were themselves bound. Is Ryan—even as he wrote—among those to whom the world was given, through whom the world was subdued? Does Ryan, perhaps, like Grafton, speak only about the European discoverers? Did he and Grafton allow their consciousness to elide or morph uncritically into the collective consciousness of sixteenth- and seventeenth-century male European elites? Do their somewhat uncritical arguments about these elites rather ironically reinscribe the sentiments of the elites? Or were they, with the subtle employment of some irony, simply "reading the texts," helping the reader to understand the issues? Surely, it is possible that I have on some points misread these scholars, but I am uneasy with their display of erudition and analysis.

What the male European elites needed in that world considered to have been "given to them" was a conceptual hook by which the "savages" could be understood—viz., assimilated and controlled. One form of such an effort, especially among the schoolmen and other men of letters, was the social-psychology and politics of antiquarianism, an interest in or even obsession with origins as (mostly unacknowledged) mirroring of the ordered traditional society. More specifically, it meant engagement in a tendentious, obfuscating, even violent, cultural politics of comparison: making exotics "read" like the "pagans" of Europeans' constructed (Greco-Roman-Christian) antiquity that somehow mirrored modern European forms of Christianity. So the "savages"—understood, interpreted, assimilated, domesticated as the "pagans" of antiquity—were placed within but on the periphery of European worlds. This was a particular form of dominance. In this way the "savages" could be accounted for in European mythic histories and collective psyches. The Others were in-scripted—brought into the European cultural circle—into the pan-European semiosphere. This inscription preserved the "mythic past" and ongoing myth-making, through making creative uses of the texts of center-formation.

But nuance is very important here: the exoticism of the "discovered" peoples with this creative reading on the part of the European elites was done in order to integrate them not so much into European society but rather into the European mind. That is, this reading was intended not so much to fit the Others in, but to explain them. Not being able to account for such peoples in the classic and sacred texts was too much of a problem for the social psyche, certainly among the elites used to defining and structuring reality for all. So this hermeneutical/reading practice, *renouvellemens*, a kind of "new science," was really a new apologetics that seemed to have gained wide currency, certainly in high circles. It was evident even among the likes of Bacon, Galileo, and Newton. They used the language of tradition to validate their various discoveries and saw themselves as upholders of tradition even as they advanced discoveries.[12]

Many of the "humanists" and scientists of the time rather easily fell back upon "paganism" as an important concept that they pressed into service to establish the clear, unambiguous category of otherness.[13] They compared themselves to the patristic fathers fighting ancient world "pagans." They put focus on origins or on the past, not the present, precisely and paradoxically because of the need to explain and legitimize the present in which the new peoples were discovered.[14] The argument seems to have been that in order for them to understand and dominate these new peoples, their past must to some extent be understood. But of course, as Ryan points out, because there is so little evidence of genuine interest in the new peoples on their own terms, Europeans pretty much made up a past about and for them.[15] And their new "past" was then fitted into the Europeans' framework of tradition, their semiosphere. As the Europeans made themselves heirs of biblical characters,[16] they mostly[17] made the new peoples their foils, that is, made them heirs of ancient world "pagans."[18] "Paganism" was used to define these peoples as the radical others because to be found outside the framework that was European-inflected Christian faith—notwithstanding the conflicts and range of differences and levels and focal points of intensities that obviously obtained among Europeans as Christians—was to mark the self as a stranger.[19] In fact, insofar as the charge of paganism (pagan = stranger) was the ultimate marker of difference, it seems that it alone had the potential to relativize the differences among Europeans. Roman Catholics and Protestants never looked so much alike as when they were compared to pagans.[20]

So the new people were most fundamentally pagans, unbelievers, and as such, could be conceptualized in the European interpretive mythic framework. This linkage was decisive: the modern "pagans" were considered beyond the pale, too different, and therefore exploitable, to be subdued and dominated as a reflection of the ultimate power of the God—by the people who understood themselves to be God's representatives in the world. Other even more bizarre rationalizations and mythical-historical theories would follow.

A triangular relationship—involving Europe; (Western = Mediterranean world) antiquity; and modern exotics as pagans—was assumed to be in place. The principal relationship was understood to be between the first two; exotic pagans were seen as an appendage, needing somehow to be worked in. But the "pagans" did not, Ryan concludes, represent the *crise de conscience* for Europeans, or an issue around which Europeans were forced to think and act differently. Change, he says, eventually came from within: from scholars "who, having assimilated classical literature, unraveled Europe's relationship with the Bible and the antique world.... Where ethnography had been an aspect of history, it now came to offer an interpretation of it."[21]

Equiano, I argue, experienced the situation described by Grafton and Ryan: he knew himself to be placed in the context of discourse that viewed the "pagan" as the non-European other, inexorably and profoundly being transmuted into the black-skinned racialized other. Among what may be argued to have been the many influences upon his story, the discourses and logics of the "new scholar"—including the schoolmen and the explorers and discoverers, the likes of which Grafton and Ryan discuss—are evident. Equiano seems to have been conversant with some of the publications—academic, pseudo-academic, and popular—that reflected some of the developments Grafton and Ryan discuss.[22] Equiano's participation in the discourse, including his letter-writing, represents a type of popularization of the discourse, a creative mix of imitation and reversal: he employed some discursive construals from the literatures of these schoolmen to make compelling his remembrances of the Igbo people as representatives of those who would be transformed into contemporary "Africans."[23] The Igbo people as Africans were represented as having antique-biblical roots in imitation of the claims of the Europeans. Equiano must have assumed that his claim about the biblical roots of the Igbo were no more outrageous and no less defensible than the arguments of the Europeans. Here was awareness of the discourse and politics that defined much of the situation in the wake of the discoveries of the other worlds. And there was a clearly conscious and bold willingness to engage in a mimetics of such discourses and politics.[24]

Most astonishing, as part of the more nuanced structuring of his story, Equiano used ancient Igbo traditions in a scrambling if not reversal of the usual arrangements and interests, including the assumption that it was natural and appropriate for Europeans to engage in all sorts of proto-ethnographic and ethnological projects on the other(s), turning the gaze upon the other(s), "explaining" the other(s), but with little if any self-inspection or self-analysis. So we have Equiano the stranger, the "heathen" and "savage," perhaps, not even really considered a respectable "pagan," whose work is creative critical commentary—part ethnography/ethnology—on European traditions and ways. In the mimetic performance that was his story, the black heathen/pagan/stranger turned the gaze on and "wrote up"[25] the white world.

In imitation of a popular performance of a "new scholar," Equiano's signifying on the white world focused—for reasons he makes crystal clear—mainly but not exclusively on the uses of the classic/sacred/centering text that was the Bible. There were other classics and centering texts, but the Bible, Equiano learned, was of special status among white men.[26] So the Bible functioned for Equiano as a kind of analytical wedge, into the center of the world, the mysteries of the world of the white men as sphere of signs (semiosphere) that he found himself needing to negotiate. Of course, he was forced to negotiate that world and its center from the periphery. He seemed to understand that he alone was no match for the center. Through his travels and experiences he must have learned that in spite of threats to the stability of the center from various forms of newness and otherness—the rhetorics and social protest among the white radical and restless explorers and humanist-scholars and religious dissenters—the center was difficult to move or destabilize; radiations outward from the center that constituted the semiosphere remained intact. Yet from his many associations he must have also been convinced that there was precedence as well as opportunity within the white semiosphere for some movement, change, and differentiation. The shape of Equiano's story seems to convey, as much as anything else, the conviction that social ferment and expressions far from the center, on the peripheries, were feasible, without at the same time imagining the end of the bounded world that was the semiosphere. The center could be moved and manipulated even if not displaced. Equiano placed himself within the currents of some of those voices on the periphery.

Equiano saw himself in solidarity with those who participated in a number of similar movements going back to the age of revolution seventeenth-century England that occupied places variously off center, those who because of their commitments to radical change were nervously and contemptuously referred to by elite and dominant contemporaries and in modern radical historiography by many negative labels, including the "many headed hydra." The image of the hydra suggested that there was not one group that had criticized the dominant center, but a "motley crew" of the biblical metaphor "hewers of wood and drawers of water."[27] This metaphor aptly captured the baseline sentiment of the mixed groups of outsiders, peripherals who at certain points in history, including the age of Revolution in England, worked together to change the world, and who could not be dissuaded from the conviction that in the Bible was legitimization for their causes, not the establishment's, with its ideology of class and social and economic structuring.

It has been argued that the Bible declined in influence in some quarters in British culture from the time of the revolution to the mid-eighteenth century.[28] But we must be careful here: such a decline probably ought to be understood in terms of a change in a certain set of practices, or in terms of openness to and acceptance of other texts as classics of a sort, less in terms of total indifference or outright rejection. If any change in terms of the Bible's place in the culture can be evidenced, no doubt among an elite minority, this change belies the reality that the Bible had already been positioned to signify the center-discourse of the culture, that is, to fundamentally shape and define the culture. A shift in attitude to it, in the handling of it as text, among elites was not by any means the destruction of the semiosphere that had already been constructed around it. It makes more compelling sense to try to understand the continuing varied, complex, levels of intense and conflicting uses of the Bible on the part of differently positioned individuals and small groups or movements—especially those on the margins, representing continuing creative social dynamism and energy, rather than the sentiments and practices of the mostly conservative and, in terms of numbers, minority elites.

Consider again Francis, the sister and mother figure of an independent congregation.[29] In spite of efforts to co-opt and silence her, it is fairly clear that her Bible was used as an instrument through which she could speak with authority about herself and to others. She was an individual forerunner of Equiano (as a black stranger, an "African" trying to negotiate the strange land that was England and its ways). And insofar as she was a part of one of those socially radical movements of the seventeenth century—in her case a radically free social movement marked by its free-spinning Bible readings—she represented a movement that was forerunner of the movements in which Equiano participated and helped lead in the late eighteenth century. So both Francis and Equiano and the movements in which they participated can be placed within the larger context of social movements that categorized England from the seventeenth into the nineteenth century.

The momentum and most powerful effect of such groups were especially evident in the London democratic movement of the 1790s, with its division into what has been recognized as three different but related camps: mainly artisans, supportive of French Jacobin-republicanism; groups of infidels and political freethinkers dedicated to moral and intellectual subversion; and an auxiliary force of lower-class religious enthusiasts, wanting overthrow of the established order. All of these types were found in debating clubs, coffee houses, pubs, music halls, and the press. These groups shaped modern England less than they wanted to, but more than they realized they had. Although crushed by government and establishment in the late 1790s, an "incorrigibile" remnant held the possibility of a regrouping and resistance as they cultivated types of *un*-bounded culture. (See Figure 3.2.)

Equiano was very much drawn to and influenced by off-center or dissenting scripture-reading formations in Britain that modeled and promised social reform, even among some radical-utopianist reform. Such formations were responses to the recognition of the larger culture as a scripture-reading formation. The latter was thought to be in great need of reform—depending on the group and its particular orientation and intensity—of a different and more intense reactivation or radicalization, and so forth.

Beyond the first two chapters of his story, Equiano consistently notes that the English defined themselves as a people by persistent reference to the Bible. So in one respect it may be enough simply to indicate that in the story he has written, in which he is depicted as "stranger" seeking to become an "Englishman," Equiano was always either in search of a Bible or exercised over the meaning of parts of the Bible. He clearly equates his engagement of the Bible with his quest to become an "Englishman." His many quotations from the Bible scattered throughout his story; his collected biblical quotations at the end of many chapters that summarize his arguments or aspects of his story-telling or as appendices; his poetry

FIGURE 3.2 Façade of the Pasadena Public Library. Tavo Olmos, photographer.

as glosses on scriptures; and, of course, his now famous frontispiece, in which he is pictured holding the Bible open to a particular passage—these make plain Equiano's investment in scriptures as part of building a strategic rhetorical-narratological bridge by which he, like most of us today, seeks to pull himself into the world of the English. (See Figure 3.2)[30]

And, of course, this relationship between the quest for the Bible and the quest for integration into British society reflects on Equiano's and others' understanding of the nature of British society, how it had been constructed and how it was maintained. In acknowledgment of Equiano's recognition of Britain as social formation, the term I use in this book to describe that construction and the politics and polity and practices associated with it is "scripturalization." It refers to more than a text, although clearly the "text" that was the Bible and those texts one might call parascriptural (hymnals; commentaries; pamphlets; prayer books; martyrs' testimonies, etc.) were certainly important sites of intense focus. But the term more broadly refers to the ideology and power dynamics and social and cultural practices built around texts. It refers to the uses of texts, textuality, and literacy as a means of constructing and maintaining society, as a legitimation of authority and power. It becomes shorthand for a type of structure and arrangement of power relations and communications of society, the ultimate politics of language. It is nothing less than magic, a powerful and compelling construction, make-believe.[31]

What scripturalization as made-up reality means is one of the important but little examined themes of Equiano's story. Scripturalization in his story is evident and presented not in terms of theorizing or philosophical or historical argument but as variations on themes and issues embedded within dramatic situations in the life of the character developed in his narrative. What readers are given, then, is a *text* in which the figure of Equiano weaves himself into the social-cultural *textures* of Britain, strategically using the nation-defining *texts* as wedge.[32] On a competitive field such a strategy would probably be thought about in terms of using the opponent's source of strength in opposition. In many moments of his story the reader finds Equiano playing such a game with intelligence, wit, and commitment.

One of those moments, quoted at the beginning of this chapter, from his chapter 11, throws dramatic light on what Britain is as a type of social-cultural formation. Equiano finds himself in Malaga, Spain, in a debate with a Roman Catholic priest.[33] Having ventured from the ship on which he was a crew member, he found himself in town and "very much shocked" by the customs of the place, including Sunday evening "bull-baiting," "the great scandal of Christianity and morals" (199). As he made his way to visit the magnificent but unfinished Roman Catholic cathedral there, he encountered a priest, Father Vincent, with whom he—we as readers are made to believe—regularly engaged over matters religious. Their conversation seems much like it was in the middle of (re-)constructed conversation. (This squares with the scripting of the place as a possible regular port of call for Equiano.) As the priest made the attempt to convert Equiano to Catholicism, Equiano made the attempt to convert the priest to his (!) (English) Protestant way. Beyond Equiano's representation of himself as the advocate of the white English

Protestant tradition (about this more below), it was his registration of what each tradition stood for that is most important here:

> On these occasions I used to produce my bible, and shewed him in what points his church erred. He then said he had been in England, and that *every person there read the bible*, which was very wrong; but I answered him, that Christ desired us to search the scriptures. In his zeal for my conversion, he solicited me to go to one of the universities in Spain, and declared that I should have my education free; and told me, if I got myself made a priest, I might in time become even Pope; and he said that Pope Benedict was a black man. As I was ever desirous of learning, I paused some time upon this temptation, and thought by being crafty (by going to the university), I might catch some with guile; but again I began to think it would only be hypocrisy in me to embrace his offer, as I could not in conscience conform to the opinions of his church. I was therefore enabled to regard the word of God, which says, "Come out from amongst them"; and I refused Father Vincent's offer. So we parted without conviction on either side. (200)

There is much here that requires attention. It is important to call attention to the assumptions on the part of both men about the two countries, England and Spain, that they represent:

The priest assumes that England is something of an unruly and chaotic world, full of people going their own conflicting ways without respect for hierarchy and authority that was the Roman Catholic church. The most troubling part of such a situation, he had learned on his visit to England, was the fact that "every person read the Bible." This was deemed "very wrong." How could truth be upheld and tradition be preserved under such circumstances? And what would happen to lines of authority if anyone decided to interpret the Bible on his or her own terms? The English situation was considered unruly, troubling.

Equiano also reported his English-inflected view by indicating that "Christ desired us to search the scriptures,"[34] and that the scriptures admonished him to judge (so the reader is made to assume) Spanish Christianity and culture with suspicion, to "Come out from amongst them."[35] How might truth be recognized and honored in society except through intense and earnest wrestling with scriptures on the part of all? How could people embody God's truth unless they are able to discern it in God's word?

The reader is presented a picture of the conflict within European society, as represented by these two characters divided into Catholic and Protestant. Fascinating and to the point of my interests in this book are the registered notions about the Bible: even as the charge that "every person [in England] read the Bible" is an exaggeration, it nonetheless makes a point about the operating perception, within and beyond Britain, about British society being woven around the Bible. Equiano's reporting of this experience makes it clear that he understands himself as a reader of the scriptures in solidarity with Protestant England, over against the (supposedly) non-Bible-centric Catholic Spain. Of course, neither the priest nor Equiano need be understood to be perfect representatives of the respective European societies; they are both Equiano's narratological constructions. Yet what they are made to voice has some powerful resonance for the advancement of a slice of historical fiction. Spain was a Catholic country—seen and experienced by and interpreted through Equiano's English Protestant labeling and understanding. England was a Protestant country—seen and experienced by Equiano under what can be considered somewhat unusual if not unprecedented circumstances. White Protestant readers who were Equiano's contemporaries would not miss the point here: given the times, the circumstances, the positioning of Equiano and his ethnic kind in society, Equiano as the protagonist, the one upholding and defending English Protestant ideology in the story must surely have been seen as an extraordinary even shocking event, requiring a double take or smile or furrowed brow: through the biblical piety and orientation of eighteenth-century English-inflected Protestant evangelicalism, Equiano, the black African from the land of the "Ebos," had indeed become "almost an Englishman." But this was possible only because Equiano had already, long before critical scholarship on the matter, correctly and astutely "read" how the English people had become a people—largely, even if not only, through their reading practices in connection with the Bible.

Few histories of early modern British society and culture would see in the main point of Equiano's little story much to gainsay in his general depiction of the conflict at the time between Protestant England and Catholic Spain. Few would argue that he had not correctly made the point that the early modern social formation that was Britain needs to be understood as one deeply influenced by the weaving of the Bible into almost every level and domain of society and culture.[36] But precisely because it seems so shocking to have Equiano—a "stranger" who is "savage and "heathen" and pagan" and then "African," and so forth[37]—depicted as the one carrying the English Protestant Bible-reading banner, what is begged here, and what goes unaddressed by critics, is the question not merely about how this situation could have involved Equiano, but how a society can come to be constituted and defined and legitimized in this way, that is, in relationship to a text, and with what ramifications. These are the twin issues that inspired this book. In this fraught moment in his story Equiano provides a window onto some of the historical dynamics, rhetorics, and politics of the formation that was early modern Britain and thereby throws light on the general dynamics of modern social formation—Protestant and Catholic.

As is mentioned above, the phenomenon that Equiano points to in his story as the framing structure of magic or make-believe that defines early modern Britain I am here calling scripturalization. This concept opens up critical historical and comparative thinking and discussion about some of the terms and dynamics and ramifications of social formation. Scripturalization as structure can be understood as reaching back in some respects to the ancient-world formations that Benedict Anderson in his *Imagined Communities* called "sacred cultures."[38] These "sacred cultures" were made legitimate by "sacral languages," what Sheldon Pollock refers to as the "languages of the gods."[39] Latin in the pan-Mediterranean and later European Christian worlds, Arabic in the Islamic Ummah, and Sanskrit in South Asia are perhaps the most dramatic examples. These sacred scripts were made—by force or persuasion—to be understood by all within the respective social worlds to be nonarbitrary and inseparable from truth. The source of knowledge and arbiter of all things important, they were also understood to be of special, if not unique origins. The extensive transterritorial use of almost all but a few texts in these languages—from those collected texts at first in simple lexical terms and then later in terms of the culturally freighted category called "scriptures" to the works of literati and scholars—these reflected and facilitated communications, commerce, the operations of government and statecraft, and social-cultural binding.[40]

With the onset of print capitalism and the possibility of the widespread popular dissemination of pamphlets, essays, and books in vernacular languages, the "sacred languages" in seventeenth-century Europe, especially in England, began to decline in importance.[41] But a few considerations are important to keep in mind: first, decline must be understood not so much in terms of lack of influence but in terms of having reached a peak of influence and done the work these languages were intended to do. Second, as Equiano's story reminds us, in spite of the early modern-era decline of the ancient- and medieval-world "sacred cultures" and "sacred languages," the languages/scripts and texts obtained; even as, or especially because, fewer and fewer persons had facility for "sacred" languages, they nonetheless remained the mystifying discourses against which other discourses were measured. Third, within European contexts Latin, the canonical medium through which the canonical text and discourses were communicated, had already established the discursive-literary framework by which European societies were bound together and the basis on which all significant communications and practices were established and justified. More specifically, Latin had already done its work of consolidating European Christendom, especially, even if not exclusively so, through the Bible. That some began to identify themselves as a people in terms of translation of the Bible into their local vernacular language(s) only made more powerfully the point that the Bible (through Latin) was a binding pan-European discursive site and instrument. Fourth, Equiano's social position—as social-cultural and racial "stranger" formerly a slave—disposed him to experience and analyze the situation differently. The already vernacularized (English) Bible that was in (center) place meant that Equiano did not need to rhapsodize about the decline of Latin; he experienced—for good and ill—the power of the English Bible (likely, but not necessarily in all situations, the King James Bible) functioning in England in exactly the way Latin had functioned in pan-European terms. It may be useful to consider Equiano's outsider position as affording him a perspective—Bhabha's lag?[42]—that allowed him to see with more detached but also more strategically interested eyes how the English world was structured, how it was centered around the English Bible.

So in the European early modern period, as the sacred culture associated with Latin was fractured and became less totalistic if not less extensive in its territoriality,[43] many more "sacred cultures"—nations with their official religions—were established. The sacred languages/scripts also exploded into many different new national(-ist) vernaculars. These explosions into various modern languages represented complex developments and dynamics: they did not represent total disavowal or disappearance of the older sacred cultures or languages. Rather, they represented some changes in self-understandings, consciousness, power dynamics, uses, and boundaries. Having been made to do a certain work, the sacred language was inspirational—viz., made to explode into several different language worlds, functioning, in terms of power relations, in much the same way.

So when Equiano the writer depicts himself in his life story debating a Spanish Roman Catholic priest on the use of the Bible, what is drawn with colorful strokes and put in sharp critical historical relief is his participation in the phenomenon of modern European vernacularized scripturalization. The latter can be understood as an early modern-era social formation translating an ancient Near Eastern, late ancient-medieval-era form of scripturalization (or ancient world "sacred culture").

But let us be clear about what Equiano offers the reader: in his story we have to do less with radical overturning of scripturalization than its development, its differentiation, and complexification. And what is most "interesting" about his story is his arrogation of his capacity and his right to interpret this phenomenon and to model the experience of it for his readers.

That is what makes the story so fascinating: it can be read as a story about peoples registering their relationships to a phenomenon that has not yet been clearly named or fathomed. As though in recognition of the nature of the "beast," that quality of being everywhere but nowhere in particular, more specifically, of being make-believe but all so real, Equiano provides not so much the history of scripturalization as hauntingly realistic portrayals of those who as actors in his narrative drama are differently situated in relationship to scripturalization—inside; outside; on the margins; directly at center, and so many places in between. These portrayals of the different actors—Equiano himself playing the lead role—in different positions in different relationships to scripturalization are also to be taken as critical-analytical observations, about scripturalization.

This chapter is focused on what scripturalization meant, following Equiano's experience of it, as social-discursive matrix. The incident with Father Vincent names rather explicitly the recognition of the discursive world that was Britain in terms of the reading of the Bible. There are other incidents in Equiano's story that reinforce this view that he has Father Vincent articulate.

In the same chapter (11), Equiano relates an incident with some "Musquito Indians,"[44] whom Equiano encountered first in England, subsequently in their homeland in Central America. In this incident, involving "white men" and "Indians" as "pagans," Equiano deftly depicted himself as being identified by the son of the local tribal king as one of the "white men." The son of the local tribal chief, along with some other youth, had been sent to England by British traders "for some selfish ends." While in England for a year the son was missionized and "baptized by the name of George." He had met Equiano eight days before boarding the sloop called *Morning Star* that was to take him home. Throughout the trip he observed the behaviors and rituals of Equiano and the white men who served as the ship's crew and finally raised a rather pointed and destabilizing question:

> How comes it that all the white men on board, who can read and write, observe the sun, and know all things, yet swear, lie, and get drunk, only excepting yourself? (204)

There is much that was going on behind this story and this provocative question. Equiano depicts the "poor innocent youth" as the other—the stranger!—in relationship to the world that he and the white crew represented. The youth had learned to speak "pretty good English." But Equiano was "mortified" to find that neither the young prince nor his companions had "frequented any churches" or been appropriately catechized. So Equiano had taken it upon himself to instruct the young man in Christian doctrine and British civilizational "morals":

> I took all the pains that I could to instruct the Indian prince in the doctrines of Christianity. . . . I taught him in the compass of eleven days all the letters . . . I had Fox's *Martyrology* with cuts, and he used to be very fond of looking into it, and would ask many questions about the papal cruelties he saw depicted there, which I explained to him. (203)

Equiano's authoritative claims about, and his possession and uses of, English scripts and some nationalizing and socializing texts and his general pious comportment made him appear to the young prince—made to speak for "Indians" as a whole—as a "white man," that is, as a complicated and puzzling black man who seemed to embody all that was assumed to be part of the world of the white men. This image in turn reflected a certain understanding, from the naïve and curious perspective of an insider, of white Protestant culture. That perspective highlights the shape of such a culture in terms of scripturalization: it appeared to be a world constructed around books.

And Equiano—heretofore in the larger story the self-described stranger—now appeared to be the insider, the quintessential Englishman. Or—to put the matter the other way round and even more dramatically—Equiano seemed quite appropriately to belong to the world of the whites on account of his Protestant-Christian-inflected ascetic piety,[45] which included his reading of the letters and books that defined the white world.

The response that Equiano reportedly gave to the young prince is telling: the crew (of white men), he made clear, is different from him because they lacked true faith—"they did not fear God" (204). His faith was registered in his ascetics of reading and prayer. His encouragement of church-going was intended to shore up the point he was making about his difference from the ship's crew: that there were others who were more like Equiano in their asceticism. His difference from the crews was also his likeness to many others, his participation in a larger phenomenon. The members of the ship's crew were the ones who were really different; Equiano showed that he belonged to the larger and more civilized Christianized white world.

The incident that immediately follows this experience also makes the case for scripturalization as structure of reality and as paradigm for interpretation of the white world that was Britain. Most important, it opens an even wider window onto Equiano's (representation of his) relationship to that world.

The incident, also reported in chapter 11, took place at Black River, near "the Musquito shore" (205). Equiano and his crew, along with "the [medical] Doctor" ("the celebrated Dr. Irving"), were engaged in trade with the natives. On this occasion, after giving "timely notice" with a stick as symbol that he wanted to visit the local area in which Equiano and company were located, the "Indian Governor" made an appearance. The Europeans often made liquor a part of the (cargo) trade with Indians. Tragically, what often resulted was Indian dependence upon the liquor. So it was not unusual for some chaos to ensue in connection with intoxication. On one particular occasion the intoxicated Indian Governor struck and stole a gold-laced hat from one of the local chiefs friendly to Equiano's company. With the ensuing chaos, the good doctor, after having tried to quell the riot, took off into the woods. Equiano felt himself abandoned but also in charge. As he reports on the situation, he began to think of what he had read "in the life of Columbus," that "when [Columbus] was amongst the Indians in Jamaica where on some occasion, he frightened them by telling them of certain events in the heavens" (208).[46] He thought to himself that the situation he now faced was parallel to that which Columbus on the field of first contact had faced. He also thought he had the same resources Columbus had—"I had recourse to the same expedient" in order to address the situation:

> When I had formed my determination, I went in the midst of them, and taking hold of the governor, I pointed up to the heavens. I menaced him and the rest: I told them God lived there, and that He was angry with them, and they must not quarrel so; that they were all brothers, and if they did not leave off, and go away quietly, I would take the book (pointing to the Bible), read, and *tell* [his italics] God to make them dead. This was something like magic. The clamor immediately ceased, and I gave them some rum and a few other things; after which they went away peaceably; and the Governor afterwards gave our neighbour . . . his hat again. (208)

There are several issues in this story to be addressed:

First, Equiano's use of Columbus's experience suggests that Equiano understood his own situation in relationship to the swarthy Other—the heathen/pagan Indian—complexly mirrored that of European dominants. Whatever the needed qualifications in explaining such thinking, it must be said that Equiano held firmly to and played with the parallelism to powerful effect. He wanted his readers to associate him *not* with the "Indians" but with Columbus (as example of a white man or of the power and dynamism of the white world). More specifically, he wanted readers to understand that only his earlier, naïve, non-Bible-reading self was like the Indians; his mature Bible-reading, Bible-interpreting, book-writing self was more like Columbus. Notwithstanding their infrapolitics and rivalries, nearly all Europeans had come to make Columbus signify heavily—as aggressive, curious, adventurous explorer, discoverer, conqueror, and reader of the rest of the world. Such association was important for Equiano's effort to establish himself as other than a stranger among his British readers, indeed, as embodiment and sensitive interpreter of the culture.

Second, the book—again and again and again for Equiano it is the book that matters. In this particular incident the book is demonstrated to be the locus of power, power that ironically only those integrated into European society can understand and wield. Part of the power of the book is its capacity to communicate—to speak to and hear those who participate in British society. So Equiano, as a representative figure of

English-ness, threatens to use, to talk to, to "tell" (God) on the "Indians," to move God to strike them dead.

Equiano compared this power to a kind of "magic." Actually, it is precisely at the point of categorizing the phenomenon as "something like magic" where things begin to get complicated. There are multiple ironies in this categorization: Who in terms of position and consciousness and sensibility would deem the phenomenon of the book that can talk and be talked to as something akin to magic? The "Indians"—in the story thought to be noble but simple-minded and gullible peoples who may be easily tricked? Is it the young naïve Equiano latent in the memory of the older Equiano of the story, representing "Ebo"/African world sensibilities? Is it Equiano the story-teller, who represents his own feelings and desperate interest in ingratiating himself to the white world? Or might it be the readers of Equiano's story, whose book fetish was dramatized in a complex set of power relations and then even signified on by Equiano? For whom does the magic of the book resonate? One of the above? None of the above? All of the above? That I along with all of his readers—from the late eighteenth century to the present day, must raise the questions without a simple ready answer suggests the power and poignancy of Equiano's narrative.

That Equiano wanted desperately to make the case for himself as one who was "almost English" is clear; it is a theme struck throughout the story. This incident with the book definitely recalls with a vengeance the flip side and radical fulfillment of the earlier (recurring) life incident (his chapter 3) in which the book seemingly refused to "talk" to him, refused to acknowledge his legitimate participation in British society. What is dramatized in this incident with the "Indians" is the transformation of Equiano to the point of being not only someone to whom the book speaks, but one who has the authority to speak to it and wield it as weapon and even authoritatively communicate awe-ful events that may be set in motion by the one who wields it. It is hard to miss Equiano's point that in this story it is *he*, not the white crew, who represents British Bible-reading society. With respect to Bible-reading/uses *he* is a white man, or the closest representation of such.

It is even harder to miss the further point that Equiano makes about British society: that it represents itself as Bible-reading culture, that it is defined by a kind of "magic," involving scriptures. This point is all the more significant in light of Equiano's efforts in his first chapter to describe "Ebo" world as a world that revolved around "magic" in relationship to the functions of the tribal priests—"Ah-affoe-way-cah," also called "magicians," "wise men," "doctors," "physicians" (42).[47] And it is striking that he subsequently used the term "magic" (and related terms, such as "spirits") again and again in his narrative—first and foremost in reference to the culture of the ship, but also in the typical setting in larger society—in reference to behaviors of white men and the general features of white culture:

> When I was carried on board I was immediately handled, and tossed up, to see if I were sound, by some of the crew; and I was now persuaded that I had gotten into a world of *bad spirits*.... (55)
>
> [A]nd *the white men had some spell or magic* that that they put in the water when they liked in order to stop the vessel. I was exceedingly amazed at this account, and really thought *they were spirits.* (57)
>
> During our passage...I also now first saw the use of the quadrant. I had often with astonishment seen the mariners make observations with it, and I could not think what it meant. They at last took notice of my surprise; and one of them, willing to increase it, as well as to gratify my curiosity, made me one day look through it. The clouds appeared to me to be land, which disappeared as they passed along. This heightened *my wonder*; and I was now more persuaded than ever that I was *in another world*, and that *every thing about me was magic.* (59)

These passages (all from Equiano's Chapter 2) led directly to the more famous passage (in chapter 3) involving the strange objects of the white world—a watch; a picture hanging on the wall; snow; and, of course, a book. These objects of the white world and the white people are variously described with the emotion-laden terms of culture shock: "quite surprised," "affrighted," "I thought it was something relative to magic," "appeared very odd to me," "I very much feared they would kill and eat me," "filled...with new surprise" "at a great loss," "astonished at the wisdom of the white people," "amazed," "had great curiosity," "I began to be mortified" (62–69).

These responses to the white world are strategic for Equiano's narrative. They reflect the culture shock of the young, nonwhite, naïve, and ignorant Equiano, to be sure. But there is more at issue: they reflect Equiano's interest in demonstrating not only that as the mature reading and writing Equiano he was not naïve and ignorant about the ways of the white world, but that the ways of the white world, just like the ways of the Indians and blacks, could be and needed to be critically investigated and explained. Such investigation could be assumed only by one who is uniquely positioned—as sort of a stranger to but with intimate knowledge of and a willingness to participate in the society. Cleverly woven together and presented as an "interesting" life story, that is, with the shortcomings and criticisms of the society deflected, Equiano's investigation was likely designed to commend itself as an apology of sort for the inclusion of the likes of Equiano as citizen in (bourgeois, book-reading, white) society.

So, again, more was at issue than what the simple development of the incident suggested. More than merely representing British culture or imitating an Englishman in the incidents with the Musquitos, Equiano, insofar as he categorized the traditions of the worlds of the Igbo and the British in terms of "magic," was also signifying on British culture. He was continuing the effort begun in his first chapter to engage in comparative religion and culture—comparing features of a white world to a black world. Given the arena in which Equiano found himself, an arena in which it was African culture, not British culture, that was dominated, held in contempt, and devalued, the comparison was intended to elevate and render valuable the former. But doing this required a critical analysis of the latter, an analysis that would result in a type of leveling.

Put in slightly different terms, the story was intended to put British culture into a critical framework and perspective—the compelling and disturbing if not singular framework and perspective that only one who had been an outsider but now is a qualified insider—"almost an Englishman"—could bring to it. In this incident the "Indians" were made to be akin to the "Africans," and Equiano represented Columbus. Equiano was like the adventurer Columbus in "discovering" what and who lies beyond the walls, the strange lands and peoples. The strange peoples in this incident were—à la Columbus, of course—the "Indians." Such identifications must have caused double takes among the first readers of the story. Equiano was playing a serious game. No matter how he characterizes and labels himself in this and other incidents in his larger story, the strange people who are "discovered" and explained are really the British. And we seem to be left with the notion that the British are the focus because of the nature of Equiano's seemingly simple imitation complex, desperately wanting and needing to become an Englishman of some type he understood and defined and sought to model on his terms.

So a bit of caution is needed if Equiano's plaintive expression about wanting to be an Englishman is to be understood. More than any other argument made about Equiano's mentality or relationship to African traditions, the construction of this controversial story leads me to think that Equiano not only claimed his "African" ancestry and its traditions, but also aimed to make sense of British culture and traditions in terms of this ancestry, vague and made up as it was, with the sketchy (textless) memories but thick sensibilities and textures. So it can be argued that in this particular story with the window it opens onto some paradoxes and rather disturbing things, including the all too easy categorizations ("Indians," "black," "white") and actions (the imitation of the white gaze; white domination and exploitation of nonwhites, including the exploitative uses of religious objects, the book that was the Bible, no less), Equiano was not so much making the simple case for becoming Englishman as he was making a compelling case for (a significant degree of) sameness/similiarity or better fluidity between European and African sensibilities and traditions. Insofar as magic, and the orientations and practices that accompany it, was found in African traditions, it was also to be found in European traditions.[48] This was adept and tricky social and cultural criticism—leveling with a very "crooked stick" (Hurston), "signifying with a vengeance" (Marrouchi).[49]

The Bible as scriptures is the site/object around which Equiano sought to advance his argument regarding the chaotic incident with the Musquito Indians. Imitating white men, he used the Bible to exploit and control. He shows the readers that he had learned some lessons quite well. In using the Bible, he was not seeking to be something other than African. He was uninterested in becoming Englishman, except insofar as he understood how little basic difference there was between the two worlds and that becoming an Englishman did not require leaping across an impossible radical divide; there were some bridges.[50] Yet what he wanted most was to help define being an Englishman in terms that were for most of his contemporaries rather counterintuitive: he stood for including being African as part of being English. This radical goal explains the need not only for a book of the sort he wrote but also his political efforts. (About this interest and the concrete efforts he made there is much more to be stated.)

That Equiano was not able or willing to countenance any such similarity between the "Indian" traditions and African worlds suggests much about the times, where he was located, opportunism, and the demographics of his readers. He clearly used "Indians" in order to argue with his primary (white, British) readers. He used them in order to establish his affinity with British ways, even if doing so meant sometimes depicting them as the greater "other," the more compelling "stranger," or sometimes even in ironic and patronizing terms as the better model of Christian virtues. The bottom line here is Equiano's strategic narratological and psychological interest in presenting himself as a credible figure within the British world. That this was done at the expense of other Others is, of course, doubly ironic and makes his story all the more "interesting."

Equiano's (re-)positioning of himself in relationship to "Indians" is controversial and complex. That it was done for the sake of narratological interests is clear enough. That the interests behind such interests were social-political, viz., having to do with black integration into British society, makes the matter all the more layered and requires comparative consideration here of Equanio's relationship to other blacks in England (and beyond). This consideration will in turn open a window back onto Britain as biblical social formation.

Now regarding blacks in England and parts of the "new world" culturally and economically connected to England, what should be noted first is the terminology used to refer to them. They are referred to variously as "poor Africans," "poor countrymen" (97), "poor oppressed Africans," "poor souls" (101), "poor fellows," (101), "unfortunate wretches" (101), "miserable wretches" (102), "poor oppressed man" (106), "poor creatures" (107), "oppressed African brethren" (224). One of the terms recurring most often, the one on which the emphasis is placed throughout the story, is the term "poor" used as both modifier and substantive. The ultimate, if not direct, source for this term is clearly the Bible. It provides a powerful emotional language with which to describe the treatment of black slaves in various parts of the Atlantic worlds, especially the Caribbean islands and the slave-holding southern part of what was becoming the United States:

> I have already related an instance of particular oppression out of many I have witnessed; but the following is frequent in all the islands.... Is not this one common and crying sin, enough to bring down God's judgment on the islands? He tells us, the oppressor and the oppressed are both in his hands; and if these are not *the poor*, the broken-hearted, the blind, the captive, the bruised, which our Saviour speaks of, who are they? (108)

With this commentary Equiano makes explicit the connection between the black enslaved throughout the Atlantic worlds and the "poor" who in the Bible are (paradoxically) privileged. "He tells us" is definitely construed as a contemporary Protestant-cultural shorthand reference to God via the Bible (understood as "word of God"). Such an expression makes perfect sense as part of the larger world in which it is believed books talk. The expression "which our saviour speaks of" is reference to words of Jesus, most likely—given the emphasis on the "poor"—from the evangelist Luke's story-telling.[51] So Equiano identifies the black enslaved with the people who are privileged by God. And he makes this identification through his exegesis of the (English Protestant) Bible.

Beyond advancing the utopian orientation in the Gospel—here particularly regarding the poor—Equiano seems also to have tried to make the point that all blacks, enslaved or free, should be converted to Christianity, otherwise they would never be (English) literate and would therefore always be poor and pathetic, outside the circle of (British) "culture": "When you make men slaves . . . you stupefy them with stripes, and think it necessary to keep them in a state of ignorance; and yet you assert that their minds are such a barren soil or moor, that culture would be lost on them" (112). This sort of argument was clever, designed to convince the reader to be open to what should be considered the compelling first step, viz. radical universal religious/evangelical conversion, in order to change society.[52]

Having impressed Governor Macnamara in London in the late 1770s, Equiano was approached by him about the possibility of being involved in "converting my countrymen to the Gospel-faith." In spite of some reservations, Equiano agreed to look into the possibilities because he understood such an effort in terms of "doing good . . . amongst my countrymen" (221). With the help of Macnamara and others, he corresponded with Anglican church officials about the possibility of getting the church's support for the effort, including his ordination as priest. From the bishop he received only "much condescension and politeness," with the note that the prelates as a body "were not of opinion in sending a new missionary to Africa" (223). Masking disappointment and humiliation and, again, reflecting what in his mind was a sense of the strategic, he refused to express the direct charge of antiblack prejudice and indicated that his recording of the matter was intended to show that important persons with some familiarity with Africa had considered the initiative important and looked to the "legislature" to give it support. The registration of the experience also reflects Equiano's strategic thinking in terms of a broad religion-based project in which black peoples are brought into the European civilizational orbit. Apart from such a project, blacks are presumed to remain mostly ignorant and unsaved and enslaved; and white dominants will then be left with corrupt hearts and—with a wink and a nod—fewer markets to exploit.[53]

After many other adventures on sea as later recorded in chapter 12, Equiano visited Philadelphia. Upon examination of the "friendly" and radically abolitionist Quakers and their "free school" for "my oppressed brethren," Equiano registered—in what is, apart from his conversion story—a rare moment of unqualified joy. The school had been established for every "denomination"[54] of blacks. Within the school the students' "minds are cultivated…and forwarded to virtue; and thus they are made useful members of the community." This was precisely the sort of project with which Equiano (and his companions in England[55]) wanted to be associated. He wanted to support such projects and see them flourish all over the Atlantic worlds. The school curriculum doubtless included training in reading arts and Christian fundamentals. Through such training the "brethren" there were assumed to be better positioned to be integrated into the larger Christian society. "Does not the success of this practice say loudly to the planters, in the language of scripture—'Go ye, and do likewise?'" (224).[56] Note again Equiano's exegesis/use of scriptures: Jesus is interpreted in the case of this contextual reading, of challenging the white Christians who are the white planters in the Caribbean and other parts of the Americas to be more humane in their treatment of black slaves, including providing them some form of education. This biblical challenge may have seemed and still does seem in terms of social reform too small a step or gesture to some. But here Equiano's very exegetical practice is proof of the potential revolutionary ramifications of the step being directed. Is it not likely that Equiano was thinking about the radical transformation that learning had effected in him?[57]

Equiano's ultimate solidarity with enslaved blacks, formerly enslaved blacks, and Africans in the homeland is reflected powerfully in his interest in depicting all of them as fellow "strangers" among or in relationship to the dominant and majority Europeans. Equiano seemed to understand himself to be in some respects one among the "poor Africans," and in some other respects he seemed to view himself as no longer holding such status, as someone who used to be but is no longer among the strangers who are the black poor. The dividing line or decisive factor in Equiano's consideration seems to be his learning to read and his conversion experience. The two experiences are for Equiano pretty much the same.

In the story Equianio tells about his life he refers to himself as a "poor" African and "stranger." But he is so only after the experience of being kidnapped from his tribal home and being transported and enslaved in the Western world and before he is converted into bible-reading Christianity. He thinks of himself in bad straits in the prior situation, that is, in terms of slavery and/as his lack of ability to read, thus his inability to understand and negotiate the world into which he was thrown. Again and again as he records his early life experiences of being tossed from one new and unexplained situation to another, from one master to another, he indicates his emotions, which were the same ones he felt in response to the various objects he had "discovered" in the white world—fear ("I was very much affrighted" [64]), astonishment ("any object I saw filled me with new surprise" [67]), amazement (68), and humiliation (69). And he makes it clear again and again that he thinks that learning to read English was the key to making the difference between continued life of estrangement and some degree of integration into the dominant society. The first talking-book story[58] occurs in the context (chapter 3) of Equiano's most acute experiences of estrangement and alienation. The message in that context is that the facility for reading the book is the key to integration into society. In the episodes that follow this story, as Equiano learns to read, he also begins to experience less fear and more acceptance by elements of the dominant society. At the beginning of chapter 4 is an emotional if somewhat convoluted summary expression of the transformation he experienced:

> I soon grew a stranger to terror of every kind, and was in that respect at least, almost an Englishman. I have often reflected with surprise that I never felt half the alarm at any of the numerous dangers I have been in, that I was filled with at the first sight of the Europeans, and at every act of theirs, even the most trifling, when I first came among them, and for some time afterwards. That fear... was the effect of my ignorance. (77)

What made the difference? "I had long wished to be able to read and write; and for this purpose I took every opportunity to gain instruction" (78). From this moment Equiano made himself a student of English letters and culture. And except for rhetorical gestures of solidarity with other blacks, he became other than a "poor African." The argument of his story is that his learning to read facilitated his personal success. Becoming someone other than a "poor African" did not alienate him from other Africans; it positioned him to see himself in the larger world with greater possibilities, including possibilities for other Africans, the great majority of whom were in his view "poor" because of their lack of facility for reading the English scripts. The point being made through his own epic life story was that reading books, especially the one that was the Good Book, facilitated integration into British society, with possibilities appertaining thereto.

In his dealings with other readers—royalty, members of Parliament. abolitionist activists, evangelicals and their opposites, state church officials, popular intellectuals, other blacks, including a special circle of black activists, and other individuals—Equiano demonstrated his understanding of the importance of reading books in British society and, for the sake of his salvation, his integration into dominant society and his personal-social and economic success. There is plenty of evidence of this understanding in the life story that he wrote, but there is also some rather interesting evidence in other sources, primarily in letters addressed to individuals and, through the newspapers, public letters that represented a joining of debates about compelling public issues (almost always in some respect about blacks, their status, and their inclusion within British society).[59]

The very fact that Equiano engaged in persistent articulate and passionate communication in the form of writing, in English—with any parties—strengthens the point that he makes throughout his story about his development and capacity for citizenship. He depicts himself on an epic journey in his quest to learn to read and be part of English society. The earlier forms of his communication, mostly letters, notwithstanding some harsh and condescending and racist responses to them, proved that he had achieved a degree of recognition in the public debates in society. Or perhaps, more accurately, they proved that he had learned how to use English book learning in order to construct a different self and position himself to fight for some things for himself and others.

What about the various addressees of the letters? What do they represent? As diverse as they are in their social and political orientations, they were for Equiano the faces and voices of the culture. What they had in common was the facility for reading and engaging books. In fact, in terms of their reading and interpretive practices they defined the meanings of the basics that he had come to accept and negotiate—such as (Western) "civilization," "culture," "Christianity," "truth." They were those to whom the books talked, those *through* whom the books talked. They were those in relationship to whom—that is, in imitation of whom—letters and books mattered. To be in some sort of discourse—including passionate argument—with them meant engaging letters and reading books, which meant being integrated into society.

It was British representations of a Bible-inflected dissenting evangelicalism that was the key bridge of Equiano's integration into British society. With the society as a fairly open and playable discursive field for many possible biblical rhetorical gestures, Equiano was able to find ways to negotiate his integration into that society. Any discerning person in late eighteenth- century Britain interested in engagement, in being influenced and of some influence, would have recognized the importance of making use of the Bible. I make again the point that arguments about the decline of the Bible in the culture by this time really miss the point: the Bible had already been made to do the work of helping to construct a culture, an order, a world of discourse and rhetorics, a semiosphere. What I call scripturalization as phenomenon was already a reality; it mattered not much that individuals inveighed against particular construals of the text or the text itself. Detractors and critics were merely reacting to a powerful reality, a reality, as Grafton helps us understand, that had been bounded by the Bible. Equiano seemed to understand this, that the power of this binding was social-psychological and meta-exegetical, meta-discursive. For this reason Equiano consistently makes clear that it was the ability to *read* and *use* the Bible—among other scripts and scriptures—that was so important for him.

In the different forms of communication in which he addressed parties on a wide range of issues, the Bible was used—creatively, passionately, sometimes playfully, always strategically. It was the rhetorical-discursive substratum in that world. It was symbol of the tie that bound persons together. It represented that framework within which persons had the opportunity to communicate effectively, that is, to speak and be heard, to negotiate that world and make themselves at home—the opposite of being "stranger." This is what Equiano observed and strove to exploit. And so it remains the case, throughout Euro-American civilization (see Figure 3.3.)

FIGURE 3.3 Litera scripta Manet ("The Written Word Endures") Librarian's Room. Dome with the central disc displaying the mural. Letters by Edward J. Holslag. Library of Congress Thomas Jefferson Building, Washington, D.C. Library of Congress, Prints & Photographs Division, photograph by Carol M. Highsmith, LC-DIG-highsm-11729.

4

"to the Britons first...the Gospel is preached": Scripturalization in the Nationalizations of White Men's Magic

May Heaven make the British senators the dispensers of light, liberty and science, to the uttermost parts of the earth: then will be the glory to God on the highest, on earth peace, and good-will to men—Glory, honour, peace, &c. to every soul of man that worketh good; to the Britons first, (because to them the Gospel is preached), and also to the nations.

—OLAUDAH EQUIANO, *Interesting Narrative*, chapter 12

THE IMPORTANT ROLE of the Bible in the making of the modern "Protestant" British nation has been firmly established in historical scholarship.[1] That the phenomenon of modern nation-formation was founded upon, refracted through, and inflected by the Bible and was widespread in Europe if not—according to some interpretive paradigms—pan-European, has also been recognized by scholars.[2] The differences in the processes of such formation notwithstanding—for example, in original motivations, in shape, character, intensity, and complexity—the uses of the Bible for the establishment of the modern European nation cannot be denied; what remains is clarity about origins, development, differentiation, and consequences.

The uses of the Bible in the modern European nationalization represented an historical stage in the uses of scriptures that took for granted the Bible as part of scripturalization as social-cultural matrix, my focus in the previous chapter. The social-psychological naturalization or social binding function of the Bible was a fundamental accomplishment, a baseline for the programs of nationalization. In the case of European nations all, scriptural sedimentation—the ubiquity and uses of the Bible in all aspects of society and culture, including the political—had (been made to) set in long before the early modern era. This was true before there were Protestant formations and nations, notwithstanding the roiling debates, popular assumptions, spins, obfuscations, and prejudices about who were the Bible readers. Before there were Protestants as we know them today, there was the far-flung always unstable but powerful Holy Roman Empire that legitimized itself through its control of "sacred" texts (and other media). The phenomenon of Protestantism should be understood as representing exploitation of the psychology and politics of scriptures for the sake of reform and other agendas. It is a mistake to argue that Protestantism invented scriptural-ism. Protestantism may have represented intensifications, but it did not invent the magic that is the subject of this book. As I argued in the previous chapter, Equiano's debate with the Catholic priest about the Bible was no more than a reflection of Equiano's interest in carrying nationalist-ideological water for Britain. It should shock no one to be reminded that in Equiano's time, and in our own, nations have shown stakes in the manufacturing and fanning of certain popular notions about many things. The critical issue is always understanding what are the stakes.

In the nationalization efforts in the early modern period, when complex social and political formations emerged that called themselves Protestants, the heretofore common European Bible was reinvented and rewritten[3] and used in order to make explicit the divine sanction of the social-political order of the new state. Of course, the relationship between social-cultural binding and political binding was complex—the biblically inflected social-cultural binding legitimized the state, and the state in turn legitimized and protected the social-cultural binding.

In Equiano's lifetime, England and much of the rest of Europe and its colonies had already begun to advance ideologies and structures of nationalization—in large part through uses (recastings and reconstruals) of the Bible. Nationalization was advanced through the mystifying authoritative offices and worldly interests of the various formations (now all too flatly called denominational groups) that had developed as part of the variegated European Reformation movement. The power and far-reaching influence of the various protonationalist-church groups were achieved through the development of explicit confessional statements that identified and oriented the holders of such statements in rather clear terms. These terms were ostensibly religious and rationalist-doctrinalist in character, but of course they effectively determined the boundaries of, as well as the terms for membership in, the civic and political unit that would correspond to the religious community.

Confessionalization[4] is now recognized among historians of early modern Europe as a representation of European reform and social dynamism—incipient modernism—around if not before 1600. It represented a playing out of some of the major internal conflicts in the Western late medieval society. These divisions have for too long among critics appeared to be only theological-doctrinal in nature, but the larger social-cultural and political ramifications are now evident to almost all students. What ensued from the agenda of confessionalization was the creation of confessional churches that corresponded to the advancement of social-cultural or protonationalist identities, in some cases even state or territorial boundaries. And each confessional church of course claimed to have discovered an "extraordinary method" of reading scriptures, certain truths that made it imperative to separate itself from the corrupt dominant status quo—Roman Catholic Church—with its claims to universal truth.

What was most characteristic of the period—among the new churches as new social-cultural and political formations and within the reform movements in the Roman Catholic church—was a commitment to the "unambiguous definition" of principles and orientations in the form of the confession (*confessio*): so the *Confessio Augustana* (1530) and *Konkordienbuch* (1577) among Lutherans; *Confessiones Helveticae* (1536, 1566) and other national texts, among Calvinists; the Book of Common Prayer (1549) and the 39 Articles (1563) among Anglicans; and the *Professio fidei Tridentina* (1564) among Catholics.[5]

Broached above in chapter 3, in connection with discussion about scripturalization in the social matrix, it is important to explore in a bit more detail how confessionalization functioned as part of modern nation-building and is related to scripturalization. Whatever else may have pertained to it, confessionalization was (and remains) about the construal and textual interpretation of the Bible. All confessional statements were assumed to be correct interpretation of the Bible, often accompanied by violent rhetorics and acts, including militarism. There could be no other type of interpretation of the Bible. Because by the time the Protestant groups emerged, the Bible had all over Europe—with very few exceptions, among some elites, perhaps—come to serve as rhetorical shorthand for the distillation of truth, it would not have been politically wise for any set of confessional statements anywhere in Europe to even be presumed to be in any respect unbiblical. Disagreements over confessional statements assumed on someone else's part a flawed approach in the interpretation of the Bible. All confessional statements were claimed to be authoritative, in (almost) the same respect as the Bible. It is important to understand that they functioned in the same way as the Bible.

Such statements were needed for a variety of reasons, not least having to do with the threat experienced by different parties seen in the conflicts around the Bible, including various culturalist assumptions about forms and styles of engagements of the Bible, the matter of what texts legitimately constituted the Bible, and of course the appropriate authoritative ramifications, especially for political dynamics, to be taken from various interpretations. In a word, what was at issue was power, with the Bible as the site of power.

Since Foucault, with his explicit theorizing, and before him, with the mostly untheorized historical-discursive soundings from the unnamed subalterns who have spoken out of their traumatic experiences, we have been challenged to understand power not so much in terms of a particular thing located here or there that can be taken up and wielded by someone.[6] Power is now more generally understood by theorists to be imbedded within and experienced through the dynamics of relationships, and wielded and felt differently in different contexts. Those who promoted the confessional statements aimed to exercise power—the power of, and to, *make-believe*, that is, to make the social collective believe certain things in certain ways, to make it accept the reality of things that are made up. The authors and guardians of the sixteenth-century confessions wanted the confessions to be authoritative statements, levers of control, shapers of the collective imagination and political will, in short, ironically, despite the contours of Protestant anti-Catholic charges about such, a kind of magic.[7]

Powerful as they were, the sixteenth-century confessional statement writers—as religious virtuosi, representatives of a particular type of elites[8]—were not always self-conscious about their own operations. But surely this does not mean that others' readings—Equiano, for example—of their operations should be uninformed. It does not make the situation and motives more or less complex that the interests of the elite inventors of realities in this case had to do—and still have to do—with religious confessions, or confessions of faith as biblical exegesis. It is not merely naïve to believe that what we mean by "religion" "transcends" or is of a different domain from the political; in point of fact, such an assumption, which aims to make us believe "religion" is above and beyond the usual dynamics of power relations, is itself the most profound effect of the power dynamics or the sometimes obfuscating offices of the magic on which this book focuses.

Confessionalization was clearly among the dynamics captured under the umbrella term "religion" for the early modern period; the term itself, with its suggestion of complex process and development (viz., -izations), seems to invite analysis precisely in terms of historical social, cultural, and political dynamics. And it thereby invites comparison to scripturalization as a complex phenomenon. I understand confessionalization and scripturalization to be in relationship to each other, with the latter providing a larger historical and conceptual framework for the former: confessionalization assumes, even presumes scripturalization, that is, a social-cultural regime based around "scriptures."[9] Scripturalization makes confessionalization possible, perhaps necessary: insofar as a society makes (textualized) scriptures the center-point around which it is oriented or—to turn the matter around—when a collective establishes a center-object as point-site for its orientation, a time will likely come when the meaning or the power and use of such center-object needs to be made more defensible or rational. Occasions for such responses may include internal differentiation or pressures from the outside. The religious wars and intrigues that destabilized Europe during the fifteenth and sixteenth centuries would help explain the development of confessional formations as modern nation-formations. If persistent violence does not settle the matter, why not try infra-ideological shifts, rearrangements, ruptures? This seems to me to be what confessionalization as one of the strategies and historical forms of scripturalization represented.

Such formations can obviously be analyzed from many different perspectives with many different methods and approaches. In spite of the fact that critics of the period acknowledge the importance of the Bible in the formation of the new religious and state denominations, just what this meant—what using the Bible meant, what the Bible itself signified—remains to be explained. Again, Equiano, as an informed and complexly situated "stranger" opens a window onto the matter.

In spite of all the social and political reforms that the reformation movements suggested or promised—including, ironically, for some groups, the boast about the freedom and authority of each individual to read and interpret the Bible for him or herself—the new religious-collectives-turned-state-churches effectively arrogated to themselves power, in the form of authority to interpret what the Bible meant for the different readers in the various new states. Or certainly, they asserted their authority to set the terms on which individuals could pursue the right interpretation. The confessional statements, which provided excellent ideological obfuscation for the official political agenda, representing in explicit terms the collusion of political and military-coercive and social-sacerdotal domains,[10] were essentially models of and rules for interpretation of the Bible. The latter was deemed important by all the colluding parties and domains, as had been the case for Catholic prelates. But, in addition to control and authority inside the Catholic church, there was also a larger set of issues having to do with the imbededness of the Bible throughout European society and culture. Insofar as the Bible had come to be the most important if not the only pan-European literary and rhetorical site in common, insofar as it was seen as the depository of ancient wisdom and canon for political and social-cultural ideology, structures, moral rules, and ethics for every situation or contingency—notwithstanding the critiques of the Enlightenment and other ongoing arguments among some elite groups and individuals—it was little wonder that change and reform-ation would lead to confessionalization. The latter represented creative and sometimes daring exegetical strategies and politics. That it was assumed that every current situation was directly or indirectly referenced in the Bible is evidence not merely of a type of human persistence and ingenuity, but more fundamentally and strikingly, of a dynamics of arrogation of agency and power that has multidirectional and multilevel and conflicting reverberations.

This dynamic of change was facilitated through language. In the case of Britain, the language that was deemed authoritative, the "language of the god" of European Christendom, the vehicle through which such a civilizational complex was advanced, was first, Latin, with the many power issues appertaining to it. Through Latin the scriptures were for many centuries experienced directly and indirectly, in hyperscholastic and multimedia popular terms, in formal public institutional and in informal private spheres. Then, for a number of reasons that need not be detailed here, it became important for many of the peoples who had been historically bound together through the Latin Bible to embrace the efforts to make the Bible more accessible, to make it "speak" to people in their own vernaculars. The success of vernacularization movements can be explained only if they are understood to have represented the interests of many—across status and class lines; across regions and territories; among political elites, including royalty and the *hoi polloi*.

What this situation depended on was making clear the authoritative "reading formation,"[11] in this case, the practice by which the nation is read into and out of the scriptures and thereby understood to be legitimate. In this situation, getting the Bible right was no longer merely a matter of reading in order to ascertain the independent truth or facts in themselves—the literary or rhetorical functions of or the historical facts or theological import behind certain passages—or for anyone's special antiquarian interest. There may have been some grudging and wary tolerance for unofficial reading practices for some individuals who were outside the box, outside the formation—university men, enlightenment writers, scientists, explorers, and so forth. But these were exceptions: what was always most important during the first wave of European nationalization was positioning, as individual or as group, within the larger ideological-political framework within which now all legitimate reading was to take place, the reading that recognized the special mystifying origins and powers and mission of the nation. This was a reading that was understood to be fundamental or critical to the security and maintenance of the nation. In such a situation—as the likes of sister Francis, John Bunyan, and Thomas More could testify, their differences notwithstanding—a particular nonsanctioned exegetical gesture or type of practice could land one in prison or lead to beheading.

In the age of the onset of the European confessional churches and their contributions to particular forms and ideologies of nationalization, there simply were no scriptures—and no interpretation of scriptures—outside the powerful framework of the nation, that is, apart from the public squares or domains.[12] But the situation was complicated, for the make-believe reality that the new formation that was the "nation" was also facilitated and legitimized by that made-up reality that was the Bible. The same mentalité or "reading" that made the people believe (in) the "reality" of the "nation" also made them, as citizens of the nation, believe (in) the "reality" of "scriptures"—of and for the nation. The one was impossible without the other. The one facilitated belief in the other. Without the make-believe facilitated by "scriptures"—among other factors and considerations, to be sure—the "nation" was only a collection of people sharing space and time. Without the make-believe "facilitated" by the "nation," the "scriptures" called "the Bible" were only collections of texts, important perhaps for some, but not powerful in absolute terms. In this situation one type of magic created and enhanced the other.

Equiano's story reflects his keen awareness that the scriptures of the English had been used in order to facilitate political binding. This awareness did not scandalize him; on the contrary, it provided him with the strategic key by which he would attempt to navigate his way through and come to participate in the society. It became the basis on which he would seek to become British. No matter his actual legal status at any particular time, Equiano reflected his awareness of the uses of the Bible in the construction of the identity and in the continuing legitimatization and governance of the nation. He makes clear his understanding of the usefulness of the Bible in terms of his participation in the ongoing work of nation-building. This recognition explains his seriousness about, even obsession with, learning to read. With the ability to read, he could see the way to being a citizen, one who could be part of the important public debates of the times. That slavery was and should be among the important issues of the day was clear enough to Equiano. Reading and writing and responding to reading and writing in public debate and telling his story he found to be the way for him to enter and have impact on such debates.

The debates were generally rhetorically framed—sometimes honestly, sometimes not—in terms of what was considered in the interest of the nation. No higher cause could be acknowledged and respected. The meaning of that good for the nation was most often argued about—in many different rhetorical keys: bombastic, literalist, doctrinalist, figurative—with reference to the Bible.

In almost every piece of writing with which his name is associated—whether written singly or with others—Equiano registered some sort of acknowledgment of and genuflection to the British nation. To be sure, much of the language—highly florid, formal, and exaggerated—is appropriate for the times and the discursive and social situations.[13] And one can hardly miss in such registrations the references to the Bible not only as the foundation but also as the entry point for participation in the nation.

Yet in some of Equiano's uses of the Bible, more than the general truth about its widespread influence in society and culture he understood to be at stake. What was often at stake was the registration of the nationalization of the Bible. Equiano needed to acknowledge his understanding of the reality of the nationalization of scriptures. He was on the outside wanting to be allowed inside. So he needed to present himself as someone who understood what being British meant. Among other things, he noted that being British meant reading the British nation in and out of the Bible, reading the nation's origins and development in the Bible, and seeing a special place for the nation in the Bible. Equiano realized that there were many obstacles to his being accepted as a British citizen or as Englishman. He also seemed to realize that such possibilities would forever elude him if he could not acknowledge not merely the scriptures in English but now, on the other side of the reformation era, the scriptures of the British *nation*.

For the sake of a closer view of the sources relevant to a discussion about Equiano's understanding of the scriptures in relationship to British nationalization, it may be helpful first to revisit the scene in which he encounters the Catholic priest. When discussed in the last chapter, it was argued that this episode provided evidence for the role of the Bible as social-cultural matrix. I should like to add that it is also compelling evidence for the nationalization or political binding function of scriptures.

In the episode with the priest, Equiano depicts himself as the standard-bearer and protector of British Protestant piety over against the priest as standard-bearer and protector of Spanish Roman Catholic piety. It is made clear that the conflict is over the Bible—more specifically, about who is authorized to read and interpret it. Equiano depicts himself as the voice of the typical British Protestant registering sentiment that in Catholic countries such as Spain the Bible either is not read, or is not highly regarded, or is read incorrectly by a few elites presuming to have special and absurd types of authorization and powers. And he depicts the priest as representative of the Spanish Catholic position that understood England to be ignorant and disrespectful of "Church" hierarchy and its stable system of tradition and authorization that secured the truth. Of course, these sentiments represented cultural and nationalistic exaggerations and prejudices; the realities were quite the contrary: England had its own traditions and systems of authorization that reached back before its reformation period and within which it framed a recognizable Anglican reading of the Bible and larger social-political formation.[14] Would not the testimony of some of the various dissenters be that they hardly experienced Britain as a society of scriptural exegetes who could read and interpret openly and freely? And regarding Spain, as had been the case in many political and social-cultural complexes that had been part of the Holy Roman Empire and its predecessors, the scriptures were, contrary to popular assumptions that remain to this day, quite important and powerful.[15] Might the truth have really been that scriptures were not irrelevant but considered too important and too powerful and volatile to be left to any but officials to interpret?

This sort of debate about the role of the scriptures in the two cultural camps, with assumptions and prejudices and stereotypes and exaggerations and ignorance, continues to rage on, even to this day. It is important, even imperative, to note here that Equiano's story is his recognition of the debate and his depiction of his own positionality and participation in it. Equiano names the Bible as the issue around which much controversy and conflict continue to turn in the cultural and nationalistic discussions, debates, politics and, it must be remembered, even wars of his times. Far from being scandalized by the debate and the rancor associated with it, and far from positioning himself as outsider to the debate, Equiano rather boldly positions himself in the context of this debate quite squarely and resolutely—as ("almost") an *Englishman*. More than anything else, it is his sentiment about the Bible that makes him so.

So the scene between himself and the Catholic priest is very dramatic and ironic: it is a realistic depiction of a fraught debate that suggests the name of the different institutionalizations of the social-cultural-political structure of "reality" built around scriptures—what I am calling in this book "scripturalization." Again, Equiano's interest is clear: he wants to position himself firmly within and speak to such a structure, at least the British instantiation of it. He wants to signify it; he wants to belong to it, but he also wants to be able to signify *on* it. That Equiano does not signify on scripturalization in the episode with Father Vincent is part of the general strategic goals of his narrativization: his arguments and strongly held positions, with some rhetorical explosions as exceptions, are indirect, subsumed under narrative form. This method makes his arguments not at all simple or straightforward; they beg nuanced critical analysis. Further, it seems important for Equiano to establish his identification with England over against what Father Vincent represented. Any Englishman would relish the opportunity to register English bona fides by taking on a Catholic Spaniard in the way depicted. The only thing possibly more delightful for an Englishman would have been taking on a *French* Catholic.

In this chapter the importance of the episode with the priest has to do with Equiano's showing whose—national—side he is on, and how this stance is proven through focus on a particular orientation to or set of assumptions about scriptures. The point of the episode is to show that, in response to the criticism voiced by the Catholic priest, not only everybody in England read the Bible but that Equiano, in drawing directly upon but not acknowledging his quotation of the passage "Christ desired us to search the scriptures,"[16] was identifying himself as Englishman: There is no "us" in the original passage; there is only Jesus' actually somewhat sardonic admonition to his detractors and skeptics to "search the scriptures" to discover the truth about his identity and his works. The word "us" is then all the more fascinating; it was inserted by Equiano or someone else in order to convey his conviction (or hope) that he is part of the collective object understood here to be the British nation. Equiano shows his readers not only that he understands what is at issue in the debate with the Catholic priest, that he is a fierce defender of English tradition, but that with respect to one of the most important criteria for inclusion in the nation as church, church as nation—faith, piety in relationship to the Bible—he is one of them. It is his exegetical ingenuity or sleight of hand that here shows him to be a good student of Protestant, specifically English, practices and politics. The capacity and willingness to read into and out of the Bible—including the reputed words of Jesus—the national British situation and sentiments were bold and telling.

There are other situations and sentiments recorded in Equiano's story that speak to his understanding of the British nation. In his chapter 12 Equiano responds in London (in 1779) to a question put to him by a Governor MacNamara, someone whom he had "served." The question had to do with Equiano's religious affiliation. In response Equiano speaks in direct and explicit terms and with pride: "I told him I was a Protestant of the Church of England, agreeable to the thirty-nine articles of that church, and that whomsoever I found to preach according to that doctrine, those I would hear" (220–221). Here the nationalization of religion and the religion of the nation can hardly be reflected more strongly. What a great student of British culture Equiano made himself to be.

A couple of issues beg further comment: first, it is clear that Equiano equates membership in good standing in the Church of England with the facility to read and understand that there are doctrinal statements, here in the form of the articles of confession, even if—as was the case among the majority population—such articles were not engaged or clearly understood. It was enough for most people to acknowledge the existence of the articles and the authority of the clergy to divine their meanings for all. Second, as the appellation itself indicates, the confession has as much to do with the assumptions about and participation in the "nation" as with the "church." The clergy, after all, were civil servants. The church was the Church of England; royalty pledged to protect the church, the church the crown; fidelity to church was fidelity to crown, and vice versa. The nationalization and territoriality of the Church of England was advanced and in Equiano's time not reversible.

After more opportunities to engage in "some more discourse on the same subject," the Governor was so impressed by Equiano that he suggested that Equiano become a missionary to Africa. As is discussed above in chapter 3, Equiano at first expressed reservations. He recalled his early evangelical efforts in Jamaica that resulted in his being "served... by "some white people" (221). He feared that he might have an experience that would subject him to the kind of abusive treatment that the apostle Paul is said to have experienced. Alluding to what "Alexander the coppersmith did [to] St Paul" as an isolated independent missionary, as recorded in a New Testament passage (2 Tim.4:14–15),[17] Equiano expressed his reluctance to accept the suggestion. What may occasion surprise is the recognition that Equiano read the New Testament passage, with the necessary minor qualifications needed to account for the differences in ancient and early modern contexts, along much the same ironic empire-accommodating, empire-defensive lines associated with "Paul" of this text (a figure who was a stand-in for the conservative empire-accommodating second-generation tradents). He showed that he was for the sake of "salvation" (from continued slave-trafficking and slavery) willing to accommodate the British "empire," that in order to advance his own late eighteenth century missionary efforts he was somewhat in sync with the official reading formation in Britain. This is ironic and disturbing in light of the fact that Equiano trafficked with dissenters of all types. Yet it may also suggest that he was pursuing with his narrative an agenda that made it important for him to register his knowledge of and willingness to participate in the British part of the (larger Western) semiosphere of scripturalization. He made it clear that he knew the rhetorical-discursive drill and that he was willing to participate in it.

After the Governor suggested that he seek ordination and promised to support his appeal to the Bishop of London, Equiano reconsidered his position. Ordination suggested authority and power; it meant that he would be an official of the church and of the state. In addition to letters of support from Governor Macnamara and from a Dr. Wallace, Equiano also presented to the bishop his person and his own letter. But the bishop declined the request, citing no real reason but only vague high-clerical speak. That antiblack prejudice determined the bishop's response apparently did not need to be made explicit.

This episode reflects yet another one of the many disappointments in Equiano's life, no matter the reasons that may be offered to explain the bishop's rejection of Equiano. This does not imply that Equiano was less committed to evangelical work, including its dissenting reformist agenda; it meant that he was very much aware of what was signified through affiliation with and representation of the Church of England. What is important for me to stress here is that the episode, especially the exchange before the request to the bishop, shows that Equiano was aware that being ordained by the Church of England required a certain level of literacy—of the Bible and the explication of such in the confessional articles—and it would have signaled dramatically Equiano's membership in British society and his representation of the British state.

In the same chapter (12) Equiano records his experience with the Sierre Leone project, which had as its agenda the settlement of the "black poor" in Africa. A sign of his stature and reputation, he was selected in 1787 to "go with the black poor to Africa," to lead a part of the project—as commissary for the government (226). But early on he astutely detected and reported problems. His charge that some principals in the project had base motives, including slave-trafficking, and were involved in corruption, abuses, and mismanagement opened up such a chaotic swirl of counter charges, including those from a powerful white banker, that Equiano, after a short time of trying his best to remedy the situation, was relieved of his duties. After a formal investigation, he was cleared of charges. The expedition went on without him. Yet he stood "by my own integrity" and remained much committed to the cause of his "much injured countrymen" (229).

Equiano's commitment to his "much injured countrymen" is much more layered than this one incident reflects. There is evidence within his narrative and beyond it (discussed below in chapter 6) that he had rich relationships with a number of Africans in England, Cugoano in particular, who, as has been indicated already, may have been assisted by Equiano with his writing. He stood in solidarity with many displaced Africans in efforts to stop the slave trade and to improve the lot of their kind.

Equiano's continuing interest in his "countrymen" was reflected next in the narrative (in the same chapter 12) in a petition he wrote in 1788 and sent to the Queen and members of Parliament. In the petition Equiano solicits "royal pity" not for himself, but for "millions of my African countrymen, who groan under the lash of tyranny in the West Indies." And he draws the Queen's attention to the fact that Parliament was at the time considering legislation pertinent to the fate of the "wretched Africans." He asks her to turn her personal generosity and compassion into a public "benevolent influence" that may lead to the Africans' elevation, including their admittance to "your Majesty's happy government" (231–232).

The communication to the Queen was included in full within the context of reflection on the brutalities African slaves were facing in the West Indies. Equiano makes reference to a climate in which legislation was proposed and passed that actually reduced the penalties against acts of brutality against slaves.[18] Then he proceeds to discuss his hopes for actions on the part of the "gentlemen in power." The comments in this section of the narrative are essentially the same as those found in the actual letter sent during the same period to members of Parliament. But Equiano seems even more interested in appealing to the members' compassion and sense of honor as part of the effort to get them to respond to the distress of African slaves:

> May Heaven make the British senators the dispersers of light, liberty and science, to the uttermost parts of the earth: then will be glory to God on the highest, on earth peace, and good-will to men.—Glory, honour, peace & to every soul of man that worketh good; to the Britons first, (because to them the Gospel is preached), and also to the nations. (233)

What follows this rhapsodic prayer is a string of quotations from the Bible that have to do with the responses of the powerful to the calls for justice for the not so powerful:

> "Those that honor their Maker have mercy on the poor. "[Proverbs 14:31] "It is righteousness exalteth a nation; but sin is a reproach to any people [Prov 14:34]: destruction shall be to the workers of iniquity [Prov 10:29], and the wicked shall fall by their own wickedness." [Prov 11:5]
>
> The liberal devise liberal things, and by liberal things shall stand," Isaiah xxxii. 8. They can say with pious Job, "Did not I weep for him that was in trouble; Was not my soul grieved for the poor?" Job xxx. 25 (233)

The purpose of this Bible-inflected paean to the Parliament is clear enough. What I think needs to be paid most attention here is Equiano's identification of the British nation with the people of God or certainly with special status and privilege—"Glory, honour, peace &...to the Britons first, (because to them the Gospel is preached)."—thus, special responsibility: "It is righteousness exalteth a nation."

In case any readers had missed the application of the point that was being made, Equiano injects the situation of the "black poor" into the biblical exhortations and challenges and into contemporary national politics: "May the blessings of the Lord be upon the heads of all those who commiserated the cases of the oppressed negroes, and the fear of God prolong their days; and may their expectations be filled with gladness!" (233)

Through his formal, direct communications with royalty and the politically powerful, Equiano revealed much: first, he showed how much he either was already participating in or wanted to invest and participate in the politics and policies of the nation. Second, he showed through his creative capacity for reading and his creative uses of the Bible in such communications that he understood one of the important ideological and rhetorical bases upon which the nation had been built, bases upon which royalty and political figures ideologized and mystified and held onto their power. It was not argued by Equiano that the Bible was the only ideological weapon used to structure and maintain the national political system and social arrangements; it was enough for him to have recognized that it was certainly one such weapon and to learn to use it. He betrays his understanding—quite obviously shared by many others—that the nation was built partly on scriptures, and that the scriptures were in ongoing terms being defined and used for the nationalization agenda.

Given Equiano's communications with powerful national figures, what then should be made of his history of communication with religious dissenters? And what light does his relationship with such figures shed on Equiano's reading of scripturalization as nationalization? It cannot be denied that Equiano continued—even after his conversion to dissenting religion—to think of himself as a "churchman," that is, an Anglican, a member of the state church. In spite of the vituperative attacks from Anglican churchmen and other statists, Equiano did not understand dissenters to be enemies of the nation. He seemed to view them as internal critics, as legitimate and necessary re-formers. Dissenters were not so much for him opposition to the nation; they represented a wide window onto the diversity and complexity of the nation, as well as its most welcome and accommodating points of entry and negotiation.

Are there consistent and specific meanings of the many different references to the nation in Equiano's narrative? Not only Equiano's tribe, but also other "African" ethnic groups and other European peoples and, of course, people of Britain, are variously referred to as a "nation"/"nations." This suggests that Equiano understood "nation" as an organized unit of peoples, on a scale of identity-formation, complexity, legitimacy, power, and so forth, with Britain, notwithstanding all the differences in orientation, organization, complexity, and scale.

It seems important to try to understand not merely why Equiano fused rhetorics about the nation with the Bible (and religious—viz. Christian life—in general terms), but also what implications and ramifications—regarding scriptures in particular—follow from Equiano's narrativation and rhetoricization of such a phenomenon. What do Equiano's rhetorics about the nation and scriptures suggest about Equiano? What do they suggest about the larger cultural and political context in which he was placed? What do they imply about his agency?

First, Equiano's stories about his engagement of scriptures make it clear, perhaps uncomfortably so, that scriptures are not merely private issue or matter or about private issues or matters. Notwithstanding his and others' rhetorics about private piety—the sometimes compelling but ultimately obfuscating mimetics of evangelicals—the scriptures that were the English Bible as Equiano encounters them and negotiates them in Britain are public texts, public matter and about public matters. That genuflections to royalty and to political officialdom were routinely made by the general population is obvious, but the point here is that in genuflecting and by making references to scriptures, Equiano was displaying some cultural intelligence, that is, knowledge of where he was, how the society and culture in which he found himself worked. That the scriptures were represented as texts, conveyed in English—not Latin!—and not just any kind of English but English that was authorized by the powerful circles of elites by and through whom certain rules of grammar were conveyed, what came to be understood as the Authorized (King James) Version, no less—all of this suggested scriptures as public domain, as national matter, including matters territorialized.

The scriptures that were in the public domains and media were always written, translated, and authoritatively communicated by *male* elites—whether clerics, scholars, or politicians. It is no accident that it was God's revelation in written texts that proved most problematic for women's historical religious leadership. The reasons are many and both simple and complicated: they have to do with matters ranging from long-held ideologies regarding women's roles in society, their restriction to the private sphere, their lack of access to training, and to public stages, and so forth.[19] Males were identified with scriptures and scripturalizing practices insofar as literacy in most societies remained the province of elite males and insofar as scriptures came to be identified narrowly with texts. And this was the default historical situation, except in some dissenting evangelical circles, in which the possession of the spirit meant the obliteration or at least relativization of difference, and women and some nonelite males arrogated to themselves the power to speak and to interpret the truths of God. They were convinced that God's ways were revealed through many different media, among which were scriptures as texts.

Although his experience should not be the only prism through which scriptures are viewed and analyzed, it is worth noting that in his narrative Equiano does not come across many women who are authoritative wielders of the scriptures. The women who are recorded as expressing generosity in helping the youthful Equiano learn to read are located only in the private household domain. Equiano had learned that engaging scriptures in public authoritative terms was a male prerogative. All those who are understood to be authorities in the public sphere with respect to the Bible are men. The window that Equiano's story opens reveals that scripture-invention, scripture-interpretation, and scripture-mystification are historically elite male prerogatives. And these male elites in many different respects work for the state.[20] They speak for it, help legitimize it, defend it as they serve as its official wizards, magicians, diviners, in precisely the same way that the magicians and physicians—"Ah-affoe-way-cah"—served in Equiano's imagined homeland. The nationalizations of scriptures and the scripturalization of the nation are complementary dynamics. The gendered privileges, mechanisms, and politics of the one served the other.

There is no evidence that Equiano sought to change this arrangement. On the contrary, just as he did not even attempt to depict himself as the Moses/Harriet Tubman in relation to black enslaved, he did not register sensitivity to the plight of women in British society. His agenda seemed rather consistently to be focused on depicting himself as someone who understood and for the most part fit into the current social arrangements. It was a dangerous game, but it seemed to be the game to which he was committed and by which he would make himself successful in his stated efforts.

Nothing bespoke nationalization more clearly than the maintenance of a mystifying ideology—of special election, the presumption of a claim of a special or unique origin, history and divine favor, a mandate in the world. Of course, such a collective orientation is difficult to create, make acceptable within a populace without a powerful mechanism of mystification or make-believe that can stand the test of time, change, differentiation, and conflicts. Such was the effect and part of the impetus behind—even if participating individuals in any historical situation remained ignorant or uncritical about—scripturalization as social-cultural and political phenomenon. Part of what it means to continue to make compelling any sort of mystification, of any phenomenon or dynamic, is a level of ignorance, or at least lack of reflection and questioning, on the part of the many. This is surely the meaning of Equiano's description of the offices of the magicians and physicians of his homeland in terms of the "extraordinary method" and "unbounded influence" of their divination and decipherment practices (42).

It was the identification and negotiation of (at least one example of) what was "unbounded influence" in the North Atlantic worlds that accounts for Equiano's treatment of the English Bible in his story. Yet it is important to understand that Equiano's focus on the English Bible notwithstanding, it was not the texts per se that were at issue, not the English Bible as (collection of) texts as "scriptures," but "scripturalization" as regime. The latter is shorthand here for the larger dynamic that structures (in a particular way, through particular means, namely texts) the communications, knowledge, and power relations in society. Such structuring is not the same as a text or texts, but it draws upon texts, textuality, and the politics around such in order to create and sustain a particular order. If it is claimed that "God" "speaks" in or through (certain prescribed) texts, there is already a magical and absurd notion requiring suspension of judgment and critical reflection. The assumption about the naturalness of such a claim reflects one's origins and/or status and orientation inside the structure; it might be said that the naturalness of the regime is tied to the nationalization of the regime. Perhaps one's origins and status as a stranger or an outsider, among other factors, may make necessary a suspension of belief and lead to the basic critical questioning about the situation.[21] This was of course Equiano's positionality and, as I suggested in the Prologue, it is in some important respects also my own and explains my claim to connection to

Equiano and his writing project. Within the sphere of the "unbounded influence" that is experienced as scriptualization as nationalization, it is a matter of importance who has facility and authority to read and interpret what "God" "says" in scriptures. All will always agree that knowing what "God"—that English abbreviation for the ultimate—wants or requires is important. All agree that God wills to reveal what God wants and requires; this is simply another way of indicating what is imperative for the society as a whole. The challenge is to find out what was the shape and secret of that revelation. So the protocol or method by which such revelation can be divined is most important.

Finally, the matter of the apparent conflict between official nationalist-public and personal-private piety interests in the uses of scriptures needs to be addressed. The window opened by Equiano's narrative clearly shows that Equiano—the "stranger," it must be remembered—understood that the two types of interests were not in conflict, were not even of entirely different spheres, but were really part of the one bounded world. They were for him seemingly different aspects of the society-defining phenomenon.

Because it is the focus of my next chapter, I shall restrain here from discussing in detail Equiano's conversion narrative (in his chapter 11). But it is nevertheless important to make the point here that although conversion narratives are in the modern Western world popularly understood in terms of personal transformation and assumed to be limited to the private sphere,[22] Equiano makes the connection between his "conversion" and larger societal and national interest quite clear. The story of his conversion seems to be as much if not more about a type of public performance or gesture that he became convinced would make him acceptable to British society, or at least a significant part of it. It was through that significant part of British society—including but not limited to evangelical dissenters and their supporters—that Equiano the stranger thought he might be accepted. This was a public and political performance.

As Equiano makes clear as he addresses public figures—including royalty—he strove, as convert, to be seen as a legitimate member of the British nation. The degree to which his conversion experience sounded and looked like the ways of the evangelical dissenters, it had to do with ramifications for radical social change for and within the British nation. Equiano's conversion as he understood it meant not a renunciation of but a particular kind of participation in the new nation that the new religious formations were advancing. More about this experience is addressed in the next chapter.

5

"...*in the Bible, I saw things new...*": *Scripturalization and White Men's Magic as Orientation*

> *...and the Lord was pleased to break in upon my soul with ...bright beams of heavenly light; and in an instant, as it were, removing the veil, and letting light into a dark place... ...and many texts were immediately applied to me with great comfort...the Lord give the reader understanding...*
>
> —OLAUDAH EQUIANO, *Interesting Narrative*, chapter 10

THE CHAPTER THAT narrates his conversion, Chapter 10, is key to Equiano's telling of his life story. As a narrative of conversion, it is anything but simple or straightforward. As should be expected, it contains many formal and rhetorical elements that are imitative of early modern-era Protestant conversion narratives.[1] There is little need to doubt that Equiano was influenced by such traditions of narration. And that all such narrations generally convey more than what lies on the lexical or rhetorical level should not be questioned. But precisely because of its rarity if not singularity among black peoples writing in North Atlantic worlds, and because of the fraught situation in which it was written and the experiences it relates, Equiano's story begs even more consideration, even more questions. Simply because of when it was written and by whom, this conversion story resists being read in simple terms. There are many discursive threads, twists, and layers. The major challenge is to figure out some of the strategies by which Equiano attempted to relate how he "saw things new" and figured things out.

Equiano's conversion chapter is of course in narratological terms about how he became the person with the perspective and sensibilities of the one who wrote the larger story. That is the chapter's overarching focus.

But the purpose of the chapter cannot be fully understood apart from seeing that it is framed by references to two black figures.

The chapter begins by making reference (179–180) to the disturbing and tragic story of John Annis, a black man who had served as cook aboard many ships. He is suddenly and tragically stolen away to the Caribbean, is (re-)enslaved, and is eventually murdered. What was the meaning of the John Annis story for Equiano? What was its meaning in the context of this chapter? Did Equiano intend to document the vulnerability and maltreatment of blacks in England, particularly in the dock, shipping, and sailing subcultures? Surely, what Annis experienced was not unique for the times; life must have been pretty precarious for all blacks in the Atlantic worlds;[2] so why the focus on him?

The chapter ends by making reference (190) to the unnamed Ethiopian eunuch of the New Testament book of Acts,[3] who was held by a large segment of early Christian tradition to have been the first gentile convert to the movement begun in the memory of Jesus. What was the point of making reference to this figure? Is it so obvious? Had it to do with what "Ethiopian" signified among blacks? Among Europeans and others who used this term to refer to all blacks, collapsing their wide range of ethnic identities into one? What was Equiano's interest and strategy? How did he come to make use of the Ethiopian? To what reading formation did he belong?

Assuming such a framing was hardly typical of contemporary white evangelical conversion narratives, what does it suggest about Equiano's agenda? Both figures are by virtue of their placement in his story made by Equiano to be disturbing and compelling. He used them "to think with"—about his own transformation from "stranger" to "African" Christian and about the larger significance of such transformation. John Annis seems to represent for Equiano the bitter sting of the precariousness of black[4] existence in the slave-trading North Atlantic worlds of the eighteenth century. The Ethiopian figure is an old one in Christian tradition, symbolizing the worldwide extension of the Christian movement.[5] Here it seems to represent more pointedly the surety of the integration into "God's children" of a person with black skin.

Equiano puts focus on his ongoing quest "to work out my own salvation...to be a first-rate Christian" (178). Other pursuits and adventures are integrated into this self-defining quest. The experimentation with or at least consideration of different associations that were part of the market of religions in mid-to-late-eighteenth-century Britain (as Equiano understood and experienced it) was detailed. That there was need for such experimentation is significant.

Insofar as he found himself in Britain, and insofar as the most powerful forces in Britain were in alliance with the state-sanctioned church, the simplest, most legitimizing association should have been the Anglican church. Equiano should have aspired simply to be a "churchman." He seems to have been so identified at the point at which he finds himself at the beginning of his chapter 10. But this identification, precisely because it represented the (slave-trading, slave-holding) status quo establishment, had to be problematic for him. As potent a social-cultural symbol as such association was, representing a certain complex degree of recognition and integration, it did not, and likely could not, guarantee him social, psychological, and physical security and grant assurances that he needed on the most important matters, especially regarding the issue of slavery, of being made the persistent "stranger." How could the church that provided ideological support for the state that enabled and profited from the enslavement of Africans be seen as a source of assurance for Africans' safety and inclusion? What did membership in the state church mean for a black person when the church approved of black slave-trafficking and slave-holding? Surely, the "stranger" would be very much disposed to the appeals of those outside the tight state-church alliance, those groups often clumped together as dissenters. The public exhortations of many among such groups included denunciations of those who bought and sold human beings as slaves. How could Equiano and other strangers resist tuning into the exhortations of such groups? Upon hearing and learning about such groups' claims about the universality of the family of God, how could blacks in Britain not be moved? Membership in a religious community other than the state church represented much more than change in tribal religious or theological orientation; it meant potential for change in social and political and economic status and in self-understanding. Change in religions affiliation in this direction represented possible change in the most basic terms—from slave to free person. Britain had long represented itself as a type of dissent from the Roman Church. But for many in Equiano's time this note was a psychically and politically precarious one to strike. The soil was fertile for more radical religious dissent and experimentation. Equiano's list of subscribers suggests that some of his readers were already disposed toward religious (=social-political) change, if not radicalism. How could Equiano not figure himself as one who had gone (religion) shopping?

That Equiano does not always make explicit what the actual stakes are for him and his (Igbo and other black ethnic) "countrymen" in terms that go beyond the (white European) religious-theological tribal conflicts is clear enough; there is an obvious reason for his not being so forthright. His readership demographic as reflected in the list of subscribers to his book was almost entirely white persons of considerable means, whether Anglican establishment or some type of formation among the dissenters. Although they were likely more or less impressed by and supportive of his writing in English, they likely did not expect him to be as forthright as well as unsettling in his registrations about the situation that obtained. It is more likely that they expected only evidence of his capacity to learn, to imitate them, and to express emotion, including making an emotional appeal to their peers for his liberty and the liberty of all enslaved blacks. But it is doubtful that they really expected him actually to write his mind. At any rate, Equiano's writing reflects his great sensitivity, his understanding of the framing power arrangements, his position in such, and the necessity to make his voice at points powerful and at other points somewhat muted and veiled, tricky—all in order to advance his agenda.

As he indicated his lack of satisfaction with membership in the Anglican church, Equiano indicates that he considered possible association with a number of other communities: the Quakers, the Roman Catholics, the Jews, and the Muslims. It is probably not productive to pursue, at least in any great detail, the reasons, such as they are, that are offered by Equiano for deciding not to join such associations. It is important to keep the focus on what was Equiano's focus, which had little to do with white tribal theological positions or even strictly with how these positions squared with their varied positions on slavery, slave-trading, and racial tolerance. Because his dispositions toward the various camps scrambled what were some likely expectations, they provoke some confusion among readers. This effect can hardly have been unintentional; Equiano was clearly up to something, which suggests the wisdom of rejecting flat or simple or dismissive readings of his conversion narrative.

Quakers, he indicates, were too silent. Not silent so much regarding a stance on slavery or in support of black peoples; indeed, as a group they very much identified as abolitionists. But it would seem that their ideological and activist-programmatic solidarity with black peoples was not enough for Equiano. Beyond the Quaker penchant for quiet in worship, it was likely the silence regarding what he wanted and needed most—assurance about salvation—that proved to be the deal breaker. He seemed to need to be verbally or ritually assured about salvation.

It is not surprising that Roman Catholics were problematic for Equiano. He was, after all, interested in being accepted into the leading European Protestant country of the time. Given the nationalistic prejudices and conflicts during the previous two hundred years or more among European countries, obstensibly mostly in terms of religious affiliation—Catholics versus Protestant, more specifically Catholic France and Spain versus Protestant Britain—the major problem with the Roman Catholic church for Equiano was simply that it was Roman Catholic. No more need be said. This prejudiced position showed how much Equiano was already on his way to becoming an Englishman.

Now regarding the Jews. They are a bit more complicated: Although their ancient story and traditions are heralded and much respected—how could they not be, given the Christian expropriation of the Jewish Bible, making it part of the Christian Bible?—they were, alas, not Christian. So in the way that Equiano, in his chapter 1, drew from their traditions, from the "Bible" (mostly) held in common by Jews and Christians, Jewish tradition could be used. Here Equiano reflected his having been influenced by the Christian supercessionism and triumphalism that made Jewish traditions only a road on the way to (Christian) truth and an inferior part of the same larger complex tradition. So conversion to the Jewish religion was not advisable; it was only to be used to think with, then (according to the most "enlightened" views of the times) simply passed by (as opposed to persecuted). Here again Equiano showed himself to think much like a European Christian.

Association with Islam was considered because Muslims were assumed—by Equiano, for his narratological purposes, and from a physical and social-psychological (romanticized) distance—to have clear and straightforward teachings, "a safer way" to salvation. It is not clear what this means. Did Equiano have direct and deep knowledge of the Muslim faith? Had he read or been taught much about the Muslims' scriptures? Had his African background included some form of knowledge about or intimacy with Islam? What factors or persons influenced his interest, translated for him perspectives and facts? Did he encounter black Muslims on his exploits in the North Atlantic worlds?[6]

Equiano despairs about not having found "among the circle of my acquaintance" any who were considered "righteous," who "kept holy" the "Ten Commandments." He felt that Englishmen of the sort he had experienced made Christianity less attractive and that Muslims, again, on the basis of some distance or, perhaps, familiarity or intimacy, were morally and ethically superior, were stricter, and more observant of scriptural codes and proscriptions. (This judgment likey had to do with intimate knowledge of Christian slave-trafficking and less so with the practices of Muslims.). At any rate, Equiano's planned trip to Turkey never turned out to be feasible; and it was likely due to the somewhat Calvinist-predestinarian perspective from which Equiano the convert to evangelical Christianity writes that forced him to argue in the end that such a trip was not preordained by God.

All of these religions had to be found wanting. For the sake of his narrative logic and structuring, all of these formations had to be found problematic in some respect and needed to be rejected by Equiano in order to set up the drama of the momentum toward the embracing of dissenting protestant evangelicalism. Also important to note here is that throughout his religious market shopping experience Equiano remarked that he was intensely reading and consulting the Bible. This is paradoxical: shouldn't the Bible be associated with all the Christians (and to some extent the Jews) and therefore be put aside as the factor that should determine which among them is valid or compelling? Of course, this question is at once too easy and too difficult to address. It shows Equiano's effort to extract the Bible—common possession of all Christian groups and with rich affinities with Jews and Muslims—from the mechanisms and protocols of authoritative religious groups and then use it as independent instrument by which all religious groups and their claims could be measured. This was, in the long history of humankind, a new concept, a particularly generic protestant modern-world sentiment and positionality. Even more poignant was the fact that it was the black stranger who arrogated to himself such freedom, having "found more heart-felt relief in reading my bible at home than in attending church" (178).

Again and again Equiano depicts himself as an ardent independent reader of the Bible as he yearns for assured salvation. Is he not then already an English Protestant? What else might the Bible-reading references and the pointed conversion experience mean?

It was actually after he was sidetracked from his serious interest in going to Turkey in order to explore the possibility of affiliation with Islam that Equiano was inspired to consider another option, one that represented a reconsideration of the dissenting evangelical movements.

Having sought out a captain scheduled to sail to Turkey, Equiano signed on as part of the crew. Perhaps, as part of a deal that was struck, he also recommended to the captain a black man named John Annis as cook. Annis was signed on and, after working on the ship for two months, he was stolen by a "gentleman" from St. Kitts, Mr. Kirkpatrick; Annis had previously worked for him as slave for many years before parting, apparently as a freedman, "by consent." The actual relationship between the two was not made clear, but it is reasonable to suspect that Annis's history with white masters was similar to Equiano's—"having known the want of liberty myself" (180)—involving a period of enslavement, then an agreement with a master to work for modest remuneration toward freedom, perhaps by purchase. It is possible that Kirkpatrick, like many other slaveholders, could not handle the notion of a free(d) black person. For reasons having to do with economic interest and simply because, as a white male in a slave-holding society, he thought he had the power to do so, Kirkpatrick hired thugs to "trepan"[7] and forcibly take Annis from the ship in order to reenslave him and sell him to another trader in St. Kitts.

Equiano's reaction to the captain and crew's response is significant: he was outraged by their cowardice and lack of loyalty to one who had worked alongside them. "I proved the only friend he had, who attempted to regain him his liberty" (180). Here Equiano shows that the incident had struck a nerve, "brought me very low": he was traumatized, clearly made fearful and anxious, as he was reminded just how precarious was black life in the North Atlantic world. He made heroic efforts to secure and release Annis, including dressing up in white face as part of a dramatic subterfuge, importuning philanthropist and abolitionist Granville Sharp for advice, and securing the aid of a lawyer who proved ultimately to be untrustworthy.

In spite of Equiano's efforts, Annis was stolen away to St. Kitts and reduced to some form of slavery—"according to custom, staked to the ground with four pins through a cord, two on his wrists, and two on his ancles...cut and flogged unmercifully, and afterwards loaded cruelly with irons about his neck" (181). Equiano claimed to have gotten some sort of direct correspondence from Annis about his condition. As unusual and hard to believe as this claim seems to be, he also indicated that some "respectable" London families served as a source of information: they reported having seen Annis in St. Kitts "in the same state"—that is, captured, enslaved, humiliated—and that he remained so until his death.

This report about Annis's experience was widely corroborated. It was in fact a famous case, reported in the newspapers.[8] What made it so disturbing for Equiano was that he recognized that he and Annis were viewed by many in British society, including some within their sailing circle, as being alike. So the treatment Annis received made it painfully clear to Equiano that his own existence was very precarious. It made him fearful and insecure, not only regarding his physical safety, but regarding the worth and meaning of his own life as a black stranger in the white world. His emotions were raw:

> During this disagreeable business, I was under strong convictions of sin, and thought that my state was worse than any man's; my mind was unaccountably disturbed; I often wished for death, though, at the same time, convinced I was altogether unprepared for that awful summons: suffering much by villains in the late cause, and being much concerned about the state of my soul, these things (but particularly the latter) brought me very low; so that I became a burden to myself, and viewed all things around me as emptiness and vanity, which could give no satisfaction to a troubled conscience. (181)

Notwithstanding the employment of the rhetorics of traditional Protestant evangelical piety—"I was under strong convictions of sin"—the words above, directly following the story about John Annis, reflect a strong connection between Equiano's fear and insecurity and Annis's experience. The "convictions of sin," that is, being "convinced I was altogether unprepared for that awful summons," "being much concerned about the state of my soul," and "suffering much by villains in the late cause" (for Annis) were all equated in Equiano's mind. In a sort of astonishing expression of euphemy and understatement—more and more like the British?—it was the "disagreeable business" involving the violence done to Annis that disturbed Equiano to the point of his needing to register his emotions in the Protestant evangelical key of "convictions of sin." He expressed his deep sentiments in a type of code—a veiling. His "convictions of sins" certainly included or were confused with his feelings of radical abjection and fear about his status as a black person in England. How could one so utterly vulnerable and alone otherwise feel?

Annis's experience, and other blacks' continuing experiences, with humiliation and violence, with the constant threats of enslavement, or with being stolen away and thrown back into enslavement—what other than "sin" or "emptiness and vanity" might describe such a situation? In historical perspective, the extent to which the human situation is thought to be disturbing, unspeakable, inexplicable, we typically turn to the domain of the mythic or poetic. The "convictions of sin," then, is understood to represent an awareness of a state of being brought "very low." In drawing on the terminology of Protestant evangelicalism, Equiano was a "sinner" insofar as he was dirtied, made the polluted other, the stranger. As he was made stranger, he was set apart, made to feel the pain of being alone, not so much physically apart from other human beings, but apart from all that is deemed meaningful in society and culture. Given all that he had endured for no reason other than his being black, represented most vividly in the immediate narrative context by the experience of John Annis, the argument or assumption that Equiano's poignant language about being in a state of sin and being converted from such was simply a reflection of conventional Protestant theology is not defensible or credible. There was little about Equiano's experience or his writing about his experience that was simple. The larger context of framing is here the key to meaning.

So disturbed and shaken was Equiano by Annis's experience that he committed himself again to leaving England and turning away from its official religious and political ideology, the ideology that gave license and protection to those who perpetrated the violence against Annis. Equiano remained interested in going to Turkey, for the reasons he had already indicated—having to do with his religious quest and out of disgust over the perfidy found in England. But he was again prevented from going there. He had signed on as steward of a ship but was in some way "prevented" from leaving by his former captain, Mr. Hughs, and others not named. His feeling about all that had taken place was summed up in his choice of a passage from the Bible: "There is no new thing under the sun."[9] He saw himself caught in a complex of strong emotions: disappointment, sadness, some anger, and resignation. He interpreted his complaints against his situation as his "travel in much heaviness" and as murmurings or blaspheming against God (181).

The situation was then set up for Equiano to relate more clearly his uses of the Bible as part of telling the story of his conversion experience. Equiano's description of his coming to a point of the most serious engagement with the Bible was told up to this point with a seeming lack of self-reflexive or deep or informed thinking about the Bible. He could, for example, inform the reader that his true sentiments are registered in the Bible and that with the Bible he could measure or judge the truthfulness of the claims of religious communities. Obviously, the story of his conversion is a narratological set up for him to reach an even higher level of knowledge. The conversion story is more or less artful but certainly a rather tendentious and freighted retrospective; it is a performance of scriptures, an artful and strategic narration of the mimetics of a type of English evangelical scripturalizing. Having rejected nonestablishment non-state-sanctioned religious associations, and having failed to escape to Turkey in order to explore the religion of the Muslims, Equiano set the narratological stage for his turn to a form of dissenting religion: British-inflected Protestant evangelicalism. This was essentially the same as turning to the Bible: "All this appeared to be against me, and the only comfort I then experienced was in reading the Holy Scriptures..." (181).

Equiano's description of what took place both participates in and exposes and I think critiques the mostly Protestant claims about the individual taking up the Bible on his or her own without the mediation or intervention of others. His story reflects for the readers the Protestant belief that one can come to the truth—God—directly through engagement of the book (presumed to be from God). But because of the acknowledged striking even shocking representation of a "stranger"—a black person—imitating the early modern European Protestant practice of engaging scriptures in such a manner, with the assumption of direct personal experience with God through the text that is the Bible, it makes continued contempt for and mistreatment of the Bible reader who is black utterly indefensible. Mistreatment of the Bible reader who is black exposes the reader to the artificiality, the culture-specific constructedness (the blanket white-ness) and the imitability of the entire practice and phenomenon. It is precisely the recognition of the culture specificity of the practice and its imitability that affords Equiano the opportunity to wrest himself from a most difficult situation, to make it work for him as he made his turn to salvation.

There are prefigurings in other parts of Equiano's book of this turn for Equiano. What Equiano allowed to be projected in the frontispiece as mimetics of scripture reading cannot be fully understood without consideration of this part of his narrative. As I discussed in the Prologue, Equiano is pictured in the frontispiece as something of a well-read lay-gentleman of the bourgeoisie, perhaps of the mold of the new evangelical who is symbol and agent of continuing social change. And the bizarre incident in Equiano's chapter 3 about the book that remains silent in spite of his importuning, which leaves an impression of estrangement from and bafflement with any book; the repeated references to the Book with which Equiano seems obsessed; the strings of scriptural quotations and allusions throughout the narrative, which give an impression of a high level of comfort with the Bible; the hymnic poetry that is suffused with biblical imagery—all of these parts of the narrative point to the conversion narrative as key and culminating part of the entire narrative. How could the book that was presumed to be the Bible (or a book related to it) come to speak to him if he had not been converted, had not become an English Protestant Christian? It simply would not make sense. Consider the "heathen" "Indians": in Equiano's story they are even further removed from British society and culture and so they are depicted as being completely unknowing about the Bible. On the other side of his conversion, however, the book, after initial silence, began to speak loudly and forcefully to him.

It makes sense that it is chapter 10 where there is the thickest registrations of and the most intensive and extensive and cleverest uses of scriptures. Through his reading, the reader is made to believe that Equiano came to the point of enlightenment and security he had long sought. The turning was slow and somewhat torturous. The salvation he longed for was liberation from abjectness. To be abject, to be enslaved, to be without a friend to come to one's aid, he came to understand that such experiences were the same as being "altogether unholy," "in nature's darkness," being a "stranger," or even being (merely) a "churchman." Through conversations with others—an old sea-faring man, and "a Dissenting minister" who invited him into an evangelical "feast"—about what the Bible offered to one in such a situation, Equiano was made to feel less alone and more secure. What the Bible represented was the site around which thinking could be explored and conversation could be had about the most poignant issues for Equiano: security and inclusion. The individuals and circles of Bible readers with whom he came in contact at this point in the narrative were most impressive and infectious precisely in that which he lacked, confidence in beliefs and a sense of belonging and being:

> [W]hen they spoke...they seemed to be altogether certain of their calling and election of God; and that no one could ever separate them from the love of Christ, or pluck them out of his hands. This filled me with utter consternation, intermingled with admiration. I was so amazed as not to know what to think of the company; my heart was attracted, and my affections were enlarged; I wished to

be happy as them, and was persuaded in my mind that they were different from the world. (184)

There it was: the big issue was security and confidence found in membership and participation within the circle of Bible readers as *free* thinkers and *free* citizens, in pursuit of happiness. It was what Equiano and Annis and so many others unnamed in the story did not have. It is what Equiano was in pursuit of, the lack of opportunity to attain which made him experience himself as abject sinner. This was not the spiritualizing of his worldly circumstances, as though looking at them through escapist lens; rather, it was an attempt to understand the circumstances in more complex terms. The reader is made to suspect that Equiano's story of his conversion burst the bounds of the genre it was supposed to imitate.

Like his story-telling, Equiano's pursuit of salvation was creative, courageous, persistent. Those Bible readers he "was soon connected" with, "the excellent of the earth," helped him to gain the "full assurance" that he sought regarding salvation so as to counter his conviction of alone-ness and powerlessness that he rather ingeniously described in the conventional Protestant cultural terms of sin and repentance. There was hardly any more poignant language for describing what he experienced. One who was signified as "stranger" could easily translate that identity into being a "sinner" in need of "salvation." So it makes sense that Equiano, presented to the reader as someone whose life was precarious, desperately needed to know "how it was possible...to know his sins were forgiven him in this life" (187). This is far from mere spiritualizing. It might more appropriately be thought of as scripturalizing with a vengeance.

The whole matter of knowing with confidence that sins were forgiven was understandably considered by Equiano (and others who participated in the discourse of evangelical piety) to be "mysterious." Equiano nonetheless persisted in asking questions of those he met. The white dissenting ministers, not unlike the "Ah-affoe-way-cah," the magicians, diviners, wise men, whom he said he remembered from his homeland, and like many such figures in cultures around the world, provided him tantalizing veiled hints of the truth, but mostly encouraged and challenged him to "read" the "pebbles," the signs, in this case, "the scriptures," for understanding and assurance. In other words, he was essentially directed to find the way to a sense of assurance with the instrumentality of the "scriptures". Did this mean he was pretty much on his own? Or did it mean that he was being directed into a particular circle?

In evangelical camps the piety, language, and ideology of individualism, correlating with the notion of personal salvation, tended to mask the reality of the operating social-political framework within which the converted lived and exercised their piety.[10] So even as they preached to one another and challenged others regarding the individualist way of salvation, they seemed to be in line with a type of determining social and discursive binding that belied their hyperindividualist rhetoric. In making reference to the "fellowship," Equiano seems to have recognized the reality of this binding and its power, and he sought to gain acceptance and participation in it.

Even more important, Equiano seems to have understood how he might make use of the binding in order to advance his agenda—"salvation" (and the number of terms that made the point in other words) for himself and for all black peoples—from slavery and its agonies and humiliations. In concrete terms, he was anxious to be part of private and public efforts—debating societies, lobbying efforts—to end the slave trade (with slavery itself expected soon to end in the wake of such a change). Equiano found himself attracted to groups committed to social change. And those making the loudest noises and drawing the most attention about radical or comprehensive change were those among the religious dissenting groups. Association with such groups afforded Equiano opportunity to address both the personal sense of abjection and insecurity and the larger social problems, including domination, prejudice, and ignorance.

We can only guess how and at what point Equiano integrated in his mind these two levels of concern—freedom from slavery and its humiliations; assurance of sin forgiven—that could be termed salvation; surely, it was the mind of the more mature reflective Equiano, the one who engages us as writer, who brought the concerns together. It was the language and sociality and politics of Protestant evangelicalism that spoke most powerfully to Equiano and which, through its most visible defensive and offensive instrument, the discursive site from which was projected both hurt and healing—the scriptures—showed him how he might empower himself.

Equiano's quest to find security that is the focus of the conversion narrative in Chapter 10 continues after the John Annis experience is related. While accepting the challenge to find answers to his questions over many issues in the scriptures, and most likely out of economic survival, Equiano again took to sea. He signed on to a ship interestingly called *Hope* (with a captain even more interestingly called Richard Strange), bound for Cadiz, Spain. On this trip, likely a result of the intensity of his quest and heightened sensibilities, Equiano seems, even before setting sail, to be more aware of and scandalized by the colorful language and behavior of shipmates. As though part of an effort to reflect some of the traditional motifs of Protestant evangelical religious conversion and world-renunciation, he seems to have isolated himself from others.[11] He had doubts about whether he should join the crew but was advised by some "religious" friends that earnest religious faith could survive the taunts of a ship's crew. For both defensive and offensive purposes, he was given by one of his new religious acquaintances a pocket Bible and a copy of Joseph Alleine's *Alarme to the Unconverted Sinners* (1673), an evangelical primer of sorts that continued to be published and distributed in the eighteenth century (189). These two gifts said much to Equiano about the ideological basis of the type of evangelicalism he encountered. That such ideology was built upon the Bible must surely have been clear to him. He would need to learn to use the Bible in order to participate in that discursive world. He no doubt also figured out that entering that world was the means by which he would be wrested from the position that held him enslaved to great anxiety and insecurity. That his thinking about everything that was happening on board was likely strategic does not mean it was either cynical or simple(-minded). Reading Equiano's interests and motives and (rhetorical-narratological) performance as layered and not simple should by now be seen as prudent. In every dimension of slavery that was imaginable and could be experienced by human beings—psychosocial abjection and humiliation; physical captivity; penuriousness; sin—Equiano wanted to be saved.[12]

But this jumps ahead of the story Equiano told. After he arrived in Spain, the defensiveness and isolation seem to have continued, so he took recourse to "many opportunities of reading the scriptures." He records that on October 6 (in 1774, according to his account) he began to "see or hear something supernatural." That evening, as he was "reading and meditating" on Acts 4:12 and exercising himself over whether salvation was a result of good deeds or solely the gift of God, Equiano saw God's "bright beams of heavenly light" and as a result began to see else everything differently:

> [I]n this deep consternation the Lord was pleased to break in upon my soul with his bright means of heavenly light; and in an instant, as it were, removing the veil, and letting light into a dark

> place [Is 25:7]. I saw clearly, with the eye of faith . . . the scriptures became an unsealed book, I saw myself a condemned criminal under the law . . . I saw the Lord Jesus Christ in his humiliation. . . . I then perceived that by the deed of the law no flesh living could be justified. I was then convinced, that . . . all that are saved must be made alive. It was given me to know what it was to be born again [John 3:5]. (190)

There is much here that begs some unpacking and analysis. I should like to try first to identify what I think is the larger rhetorical and ideological context of what is considered to be the core of Equiano's conversion story, the very real narratological moment of his turn. The reader should find interesting and puzzling in this context the passing reference to Acts 4:12 as the passage that Equiano was mulling over just before the explosive experience of conversion (189).[13] This is the passage that is highlighted as part of the frontispiece of the first edition of the published book. And note also that this passage is actually quoted at a later culminating point in the conversion narrative (192). Clearly the passage is significant for Equiano: it was likely the key passage for his self-understanding as convert to Protestant evangelicalism. It reflects the conviction that there is but one means by which salvation is experienced: faith as conviction.[14] This conviction makes plain Equiano's interest in seeing that the playing field is thereby leveled, that *all* can participate and *all* must participate on the same basis. The gates are open to black strangers. The second reference to, and the actual quotation of the Acts passage serves to round out the conversion narrative. It is clear that this passage is the point around which Equiano built his conversion story.

But in the first reference to Acts 4:12, just before the narration of the conversion experience, Equiano does not immediately turn to this passage in detail; he seems to want to build up to this focus. At this point in his storytelling he skips over the Acts passage and includes a string of other biblical passages that reflect a fairly conventional evangelical rhetorics of conversion experience.[15] Given his status and given the demographic of his readers and his assumptions about his potential subscriber-readers—mostly establishment church members or evangelical dissenters—Equiano may have thought it appropriate or even necessary to include such language in his story. (Of course, such language has generally annoyed those readers outside of this confessional circle and those, whatever their disposition, who are unwilling to dive deeply into the ways in which Equiano makes scriptures and scripturalization work for him. Such deep diving is what I claim in this book to be modeling and challenging readers to do.)

Although the language about the conversion experience, in imitation of traditional conversion narratives, suggests suddenness and spontaneity, critical readers know that it was surely over a period of time of struggle and anxiety that Equiano came to understand himself first as a sinner and then as a believer. The timing is collapsed for the rhetorical effect of registering the miraculous. At any rate, another aspect of the miraculous was the radical tenet held by evangelical groups, that as *all* human beings are sinners, *all* have opportunity to be saved. So Equiano recalls that he began seriously to take up such a belief as a path to becoming more assured of salvation, insofar as salvation was understood to come from God alone. This "experience"—actually, very likely, the slow-to-come, very difficult to realize insight or recognition—seemed to be the answer to the anxiety over abjection experienced by Equiano. This explains his melt-down and weeping over "my poor wretched state." It was a rather profound recognition of the situation he and Annis and other blacks faced in eighteenth-century England and the salvation from which he was now convinced had been given him without condition.

Equiano's conversion must be considered an assertion of his having been "set... entirely at liberty." But of course, out of respect for the assumption that Equiano's narrative is complex, we must ask what he thought such liberty was all about—liberty in relationship to what? Liberty from what? To what end? What does "entirely" mean here? His use of fairly traditional rhetorics of evangelical conversion—"removing the veil;" "I saw myself;" "I then clearly perceived;" "It was given me at that time to know;" "I was sensible of"—puts the emphasis on cognition, consciousness, enlightenment, and so forth. This is the point at which Equiano comes to see things differently. It is also strikingly, disturbingly imitative of traditional Western Christian conversion narrative and peroration. It is in his conversion narrative and peroration that Equiano seems paradoxically to be at once most imitative of evangelical (British-inflected) rhetorical gesturing and performance, and at the same time most critical of it, if not resistant to it, certainly, a creative agent in relationship to it. It is in this section that focuses most directly on the conversion experience that is found the most concentrated representation and intense engagement of scriptures. And it is in this section where there is the most intense engagement of scriptures that Equiano demonstrates most profoundly his mimetic arts or performativity and agency.

What is the import of Equiano's glosses on the rhetorics of such a narrative? What agenda was behind the mimetics of the conversion narrative? Beyond the conventional one, what messages did Equiano intend to convey to his readers? Might he have intended to use the conversion narrative for strategic purposes, to encode a special message inside an already culturally encoded message? Equiano seems to have understood his conversion in terms of his coming to a point of wresting himself, or in terms of the narrative voice being wrested, from the positionality and consciousness of the stranger who was a slave. He had been the stranger who had been the slave who had been literally and ideologically bound by a structure with clear lines and protocols of power that left him marginalized and quite vulnerable as outsider. He seems to have understood this marginalization and lack of power not simply in terms of political or economic or social or religious (= establishment church) interests, but as the fusion of all of these domains as they overdetermined him and left him voiceless.

The matter of voicelessness or silence takes the reader back to the profound meaning of Equiano's use of the [non-]talking book incident (in his chapter 3; discussed here in chapter 1) and thereby provides a window onto a different nuance to the typical evangelical conversion story. Before conversion, before coming to a point of seeing and knowing things deeply, it could hardly be expected that the book that was the Bible would speak to Equiano. On the other side of conversion, however, Equiano is bombarded with bright beams, is allowed to see and know special things, and the "word of God" is not simply read, is not simply heard, but becomes "sweet to my taste, yea sweeter than honey and the honeycomb" (190).[16] (Here is registered dimensions of experience with the text that go beyond the usual dimension of the oral/aural). What is at issue here is Equiano's recording of the dramatic reversal of the non-talking book story: his transformation means he is positioned not merely to read and be read to, speak and be spoken to; he in fact becomes intimate with God, "sensible of the invisible hand of God." He thereby became like the priests, magicians, and doctors of his people (as described in chapter 1), a powerful "calculator" of *his* times, one who had come to possess "extraordinary methods" of "discovery." This represented a subtle and creative and subversive confusion of assumed African (Igbo) traditional and British evangelical orientation, sensibilities, and epistemics.

According to the ideology of the evangelical world with which Equiano was in conversation, all human beings are corrupt and exist in a wretched state. But it is fascinating that in this context Equiano highlights "the Ethiopian" mentioned in the book of Acts (8:26–39) as the second black figure in his conversion story. What was Equiano doing with the Ethiopian figure? What were the assumptions and terms of his use of this scriptural figure? I suggest that it can hardly be the case that this figure was highlighted because he was considered by Equiano or by anyone else to have been more morally or ethically deficient and more in need of salvation than any other person. We are probably closer to Equiano's use of the figure in seeing him represent what the original text-source, and later Christian traditions, including modern and contemporary exegetical discourses, would have us think the figure represents: radical otherness embraced.[17] Of course, there is great irony in this reading because this radical other, this ancient world "stranger," was so in the ancient context only from the assumption of the political-ideological perspective of (the Roman) empire as center. Ethiopia was ideologized as the periphery; the black body was ideologized as the radically different, the barbarian, located at the far southern fringes of the empire and of the (Greco-Roman-determined) civilized world and was overdetermined, overtroped, and often romanticized.[18] This perspective is clearly registered in the ancient Christian writings. Oddly or paradoxically enough, it reflects the mimetics of one of a number of ancient urban petit-bourgeoise, dissenting groups, subversives—"enemies of the Roman empire"[19] (as defined by the prejudices and sensibilities of the establishment of the Greco-Roman empire).

Equiano may have intended the reader to pick up on the radical otherness that the Ethiopian figure represented. But he seems to have wanted the figure to represent something beyond the acceptance of difference as sign of the sensibilities and universality of primitive Christianity. The latter represented an apologetic politics that at the same time betrayed the fact that very few in that circle were black.[20]

Because Equiano was a black person and as such signified the stranger-as-slave in the early modern period of the North Atlantic world, his interest was necessarily different from, even as it was somewhat imitative of, primitive Christianity. At issue for him was the squaring of historical Christian apologetics with his status as black person-as-stranger-as-slave. Christianity could hardly be made sense of or be embraced unless it could in some sense be understood not merely as the movement that encompasses Ethiopia on the periphery of empire, but as a movement fundamentally defined by, reflected in, and refracted through the black made stranger or abject figure. So Equiano decontextualizes[21] Christian scriptures that they might be (re-) activated as scriptures by and for the eighteenth-century black stranger. He essentially invents a different scriptures—one that is not a white Bible, the carrier of the white positionality and sensibility, but a voice that recognizes and affirms his being. This voice that spoke to him was, odd as it might seem to a stranger to white men's magic, a text. It was something that he did not and likely dared not name, but it was what functioned as, and what I might here name, African(ized) scriptures.[22]

So the Ethiopian is figured by Equiano ultimately not as the black "stranger" outside the Christian movement who is through white men's greatness of converted heart finally included, but as the one who embodies the Christian movement. He is not the peripheral figure of the world shaped, and geographically determined, and somewhat romanticized by, the Roman empire, and by extension into eighteenth century Britain, contemporary white discourse; he is made to be the (early) modern-world personification of the "wretched poor," "the poor Africans," "the oppressed natives of Africa," "the much wronged people of Africa," "the poor injured Africans"—the ones not only who find salvation but for whom salvation was created. It is this figure, "willing to be saved by Jesus Christ," the one to whom self was "obnoxious," the one who had not claimed to be a performer of "good works," who is redefined and made the Christ(ian) figure by Equiano.

Equiano's association with the Ethiopian went further: as Equiano had understood himself as one who had "spots," as one who was black, the Ethiopian was also defined in this respect. But there was much more at issue here than pigmentation of skin. Being black meant for Equiano much more than the rhetorical play around color symbolism that with its nonetheless serious effects and origins in Mediterranean antiquity, including Jewish and Christian traditions, was extended into the modern eras.[23] This play is registered in the famous passage from the prophecy of Jeremiah

> Can Ethiopians change their skin
> or leopards their spots? (Jer 13: 23)

and from which the fraught term "spots" is derived. The rhetorical question and the traditions of sayings behind this passage point to a phenomenon that is understood to be absolutely immutable by being compared to the dark spots on a leopard. Equiano understood that the darkness of skin in the North Atlantic world into which he was "born" and against which he had to struggle as a "stranger" had come to be understood as a mark of humiliation. Equiano highlighted the Ethiopian of the Christian tradition who had come to be represented as part of an ideological-apologetics invested in an agenda of immutable othering. Of course, this troping of the Christian tradition—here is the rub—was not developed out of the actual experience of an actual Ethiopian or black person of the time; it was built around romanticized but nonetheless clever missionary propaganda on the part of nonblacks. "Look how powerful we are—the reach of our message extends to the ends of the Roman-determined ends of the earth, even to the radical other!"

Equiano's use of the trope, on the other hand, was based on the actual experience of black peoples. Positioning himself critically within such Christian rhetorical traditions, Equiano decontextualized the Ethiopian: he identified the Ethiopian, and all Africans, as dark-skinned peoples, with the abjection of black peoples who were forced into slavery within the dominant Christian societies of the North Atlantic world of the late eighteenth century.

Equiano's identification with the Ethiopian was bold: it transvalued the "spots" associated with the leopard and with black peoples from an ostensibly unnamed amoral defining characteristic or mark of identification of one people—without serious or self-reflexive attention to the politics and psychological dynamics that may have been reflected and the racist logics that would be supported by such a move—and made them into a mark of morality or character definition of all of "God's children." Readers from antiquity and from the emerging modern world making use of such rhetoric were expected not to think much about how real Ethiopians are referenced, except in the sense that they were associated with dark skin. Negative valences were downplayed.[24]

Equiano's change in the charge of the trope suggests that his agenda had to do with addressing directly the negative valence of blackness around which so much of the early modern North Atlantic world was bound together. According to his exegesis of the pertinent texts, "spots" are not simply a matter of a somewhat neutral defining physical characteristic. Now in the world in which "Ethiopians" have been "discovered," have been brought close and subdued and humiliated, "spots" are flaws, shortcomings. So drawing on, imitiating, but also tweaking early modern European Christian evangelical tropicalizations, we have Equiano at play: If all, without exception, had "spots," that is, human flaws, then all, without exception, were in the same fundamental human condition and in need of the same salvation. In societies that were being built on the stolen labor of the black body, sharply contrasting the latter with the free body that is associated with the people who have become "white," this assertion by Equiano represented a radical leveling, a social-psychological unbinding, freeing. What the Ethiopian comes to represent is not so much the strange and exotic black body, but the body that all humans carry about, with its flaws and beauty. The Ethiopian is still used to think with, but with Equiano he is no longer the distant romanticized figure; he is everyone.

That this interpretation is fraught with interpretive minefields is clear enough. The fall back into essentialisms can happen quite easily. I need not defend Equiano here; I need only to make the argument that his point seems to have been to take the Ethiopian out of an ancient-world tropicalization in which he is exotic into a more complex modern-world tropicalization that includes persons who actually speak.

Equiano's interpretive play with the Ethiopian was a critical response to the binding that was one of the effects of scripturalization. Equiano seemed not only to have figured out what games the dominant culture had been playing with scriptures, especially as regards the issue of slavery and the treatment of black peoples in general, he seemed aware of what game he might play in the engagement of scriptures in order to free himself from the negative effects of the binding, in which black skin color had been made to signify strangeness, the margins, absence. It was a tight box held together by discourse. So discourse was picked up as instrument of salvation from the box.

As an effort to explain what may have been Equiano's agenda in drawing upon the conventional conversion narrative, I return here to the point made above regarding the specter of Annis in Equiano's consciousness. What seems to have struck Equiano was Annis's experience of being stolen away and subjected (again) to slavery. This put him, along with almost all blacks in the North Atlantic worlds of the early modern period, in a "poor wretched state," a state defined by insecurity and anxiety about when one might be stolen away and killed or, worse, forced into slavery and humiliation. It was this type of experience that haunted Equiano and influenced his re-presentation of his conversion experience, with its primary focus on salvation from the "wretched state." Equiano was "set... at liberty" only when he had figured out that there was direct and powerful connection between affiliation with a particular kind of community, the "fellowship" or chapel-like gathering of dissenting evangelical "believers," and his sense of security. This security was based on the particular community's acceptance of the oft-repeated[25] declaration in Acts 4:12 (and several parallel declarations) that only in Jesus was there salvation. Equiano had come to believe that the subjugation and anxiety and aloneness that he and Annis and so many other black peoples had suffered could be alleviated through affiliation with the community that defined itself by the claim that only in Jesus can all be saved. The categorical absolute in the claim represented a level social playing field: salvation was to be facilitated by *one* clear single source and effected by *one* set of terms. And without exception *all* persons, *all* groups of humanity, could secure the benefit by such terms. Period. Equiano got the point.

The notion that all groups of humanity, without exception, could be saved was for Equiano clearly the main point to advance and defend. That this meant the inclusion of the stranger who was black was obviously the point that he wanted to emphasize. So powerful and controversial, so potentially unsettling and hard to fathom, was this notion of the inclusion of the black stranger in God's family that Equiano set up his glosses/commentary, on the Bible and on the traditions' uses of the Bible, with a special rhetorical strategy in order to explain the special implications and ramifications to the reader.

For Equiano the focus of revelation of truth had shifted: the very idea of the inclusion of the black stranger was the deep mystery of the universe, an almost "unspeakable" matter, one that had heretofore been known to only a few. Equiano obviously understood himself as one of the few who understood the truth. The "veil" had been removed (190)[26] so that he could understand what was really at issue. The mission of his narrative was to inform readers about what had been revealed to him as convert, as "wise man," again, not unlike the wise men he described as having been part of the traditions of his homeland.

The rhetorical strategy Equiano used was to signal to the reader the mysterious truth about the inclusion of black peoples in God's family and, even more difficult to fathom, the truth about the black person as the figure of divine presence in the world. Repeatedly in chapter 10 Equiano makes direct reference to the reader, winking and nodding about these matters. These references—"May the Lord give the reader an understanding in this" (191); and "May God give the reader a right understanding in these facts!" (192)—signal that something significant is being pointed out. In each case,[27] Equiano has put focus on the mystery of his salvation and what it means in terms that go far beyond him and his time and circumstance. In imitation of the claims of those in Christian and other traditions, including Igbo traditions, Equiano claims to have privileged insight into the matter of God's designs for black peoples' destiny in the world. But this insight comes through the "extraordinary methods" involving his wrestling with English scriptures. How poignant and paradoxical is that? The nods and winks to the readers signal the special insight to which Equiano—now as biblical scholar—lays claim.

In the first nod and wink to the reader, the context of discussion is about his independent reading of the Bible that led him to salvation and to an understanding of its import:

> Now the Bible was my only companion and comfort; I prized it much, with many thanks to God that *I could read it for myself*, and was not left to be tossed about or led by man's devices and notions. The worth of a soul cannot be told—*May the Lord give the reader an understanding in this*. Whenever I looked in the Bible I saw things new, and many texts were immediately applied to me with great comfort; for I knew that to me was the word of salvation sent. (191; italics mine)

Here Equiano made a poignant confusion between salvation of the soul in terms of the conventional spiritualizing of Western Christian theology and the salvation or "worth" of the "soul" that is a powerful ironic allusion to the monetary value of the slave as nonperson in the modern slave trade. The notion of "worth" here is made to echo Matt 16:26 (= Mark 8:36) in which Jesus is depicted asking pointedly, "For what is a man profited, if he shall gain the whole world, and lose his own soul? Or what shall a man give in exchange for his soul?" Here conventional theology makes Jesus' question a matter of weighing monetary loss over against spiritual gain. Equiano's recasting of the question into a declaration retains the point of the message in the passage about the greater worth of the soul. But here's the rhetorical rub for Equiano: his turning of Jesus' question into a firm declaration goes further by linking the matter of the worth of the soul back to the experience of Annis. In the quotation above, just before the declaration about the worth of a soul, Equiano makes another statement about his being able to read the Bible "for myself." In this statement is reflection of his power to withstand being "tossed about or led by man's devices and notions" (191).

These statements in juxtaposition add up to a statement of defiance and resistance—against the enslavement and humiliation of black peoples, and against the reading and uses of scriptures that would support the enslavement and humiliation of black peoples. The free application of the Bible to one's own situation—"immediately applied to me"—should be understood as an expression of freedom and social power in the most comprehensive and radical terms. What might someone who had been a slave, who had lived under constant threat of being returned to slavery, who had witnessed others of his kind subject to humiliations and sufferings far worst than his own, what might such a person mean by indicating that he was reading the Bible "for myself" and was thereby no longer "to be tossed about or led by man's devices and notions"? What else might he mean by following such a claim with the declaration that "the worth of a soul cannot be told"? And what if the one speaking had been enslaved and exploited by others who were good—Protestant Christians—and English gentlemen?

We many never fathom all aspects of the meaning of Equiano's glosses on the New Testament passage, but it is clear that he means by his rhetorical moves much more than the literalism and spiritualizing that usually subtend what may be thought of as traditional un-self-critical piety. To read Equiano in that key would be a mistake. But another mistake in interpreting Equiano here must also be avoided: the assumption that he only uses forms and traditions at hand, without conviction, that he does not take seriously religious language and religious piety, that for him everything was, as much as eighteenth-century Britain would allow, a matter of deconstruction.[28] It seems to me that Equiano did indeed deconstruct Western Christian rhetorics and practices; such deconstruction explains the nature of his conversion. But this means he needed to engage quite seriously the traditions and practices that defined the world into which he was thrown. In Protestant Bible-reading Britain, this made signifying on scriptures—the engagement of and critical play with the Bible, not necessarily the usual matters of debate around meaning of texts)—a matter of much seriousness.

Equiano's Bible reading afforded him opportunity to apply the biblical language of the worth of the soul to his own situation and the situation of most blacks in England. His being able to read the Bible led him to the salvation of the soul as confirmation of the soul's worth. No soul that could be saved by God could be seen as unworthy and subject to humiliation and enslavement. That is the mysterious truth and powerful logic that he wanted to let the reader in on:

> Sure I was that the Spirit which indited[29] the word opened my heart to receive the truth of it as it is in Jesus—that the same Spirit enabled me to act with faith upon the promises which were precious to me, and enabled me to believe to the salvation of my soul. (191)

In Equiano's view enslaving and humiliating one who read the Bible for himself, who "saw things new," who was convinced that his soul had been saved and therefore had "worth," was undermined. The one who would no longer be tossed about regarding spiritual things could hardly assume that there was any divine legitimization in his being tossed about by the vagaries of slavocracy: "I was "persuaded that I had a part and lot in the first resurrection, and was enlightened" (191–192). This was arrogation of freedom, of every kind, in every domain..

The other nod to the reader occurs in the same context of Equiano's commentary on the import of the conversion. Near the end of the conversion story the categorical formation-defining declaration from Acts 4:12—"Neither is there salvation in any other... but only Jesus Christ"—is now actually quoted (192). Immediately following this quotation is found the other pertinent wink and nod to the reader—"May God give the reader a right understanding in these facts!" The "facts" had to do with the two issues raised in the declaration: one, that only through Jesus was there salvation; and two, that the requirement for salvation was universal, that it applied "under heaven among men." The same requirement was for all, including black peoples.

It was the import—"the right understanding," the right application, the profound implications and powerful socio-political ramifications—of these "facts" that Equiano thought mysterious, and so he sought to turn the focus of his readers to such. But what follows is not Equiano's explicit argument about what are the ramifications of the "facts," but another scriptural quotation, one that is epexegetical of the earlier quotation. This tacking on of another scriptural passage might suggest an even greater sensitivity on the part of Equiano that conventional language here fails to communicate what is at issue. The thinking may have been that only more scriptural language would open up the mysterious issue (salvation for all) at hand.

The other passage is from a fairly obscure New Testament text: the second-century pseudo-Pauline letter to Titus. The text is a polemical parenesis written to a young pastor who is assumed to be the historical Titus who was a co-worker of Paul (2 Cor 8:23). This young leader gets advice and counsel from the great missionary preacher. Exegetical analysis and history of religions research have pretty much established that the background of the "letter" to Titus involves (among other issues, to be sure) conflicts in the second-century missionary field (supposedly on the island of Crete) over differentiation between fairly moderate and radical orientations to the world outside the community of believers. So "Paul" wrote to "Titus," counseling the latter to beware the radical ascetics and world-denying ideologies associated with "opponents." These "opponents" were considered threats because of what was considered their unqualified condemnation of and ultimate characterization as pollution of those who disagreed with them, were not like them. These radically ascetic, hyper-judgmental, super-sectarian types "Paul" counseled "Titus" (ironically?) to denounce: "they must be silenced... rebuke them sharply... They are detestable, disobedient, unfit."[30]

Whether Equiano understood the historical backdrop to the letter to Titus in precisely this way is not clear; *religionsgeschichte* was yet to be born and its precursor discourses would have given little space to it in the Britain—even the ivy-walled university parts of it—of Equiano's time. But it seems clear that he understood that the "Paul" whom he quotes, using the (King James) English version of the Bible, was counseling the young pastor to beware of and to condemn certain parties associated with certain behaviors and ways of thinking: "To him that believeth, all things are possible, but to them that are unbelieving, nothing is pure."[31] Equiano makes a change in the passage so that "To him that believeth, all things are possible" replaces in the English "To the pure all things are pure." This version may reflect Equiano's interest (and perhaps the interest of those who influenced him) in refocusing the issue, putting it on faith rather than purity. But the second part of the passage as Equiano quotes it—"but to them that are unbelieving nothing is pure," Equiano changed from "but to the corrupt and unbelieving nothing is pure" in the original. One can see here again that Equiano drops the emphasis on the controversy around purity. He seemed to be focused only on one issue: he makes "Paul's" exhortation turn around the difference between those who "believeth" and those who were "unbelieving." The former Equiano understood to be those who saw that "all things are possible." The latter he associated with those who held that "nothing is pure."

Equiano took up the Titus passage because he sensed that it reflected a major conflict in the ancient setting. This conflict he decontextualized and used it to apply to his situation. That is, he set up the conflict as a means of throwing light on the issue of his time, specifically the issue having to do with judgment about who in the eighteenth century is found acceptable to gain salvation, to be admitted into the family of God. Those in Equiano's time and situation who "believeth" that "all things are possible" are those who see that God has accepted all into the family. Those who are "unbelieving," who think "nothing is pure," are associated with the radicals of "Paul's" time whose vision of the family of God is narrow.

Equiano associated the "nothing is pure" ideology with those who did not accept the "worth of a soul." The latter were in his thinking among those who did not acknowledge the humanity of peoples with black skin. That Equiano holds forth against such attitude makes sense: it was precisely this sort of ideology that produced in Equiano so much anxiety and fear. It was an ideology that in the time of pseudo-Paul was advanced by recourse to the politics of the remembrance of the apostle. Who in succeeding generations would be most concerned to possess and control the memory of the apostle? Who indeed. In Equiano's time the politics of remembrance were engaged through creative use of scriptures by those deemed authorized.

In the early modern era, all European nations, contoured and defined in so many respects by the formations that were scriptural religions and notwithstanding the forces and challenges of the Enlightenment, very much needed issues having to do with inclusion and human dignity and rights to be adjudicated through uses of scriptures, now understood as their own protonationalist divining object, mirror, tool, weapon, and fetish. All of this means that Equiano could not have possibly ignored analyzing and assessing the ways of dominants; and he could not have avoided taking up the major fetish of the dominants—the Bible as scriptures—as a means of surviving and freeing himself. He needed to use scriptures to clue his readers, readers of the Bible all, about how and what the Bible (now) "speaks" to him about the matter of inclusion in God's family. Only those who do not believe think that "nothing is pure," meaning for Equiano that black peoples are not included; those who believe come to see that all things are pure, that is, that all peoples are included.

The salvation that Equiano sought and which he had slowly and finally come to secure was thought about in terms of an unbinding. It was an unbinding from that "poor wretched state," that situation by which he identified himself from the beginning of his story-telling. It would seem that the whole point of his story was to re-present his transformation from abject figure to a member of God's family, with rights and privileges and, most important, a sense of security and affiliation.

The whole point of the conversion narrative—beginning with focus on the tragic experience of Annis and the chronicling of Equiano's struggle with anxiety, fear, and insecurity in light of Annis's experience—shows Equiano's quest for salvation, being delivered or wrested from the wretched state of enslavement and from being a persistent outsider. This fraught and burdensome status obviously served well some basic political and economic interests. Equiano made himself aware of the ideological substratum that provided legitimacy for such interests, or at the very least did not severely question how such interests were supported. He understood that it was the uses of scriptures (among other things) that made it possible for the political and economic interests to be supported so powerfully. Of course, among some interpreters, the selective decontextualization of some passages was made to support modern-era forms of black enslavement. Along with dissenting evangelicals and some politicians, Equiano privately and publicly debated such interpreters. But what seemed most troublesome was the use of scriptures hinted at in Equiano's conversion chapter: the use of scriptures to render his tribes-people spotty, strange, marginal, dirty, flawed, polluted. It was this sort of overdetermination that he thought very problematic, a binding. Conversion as reorientation to and affiliation with the converted, facilitated by the engagement of the Bible, was for him the needed unbinding, the instrument by which one might engage the world on stronger terms, the garment one might put on so that there might be protection as one tries to negotiate the world.

6

"*...take the book...and* tell *God to make them dead...*": *Scripturalization as White Men's Hegemony*

> *Recollecting a passage I had read in the life of Columbus, when he was amongst the Indians in Jamaica, where, on some occasion, he frightened them, by telling them of certain events in the heavens, I had recourse to the same expedient, and it succeeded beyond my most sanguine expectations. When I had formed my determination, I went in the midst of them... I pointed up to the heavens... I told them God lived there, and he was angry with them... and if they did not leave off, and go away quietly, I would take the book (pointing to the bible), read, and tell God to make them dead. This was something like magic.*
>
> —OLAUDAH EQUIANO, *Interesting Narrative*, chapter 11

THE PASSAGE QUOTED above is from chapter 11 of Equiano's narrative. It is the same chapter in which Equiano depicts himself in Malaga, Spain, in conversation with the Catholic priest, Father Vincent. But given the more immediate focus of this chapter (power), the more important context for the passage has to do with some events (discussed above in chapter 3 but with a different focus) that took place elsewhere among the "Musquitos." Equiano relates events that unfolded in connection with a "new adventure" that he signed on for at the request of the "celebrated"[1] Dr. Irving. Having purchased a 150-ton sloop, Irving wanted Equiano to join him in setting up a slave plantation in Jamaica. Equiano indicates that, after some conversation with friends, he accepted the offer, with the commitment to use the time as opportunity to advance his missionary work: "knowing that the harvest was fully ripe in those parts... I hope to be an instrument, under God... bringing some poor sinner to... Jesus Christ" (202).

Even before embarking on the trip he was able to turn to his stated interest and set the tone for the narration of the adventure: he began to evangelize four "Indians" he met through Dr. Irving, among them the son of the king of the Musquitos. He and his companions had been in England for twelve months, having been caught up in complex economic and political schemes. They had been brought there by traders "for some selfish ends" (202).[2] The prince had been baptized and given the name George and taught "pretty good English," but, according to Equiano, had not been sufficiently catechized. So on the way to Jamaica Equiano set out to teach the prince English letters and basic British-inflected Protestant ideology ("doctrines of Christianity"), complete with that book that next to the Bible was in Protestant England most cherished, *Fox's Martyrology*.[3]

Equiano's catechetical-propaganda program seemed to work fairly well—until the "poor heathen" was taunted by ship crew members, "true sons of Belial," about the prince's newfound Christian piety. This taunting caused the prince to go into retreat, refusing to "learn his book" or associate with crew members. In a state of confusion about white sailors' taunting him for engaging white ways taught him by a black man, he directed to the Equiano of the narrative the question that the (mostly white) readers no doubt had in mind (with some qualification for differences in context, to be sure) about Equiano the writer: "How comes it that all the white men on board, who can read and write, observe the sun, and know all things, yet swear, lie, and get drunk, only excepting yourself?" (204).

The answer given by the narrativized Equiano—"they do not fear God"—reflects conventional British evangelical piety and is not really a direct answer to the question. But Equiano the writer has already made the much more important issue: the association of whiteness with Christian piety and doctrine and with English reading and writing, and its puzzling representation by a black man. The paradox that this representation causes is voiced, from the perspective of white dominants, by an "Indian," an *other* Other. Of course, what Equiano has done here is to shock readers into rethinking what face can be associated with Christian doctrine and piety. Can a black face represent such? It is through the unwitting, disturbing testimony of the "heathen" "Indian" other as well as the white crew members that Equiano's black face is declared representative of

Christian piety. English reading and writing continue to be associated in the minds of all with white persons; but Equiano's rendering of this incident was intended to shock and destabilize such assumptions and force reconsideration to the point that the tribal representation of Christianity is thrown into confusion.

Equiano continued to represent himself in chapter 11 as a transgressive figure who causes double takes and confusion. He depicted himself accompanying Dr. Irving reaching Jamaica and being very much involved in the purchasing of human beings—as slaves!—for the establishment of a plantation. He makes the point that he chose as slaves "all of my own countrymen, some of whom came from Lybia" (205). The reference to "Lybia" begs consideration, but I will refrain from addressing it in this context.[4] Most important here is the fact of Equiano's involvement in slave-trafficking of black peoples, even as he registers his identification with them as a person of African descent. He presents himself as a black Christian evangelical with missionizing commitments who also facilitates the purchasing of black peoples as slaves for a white-owned plantation system. White men, indeed. No wonder the "Indian" prince was confused. He spoke for many: the world seemed upside down: the black stranger assumed the speech and practices of white men. Equiano the writer must have expected readers' heads to turn rather violently, if not explode.

But such bizarre incidents seemed only to be a narratological setup for the most dramatic and poignant depiction (in a particular qualified yet unnerving sense) of Equiano—as a white man. The narration continues: having sailed from Jamaica to a place called Cape Gracias a Dios on the Musquito shore,[5] Equiano and company engaged natives on what seems like the usual terms of first contact between Europeans and Others, with the usual perspectives and sensibilities of the Europeans—"we used them well"; and cargo goods, alcohol among them, were offered for exchange. The natives offered to help clear the land for the plantation (205).

As a part of the narration of the contact with the natives in the area, Equiano took a slight rhetorical detour to describe them:

> I do not recollect any of them to have had more than two wives. These always accompanied their husbands when they came to our dwelling, and then they generally carried whatever they brought to us, and always squatted down behind their husbands. Whenever we gave them any thing to eat, the men and the women ate separate. I never saw the least sign of incontinence amongst them. The women

are ornamented with beads, and fond of painting themselves; the men also paint, even to excess, both their faces and shirts; their favourite color is red. The women generally cultivate the ground and the men are all fishermen and canoe-makers. Upon the whole, I never met any nation that were so simple in their manners as these people, or had so little ornament in their houses. Neither had they, as I ever could learn, one word expressive of an oath. The worst word I ever heard amongst them when they were quarreling was one that they had got from the English, which was, "you rascal." I never knew of any mode of worship among them; but in this they were not worse than their European brethren or neighbours, for I am sorry to say that there was not one white person in our dwelling, nor any where else, that I saw in different places I was at on the shore, that was better or more pious than those unenlightened Indians ....The natives were well made and warlike...they seemed to be singular, in point of honesty. (206–207)

All readers will note in Equiano's description here something familiar: not only is the description in substance similar to the description of the Igbo that Equiano provided at the beginning of his story (chapter 1), it also reflects the same general tone and assumptions that he reflected in that earlier context. Like the Igbo, the Indians are held to be a noble, hard-working, and pious or continent "nation." Like the Igbo, the Indians are simple in their manners and customs. And like the Igbo, the Indian worship traditions, seen through the lens of British Protestant evangelical traditions, are understood to be odd or nonexistent. Such observations and comparisons gave Equiano rhetorical opportunity to excoriate his immediate company—of mostly white British-identified crewmen, it must be assumed—with religio-cultural perfidy. That he thought that there was "not one white person in our dwelling...that was better or more pious than those unenlightened Indians" indicated that he was conscious of engaging again in a complex and delicate comparative (religion/culture) analysis. In such analysis white, black, and Indian worlds are at once seen as separate, with black and Indian traditions devalued and held in contempt according to British standards but also confused and collapsed and made malleable, with the potential for culture-switching. Indians and blacks are compared to each other in terms of work habits; blacks and whites were in chapter 1 compared to each other in terms of common roots in and affinities with some ancient Jewish traditions; and "whites," as was already indicated, were considered disappointing and poor exemplars of the Christian religion and British culture. Of course, the black and Indian characters in this incident, because of their lack of socialization into British Protestant piety, are thought by Equiano to be needing enlightenment. But the larger point is that all can fundamentally be made to be like those of another social category. Blacks and Indians can be made, through the conversion/socialization process to which he adheres, "white." These complex comparisons and juxtapositions place Equiano in positions of affinity and tension with all the social categories named. He depicts himself as being at the same time the center of, outside, and above these categories, representing the dynamics and reality of trans-formation.

Yet as the continuing narration seems to indicate, Equiano's orientation is determined by that of white Protestant evangelicalism.[6] The most dramatic and disturbing registration of such consciousness was yet to be depicted in the narrative. Feeling safe, Equiano and his company set up camp among the peoples of the honest and amiable "nation." The company had heard about but not yet encountered the great and powerful man who was the "Indian governor." The latter, we are told, traveled in high style among the peoples in different districts and provinces in order to hear and settle differences. Having heard about the encampment of Equiano's company, the governor sent notice ahead, with a stick as sign, about his intention to visit. In response, Equiano's company sent him some of the usual items of first contact: rum, sugar, gunpowder. In the flesh, the governor was, according to Equanio, not at all "a grave reverend judge, solid and sagacious," but instead loud and rather crude. He was full of the liquor that Equiano and his company had supplied. As such, he seemed already to have been manipulated by and was in part a creation of the world Equiano represented. In terms narratological and political he was being set up for what was to come.

It was when the drunken governor struck and took the hat of one of the local native chiefs that things got out of hand. Chaos and confusion ensued. Dr. Irving made what seemed to Equiano a feeble attempt to calm things down. He proved to be unsuccessful, and out of frustration and panic he escaped into the woods. As Equiano tells the rest of the story, he was left to exercise leadership and come up with a "stratagem"[7] (208) to deal with the situation. The reader is then led to the comments that were quoted at the beginning of this chapter, comments in which Equiano recollects a passage from his reading about Columbus's adventure with "Indians in Jamaica." A short detour is in order.

The specific incident to which Equiano alludes took place during Columbus's fourth voyage. The incident was not recounted by Columbus; it was, like so many stories about his experiences, recorded and embellished by admirers and tradents. Among these were Diego Mendez de Segura, who sailed on the fourth voyage with Columbus and is described as majordomo and arch-defender of Columbus and traditions around him;[8] Ferdinand Columbus,[9] the second son of Columbus, a learned man who wrote a biography of his father; and Bartolome de las Casas, Spanish Dominican priest who wrote a history of the part of the world that Columbus "discovered," including the havoc it wrought.[10]

According to Mendez and Ferdinand, the backdrop to the incident is as follows: Columbus and his party found themselves in Jamaica shipwrecked without food and supplies. Columbus dispatched a small company to go to Hispaniola for help. Through bartering and flattery, trickery and bullying, Columbus and his crew ingratiated themselves to and manipulated the natives. For a long period they depended upon the natives for food. But the trickery and rewards of the exchange system wore thin. So according to Mendez:

> [T]he Indians became disaffected and would not bring food as before. [Columbus] caused all the caciques [native leaders] to be summoned and told them that he marveled that they should not bring food as they had been accustomed to do, knowing that, as he had told them, he had come there by the command of God and that God was offended with them and that on that very night He would show this to them by signs which He would cause to appear in the heavens. And as on that night there was an almost total eclipse of the moon, he told them that God did this from anger with them because they did not bring food. They believed him and were very terrified, and they promised that they would always bring him food.[11]

In terms of the sensibilities that characterized his world, Mendez seemed to have exercised some restraint in the recording of the incident: he held back from taunting or registering contempt for what from his perspective was the ignorance and weaknesses of the natives. Instead, he focused on the resolve and courage of Columbus.

Ferdinand Columbus added a few other details and perspectives, especially regarding the belief in God—the ample amount displayed by his father (and also obviously held by him), the utter lack of it displayed by the natives. For Ferdinand such belief meant power. His father, he judged, possessed a great amount of it, and the natives registered only fear and incredulity:

> As for the Indians, God was very angry with them for neglecting to bring us food for which we paid them by barter, and had determined to punish them with famine and pestilence. To convince the incredulous, God would send them a clear token from Heaven of the punishment they were about to receive. They should therefore attend that night the rising of the moon: She would rise inflamed with wrath, signifying the chastisement God would visit upon them... at the rising of the moon the eclipse began, and the higher it rose the more complete the eclipse became, at which the Indians grew so frightened that with great howling and lamentation they came running from all directions to the ships, laden with provisions, and praying the Admiral to intercede with God that He might not vent His wrath upon them, and promising they would diligently supply all their needs in the future. The Admiral replied that he wished to speak briefly with his God, and retired to his cabin while the eclipse waxed and the Indians cried all the time for his help. When the Admiral perceived that the crescent phase of the moon was finished and that it would soon shine forth clearly, he issued from his cabin, saying that he had appealed to his God and prayed for them and had promised Him in their name that henceforth they would be good and treat the Christians well, bringing provisions and alleles they needed.... Perceiving that what he said was coming true, they offered many thanks to the Admiral and uttered praises of his God as long as the eclipse continued. From that time forward they were diligent in providing us with all we needed, and were loud in praise of the Christian God. For they believed that eclipses were very harmful, and since they were ignorant of their cause and of their regular recurrence and did not suspect that men living on earth could know what was happening in the sky, they were certain that his God had revealed that eclipse to the Admiral.[12]

These accounts of the incident, with their shades of differences, share the perspective regarding the dominant power of the world of white folks. In this instance the dominance was reflected in the "signs" or "tokens"—part of a system of their world's "magic." The magic entailed control of the heavens, including the moon. Columbus is understood to be in direct communication with a powerful god who controls the heavens. Communication with the gods produced a kind of knowing that was a form of power that could be called upon and demonstrated anywhere and seemingly for any purpose.

It is not likely that the incident was ever intended to illustrate anything other than the dominance of the white men and their world represented by Columbus. This dominance seemed to turn not around the expected weapons of war, but around a special item of cargo, knowledge, secret knowledge of the ways and will of the gods. Columbus is depicted as knowing things that the others, the "savages," did not and could not know. It is this special knowledge about the gods that the natives reacted to with such awe and terror, as if it were some kind of magic. As magic, this knowledge was understood as power.

Of course, the backdrop to this incident was the threat that the natives represented. The latter were in the real position of power. They had the advantages of being on their home turf; Columbus and his party were the intruders, in this case shipwrecked and without the means to overwhelm the natives in the usual terms of power. So in this situation the white men needed a trick or "stratagem" whereby the natives could be made to mis-recognize their own powerful position and be rendered somewhat befuddled by the claims and wizardry of the white men. In short, in order for Columbus and his crews to survive the situation, the natives had to be made to misperceive the power situation; they had to be tricked into believing they were not powerful but ignorant and weak. Here the mechanics of power were clearly discursive and ideological. Is this not really the baseline for the maintenance of power?

Although the incident that Equiano records did not involve an eclipse of the moon, it is clear enough on what basis he recalled and made use of the incident involving Columbus. His experience with the Musquito natives involved precisely the same sort of power dynamics that were reflected in the stories about Columbus. Like Columbus, Equiano was away from his home turf. The "Indians" were in a commanding position, and some of them, full of the confidence that meeting strangers on home turf may inspire, and no doubt,full of the alcohol supplied by Equiano's party, appeared to be threatening. Also like Columbus, in order to address the situation, Equiano thought of a "stratagem." I take this term (or its equivalent), actually found in at least one account of Columbus and in Equiano's story, reflects Equiano's reading of Columbus's experience as revelation, even celebration, of Columbus's connivance. It is also Equiano's recognition of his need to imitate the legendary Admiral and explorer. The point in all these contexts—Equiano's narrative; the mythic accounts about Columbus; and the larger situation of contact between Europeans and the "savage" Other—was to figure out how to manipulate the natives and destabilize their position of power.

This means, of course, that in the incident with the Musquito natives Equiano not only invoked but identified himself as Columbus, the historical legendary figure who discovered and conquered the worlds of the "heathen." In his engagement with native "Indians"—other peoples of color—Equiano identified with the white man. This identification is rather complicated: Equiano does not mean by it that he is self-loathing and wishes to be some type of human being—white—other than what he is. He does not mean by it that he has fear and contempt for these "Indians". And it does not mean that his perspective on the world has been hijacked or manipulated by white dominance. These meanings, as difficult and disturbing as they are, would be too easy. By this point, all readers of the narrative will have learned that Equiano is far too clever as writer and that more is usually at issue.

Drawing on Columbus as symbol of the power of the white world and as the one who, as the stories go, came up with the actual "stratagem" is really part of Equiano's larger narrative strategy. The "stratagem" referenced in the story about Equiano's exploits with the Musquito natives is layered and complex; it requires reading that matches the cleverness of Equiano's composition. Equiano seems to want readers to compare him to Columbus, but only insofar as he demonstrates the kind of power and authority that is associated with being white. The type of power at issue in this case is knowledge, or more broadly and poignantly, a power play that is reflective of, presumes, and draws on a larger structure of hegemony that is ideological and social-psychological in nature.

Insofar as Columbus is depicted as someone in communication with the god who controls the heavens, he is seen as powerful. His power is understood to lie not in any object but in the knowing itself or rather in the capacity to communicate with God and so to know God's way. Equiano seems to recognize as much as he depicts himself as man of power in relationship to the Musquito natives. He understands his power over the natives to lie in his capacity and authority to communicate. Communication here means not merely passing along basic information, but being able and authorized to speak to God and to communicate what God says. And as the narratived Equiano has already discovered (in the non-talking book story of chapter 3), according to the assumptions of British Protestant evangelicals, God talks now mainly through the book—the Bible—as the most important symbol of power: "I would take the book... the bible... read, and *tell* God." (208).

In this claim to power there is the assumption that the natives are ignorant and credulous, easily frightened and manipulable. It is all the more fascinating to note that Equiano used the same descriptors regarding incidents earlier in his life. He described himself as being, before enlightenment, almost always terrified and shocked by the ways of the white world.[13] And the people he claimed as his own people, the Igbos, were described in his chapter 1 as being prone to believe things that were incredible and superstitious. They were described as being under the sway of magicians and wise men. Surely the point was to make description of the Musquitos evoke the description of the Igbos and to make the reader understand the two peoples as not being enlightened by (Protestant evangelical) truths.

Given Equiano's "strong analogy" of the Igbo to the ancient-biblical-world Jews, his speculation whether "the one people had sprung from the other," no doubt in imitation of world European Christians' penchant for comparing themselves as such,[14] Equiano must have considered all peoples, including all groups of Europeans, to be subject to the magicians and wise men of their respective worlds of magic. In light of such a "strong analogy," should we not wonder whether the ancient Jews were not in Equiano's mind also subject to such forces? "Like the Israelites in their primitive state, our government was conducted by our chiefs, our judges, our wise men and elders" (44).

Now if most peoples, including Jews and Europeans, are subject to magicians and wise men, surely so the "heathen." In other words, Equiano seems to have projected from his own experiences of British culture some things about Igbo and Musquito culture. His and Columbus's engagements with the heathenish other were based on their own experiences and observances of such phenomena. There certainly had been European folk traditions that were characterized as "magic."[15] But even more to the point for Equiano, with his rather special positionality as black stranger who belied so many of his experiences, the dominant arrangements and relations of power in Britain and throughout Europe that had come to disdain the folk traditions and their orientations to "magic" nonetheless could be thought about in terms of "magic." These dominant arrangements of power, after all, included evangelical Christianity and its orientation to biblical interpretation.

It would appear, then, that Equiano read and used stories about Columbus to think with, to model himself and to act on. The perdurance of the incident in the memories and constructed stories about Columbus suggests its poignancy, that it captures a truth that is, perhaps for some, an embarrassing truth about how the dominant center European world is constructed. And, of course, Equiano as the black stranger disturbingly positions himself—through his writing, no less—to remind readers of such truth and to make use of such a truth in order to destabilize his (bottom-link of the chain of being) position as well as the larger general situation. He was not so much trying to be white as he was demonstrating how power worked in the dominant world of the Europeans. He was imitating and signifying on such systems and arrangements. I assume that Equiano, like "Columbus," assumed that certain tricks that work at home, among the hoi polloi and even those above them, might, with some modifications, work abroad among savages and heathens. Their manipulations rested upon crude but clever assumptions about societies, about social psychology across cultures. In imitating "Columbus," Equiano was showing that he knew how power as understood by the Europeans could be worked. He depicted himself not so much as a white man for the general sake of assuming another identity but as a man using power. The power was understood by him and by all others within the white world as white men's magic.

What begs further consideration is the nature or type of power or magic that Equiano depicts himself displaying. Some observations are first in order: whatever else may be at issue, the power that Equiano imitates and wields is assumed to be basically ideological and social-psychological in nature. It is assumed to be a matter of positionality and structure of relationships. And it is certainly understood that "it" can be extended beyond the borders of the homeland nation.

Of course, Equiano does not use the term "power." He uses instead the term "magic" in order to convey what is at work.[16] The one concept stands in for the other. The term "magic" may simply be used to capture the essence or nature of operations of something that is confusing or puzzling. That power aptly names what is at stake for Equiano is clear enough through a reading of his story. His entire story is really about the quest for power that he associates with white men. He depicts himself as one whose life represents dramatic changes in terms of such power: from abject powerlessness, as a slave, to one who, as in the incident with the Musquitos, represents a European version of Christian faith and wields power in the tradition of one of the most legendary of white Christian men. So insofar as the power is white men's magic, Equiano understands his quest to be to pursue and obtain white men's magic.

Equiano understood that there really was no object or thing that contained power in either his or Columbus's situation with the natives. All Columbus had, all that Equiano had, was a suggestion, an idea, an image. What was traded on or exploited was the very idea, shared by natives and Catholic Spanish and Protestant British alike, of an anthropomorphized god who through various media and in various ways talks and listens to certain human beings. The latter are thereby rendered powerful. Their power is evident in and tied to the communication or the authority or ability to participate in such communication, thereby structuring certain relations.

But such an arrangement turns around a type of suspension—of doubt regarding the truth of what is faced. And it involves accepting certain assumptions about reality. It is not a heavier burden to believe that strange-looking and strange-talking "men" who arrive on one's shores from a distance are mysterious and powerful. It is not a stretch to accept that such men are in communication with forces that are unknown and potentially threatening. And it is very understandable that a group would give respect to one among such strange men who holds forth and declares with a sense of authority in ways similar to an indigenous magician or wise man might have. It is also unsurprising that one would give pause when such figures claim that they had spoken to and heard from a god regarding the causes of unexpected outsized events such as the darkening of the moon or regarding the explicit threat of death against one's company. This was the assumption and orientation of most traditional societies. What "Columbus" and "Equiano" are depicted as having done is exploit the social psychology—with its fears, expectations, and hopes—of a particular context and time. That is what magicians do. Therein lies their power. That is the work and effect of the Wizard of Oz.[17]

The magic and sleight of hand of the Wizard of Oz are now understood as quite common, especially in the fraught contexts and time periods of first contact, extending from the fifteenth to the nineteenth century. The experiences of contact between the West (Europeans as travelers/explorers/merchants/conquerors) and the Rest, (the "discovered" savages/

heathen as the Other) represented a kind of stage that inspired the production and performance of what Equiano discovers as white men's magic.[18] It was in the contact zones that difference was discovered, interpreted, and negotiated; or out of a sense of fear covered up or undermined or exploited. Focusing on the past two hundred years or so of contact zone experiences in her fascinating and sometimes disturbing book, an anthology of indigenous peoples' stories about "white men," Julia Blackburn's *The White Men: The First Response of Aboriginal Peoples to the White Man*,[19] provides perspective on what may have been at work in Equiano's story telling. Told by those who encounter strange intruders from unknown places, the stories in Blackburn's book establishes some aspects of the social-psychology, the anxieties and fears that condition the responses that have been noted among aboriginal peoples in such situations:

> It is as if creatures from outer space were to land in one of our cities. The news of their arrival travels at a desperate speed from place to place, from country to country. The simple facts of the situation become immediately confused with the private fears and imaginings of each individual who hears what has happened, and soon many wild and contradictory stories are in circulation.
>
> There would be those who believe that the arrival of the white men must be a sign presaging the end of a troubled world, and they then realize that they have been expecting such an event for a long time. Others would perhaps trust that these are benevolent intruders who have been sent to help the human race and bring a new golden age into being. One person becomes hysterical and the mood infects a whole group, because this is a time of mass responses. Even if these strange creatures travel about very little and do no harm to their hosts, just the knowledge of their existence forces people to reassess completely their sense of their own place within the universe. (26)

Among the responses she records in the book is one that involves the devolution of power of the kings of the Ambo in what is present-day Namibia and Angola. After the 1861 ritual murder of Haimibili, the greatest of the Ambo kings, each successive ruler became less and less powerful until the last king, Mandume, was killed in 1917. What then followed was a succession of local and regional headmen who over time came to be ruled by white colonial government officials. In response to this situation, the prophet Muselanga included prophecies in a layered poem written over a period of about twenty years, from the 1870s to the 1890s:

> **Something strange is creeping over the waters;**
>
> Foreigners creep in to the country.
> It was far, it comes near, it is here.
> People start to walk.
> Perhaps an omuhama tree will fall across their path.
> The strange people come from a distant country,
> They come with different words.
> When they are talking they should be listened to.
>
> I walked and walked through the country
> And I saw the kraals of the nobles.
> I walked a second time through the country,
> I did not see the kraals of the nobles.
> Bu white men's houses I have seen.
>
> Oejulu! I do not see the kraal of the King.
> I do not see the kraals of the nobles.
> Only the kraal of the woman Naminda I see.
> White men's houses I see in what were the fields of Haindongo.
> Houses I see like white millet meal.
> The world will end, it will end completely.
> The King will die, he will go underground to the palace of the frog.
> I will go away from here, I will go underground into the hole of the bees.
> I will go in a clothing of earth
> For I have cursed the King. (38–39)

The point to be taken from such prophecy is that the presence of white men brought on chaos and anxiety. The strange thing is also the problematic and fearful thing. The continuing presence of the white men provides opportunity to reflect on what makes for their strangeness.[20] A provocative representation can be seen in an image (see Figure 6.1) painted onto the henta boards from the Nicobar Islands, located southeast of the Indian subcontinent.[21] A white man is depicted as a ship's captain who juggles and is otherwise surrounded by many objects, goods of cargo, including an umbrella, a pipe, a compass, a telescope, a light, a clock, some

FIGURE 6.1. A white man as figure of the god Deuse, standing among trade goods on the henta boards from the Nicobar Islands. Werner Forman Archive/British Museum, London.

furniture. With so many objects that put so many things in motion to such powerful effects at his command, the white man is considered to be the embodiment of God (Deuse).

What do these responses suggest? It is apparent and understandable that in the contact zone, in confrontation with the sudden and dramatic appearance of strangers, the indigenous peoples register anxiety and a sense of being threatened, even overwhelmed. Showing up from distant lands—and with "cargo," no less—is itself a display of power. It makes sense that the speech—the proclamations and threats—of the white-faced strangers under the dramatic circumstances of first contact would be taken seriously and warily.

But these responses and many others in the forms of images and testimonies make clear that indigenous nonwhite peoples did not simply react monochromatically or only in fear and with a sense of intimidation. Such flattening of perspective is obviously needed for the establishment of the "savage systems"[22] of subjugation that whites established and maintained. The images and so much more in forms of expressivity make clear that indigenous peoples not only thought in layered and complex terms about these white-faced strangers, they also used them to reflect upon themselves and their situation in the world. They wrestled with the meaning of white men in their world, using them as touchstone but going beyond the literal presence of a group.[23]

I think it is clear that "Equiano" (the simple character in the contained little story; the writerly Equiano who is a more complex figure will provoke below another interpretation) and "Columbus" (the legendary, not the historical figure), representing the "white men" in the contact zone, did not care to reveal the truth about the layered thinking and capacities of such people. They preferred their indigenous peoples to be remembered as simple, flat, ignorant, superstitious. This is the prejudiced view of such peoples that we as equally flat and prejudiced contemporary readers have accepted. That such acceptance of this view is our history and is ongoing is a disturbing fact that is everywhere evident and need not be elaborated on here.

Now, regarding the perspectives of the white men, it is evidently the mixture of fear, curiosity, and headiness if not arrogance from the success of having shown up that leads to an assumption about superior power. As the competition in all arenas—military, political, economic, cultural/religious—continued unabated among nations of early modern Europe, it extended into exploration and expropriation of other lands. And that such interest led often to trickery and manipulation in addition to violence few would deny.

But it may surprise some if I argue that it is not easy to probe further the mind of the white men in interpretation of the situation. Precisely because of their consistent aggressive and systematic efforts to subjugate the indigenous peoples, in spite of their penchant for describing the others, their self-probings are not easily available. We can get only some indirect glimpses of what white men were thinking and feeling in the story about Columbus and in Equiano's story. What is needed above all is testimony that is the registration of white men's self-reflexivity and self-probing, sentiment far beyond the typical promotion of the superior power of white men or the subtler but even more insidious unreflective and unmarked whiteness, that claims to be universal.

Anthropologist Michael Taussig, ever the risk taker in the field and in theorizing, provides fascinating testimony. I have already referred to his *Mimesis and Alterity: A Particular History of the Senses*, in which he challenges his (assumed mostly white?) readers to consider the "mimetic faculty" as performed by peoples of the "Third and Other worlds"—a result of their forced contact with the "First World"—as portal to the sensibilities and minds of all involved.[24] The mirroring that is "mimetic excess"—"mimetic self-awareness . . . turned on itself, on its colonial endowment"

(252)—ruptures and destabilizes all identities and all knowledges. In this situation, argues Taussig, "mastery," the manipulation of canonical knowledge, is not possible. In the ongoing fraught histories of contact, dominance is "mirrored in the eyes and handiwork of its Others." This is of course an "unsettled" and "unsettling" situation, "a Nervous System, because the interpreting self is itself grafted into the object of study. The self enters into the alter against which the self is defined and sustained."[25]

Taussig indicated more precisely what the "Nervous System" might augur in his poignant reflection on one of the images that he discovered in Julia Blackburn's book *The White Men*. The image was a photograph of an Igbo mbari shrine[26] (see figure 6.2).

Taussig's reaction to the image is very significant: it is for him a site on which can be reflected different but related levels and types of awareness: of the freighted critical response on the part of nonwhites to modern-era contact between whites and nonwhites; of the response on the part of whites, including himself, to the nonwhite response. His honest, disturbed, and disturbing reaction is quite moving:

> He frightens me, this African white man. He unsettles. He makes me wonder without end. Was the world historical power of whiteness achieved, then, through its being sacred as well as profane power? It makes me wonder about the constitution of whiteness as global colonial work and also as a minutely psychic one involving powers invisible to my senses but all too obvious, as reflected... by this strange artifact. I know next to nothing of the "context" of ritual, belief, or of social practice in which an older anthropology... would enmesh this African white man, "explain "him (away), "Africanize" him (as opposed to "whitenize" him). All I have is the image and its brief caption, and I am my own gaping subject of analysis, for it is precisely this fractured plane of visibility and invisibility that constitutes the impact of the image on an uncomprehending West now face to face with itself, bursting the earth. For the white man, to read this face means facing himself as Others read him, and the "natives' point of view" can never substitute for the fact that now the native is the white man himself and that suddenly, woefully, it dawns that the natives' point of view is endless and myriad. The white man as viewer is here virtually forced to interrogate himself, to interrogate the Other in and partially constitutive of his many and conflicting selves.... Such face-to-faceness no doubt

FIGURE 6.2 A white man. Mud sculpture that was part of sacred Mbari house, made by Owerri Ibo of Biafra. Situated in Umuedi Ofekelem, Nigeria. Photograph by Herbert M. Cole, 1967.

> brings its quotient of self- congratulation. "They think we are gods." But being a god is okay as long as it isn't excessive. After all, who knows—in imaging us as gods, might they not take our power?[27]

We are not used to having such testimony from the normally unmarked white man. Might Taussig's response, insofar as it represents heightened awareness of the influences of the ongoing contact between whites and nonwhites, help us all think about our own perspectives? And might it represent the sensibilities of white readers that Equiano had sought to influence in this narrative? There is much in these words that could be analyzed.

But I should like to focus on what it may mean to an effort to understand what Equiano was up to in telling the story about his encounter with the Musquitos. Insofar as he wanted his narrative to disturb the readers' sense of the immutability of social categories, this story does precisely that. And Taussig's response insofar as it reflects destabilization and defamiliarization of fixed categories and arrangements would seem to be the type of response Equiano wanted from his readers.

There is something a bit ironic and puzzling about the fact that throughout his story Equiano calls himself a stranger—in relationship to, that is, outside of, the white world that was England. The story essentially turns around his efforts to transform himself from stranger to successful insider, "almost an Englishman." Yet within the story Equiano is also depicted as stranger—in relationship to a world far away and quite different from England, a world in which the natives looked more like Equiano than those with whom he traveled and those left back in England. How was it possible for him to be both? Creative narrative development and the time change that it forces make this circumstance plausible for the reader. His readers are presumed to assume, even though some already knew him as a person, that Equiano the character was as a black or Negro a stranger, a radical other, to them. But as the readers are made to experience Equiano as writer, encounter the complex and puzzling development of Equiano in the story, they also develop in their their psychological assumptions about the character and about the larger issues to which the character points. Equiano's change is from stranger to whom all things English are alien and frightening to one who is an insider who can define, defend, and represent Englishness.

This change is somewhat fraught with difficulty. Equiano clearly wanted his readers to see him as a type of Columbus, as a man who represented power, mastery, and control. What better way to represent Englishness than to be seen exerting power far beyond the shores of England and in imitation of the legendary Columbus no less?[28] He wanted his readers to find convincing the story of Equiano facing the Musquito with the projection of power, that is, power understood to reside in, among other things, literacy, the book. This required suspending belief so as to see Equiano not so much as white man but as man wielding the power of white men's magic. The sort of magic wielded was ideological and psychological mastery in nature as well as geo-spatially—it could be wielded anywhere. This meant that notwithstanding the highly unusual circumstances, even counterintuitive thinking—that is, a black man assuming leadership role over white men who make up his crew as he confronts nonwhite peoples on their home turf in a situation of decided disadvantage for him—Equiano depicted himself as representative of a burgeoning imperial force that was defined by white men. He had to be convincing as a wielder of white men's magic. He had to make his mostly white readers forget racial difference and its assumed hierarchialization and see him as one who represented them in this incident.

What needed to be represented above all was the mandate for expanding the ways and traditions of Europeans, in this case, the British. This meant that Equiano had to make his readers understand that the traditions and systems, the ways things were ordered in Britain, needed to be established as authoritative and powerful, to the extent that they could be tested far beyond the shores of Britain. This was the workings of empire—ancient and early modern. Among the different forms of power—ideological, economic, military, political[29]—it is the ideological, not the military, that has proven to be most effective in maintaining hegemony.[30]

The magic in the world Equiano confronted was displayed in convincing others that the white world was powerful, overwhelmingly so, and in every respect, to the point that guns were not usually required in order to subjugate. The subjugation of the type hinted at in Equiano's story, and that actually obtained in the world he knew, required some strongly and consistently held assumptions among white men. There must have been an awareness of Britain as a bounded culture, a discursive formation or semiosphere of a sort,[31] constructed around a type of logonomoic system[32] in which discursive practices are tightly regulated and naturalized; certain things go and come "without saying."[33] Control was needed for the sake of both internal and external power dynamics. All those within the empire or part of the regime had to understand that what made it work was structure, recognized hierarchies including not only social status and rank but even more fundamentally—even as (the particulars of) social status and rank are changed if not undermined—language/discourse as the baseline vector. Thus the politics of language/discourse/knowledge emerges as key "stratagem" in the formation of modern world hegemony.

Such control was in place long before and after him, to be sure, but it was John Locke who, with his argument regarding the need for the "purification" of language, helped identify the key challenges as well as strategies in the modern ideology and politics of language use. Locke was the most important theorist of modern language; he primarily provided the language about language use. By "purification" Locke meant language that was transcendent, that is, untethered to the Babel of local and individual interests that allow words to be used according to the moment and current and traditional sensibilities, the "cheat and abuse of words."[34] In "The Epistle to the Reader" in his *Essays Concerning Human Understanding*, Locke makes it clear what occasioned his writing and how such occasion reflects the disturbing situation:

> [F]ive or six friends meeting at my chamber, and discoursing on a subject very remote from this, found themselves quickly at a stand, by the Difficulties that rose on every side. After we had awhile puzzled ourselves, without coming any nearer a Resolution of those doubts which perplexed us, it came into my Thoughts that we took a wrong course; and that before we set ourselves upon Enquiries of that Nature, it was necessary to examine our own Abilities, and see what *Objects* our Understandings were, or were not, fitted to deal with.[35]

Locke here confessed that advancement in "discoursing" was impossible because, as he would go on to argue, there was no shared, no universally recognized understanding about or rules of language use. It seems that in Locke's view what was desperately needed was rules in the use of language that would effect its transcendance, its deliverance from the "chains" of traditionalism. Language needed to be (re-)constructed and used in universal terms, in terms that would effect and reflect its decontextualization and deprovincialization.

Of course, such universalism came at a price: it ironically meant for Locke and (other language and political theorists) that only an elite, only high-status white men, who would be properly trained and socialized, could be considered legitimate practitioners. Only certain properly trained persons could be considered proper users, speakers, and writers. The power dynamics of such arrangements are quite real: it meant that only legitimate language users, speakers, or writers would compel respect in the various social domains. So the theory that aimed to make language usage universal, to make it make sense apart from the chains of local and individual traditions and quirks, to wrest it from even the elitist medieval world of tradition, with its chains of intertextuality and high rhetorics, gave way to the modern world and with it yet another regime, in this case a "metadiscursive regime."[36] This regime works through a "rhetoric of control":[37] it represents an effort to establish samenesses in public communication: who can speak and write with authority and legitimacy; what one can say or write; how one speaks or writes. In terms of the epistemic, it is an imperial reach. It makes incontestable a part of "the horizon of the taken for granted,"[38] that which otherwise would be understood as a matter of coercion. The sleight of hand that is the "rhetoric of control" makes the violent claim about universality and transcendence and the natural out of a particular worldly orientation. This "nonagentive"[39] power—or magic—of white men is experienced as being beyond the reach of most humans. It is presented as being outside the normal realm of institutional power dynamics, encompassing all physical and social-cultural borders. But as violent as dynamics of control appear to be, it is important not to lose sight of the fact that they actually turn around the politics and social psychology of language.

The use of language for control is far more efficient and insidious. If, as is indicated above, the first stage in the process of control is to convince the many that only self-styled elites are the ones who can be taught to use language correctly, that the "vulgar," the "swinish multitude"[40]—poor landless males; most women; and savages and barbarians—need not bother to speak, need not be heard or respected by elites, the second stage entails the elites' seemingly contradictory gesture toward the vulgar. Thinking themselves heroic and charitable, the elites deign by the early nineteenth century to begin to teach the vulgar the rules of the language game precisely in order to control them, to teach quietude, the importance of following the rules. In this stage, in which the vulgar are imagined to be a part of the system of education, there is evident something of a shift in thinking, from emphasis on "general" and abstract knowledge to "useful" knowledge. But the politics of this shift is consonant with the elites' firmly held notions about language: that its origins are arbitrary and general, artificial, not originated or produced by "mere people," but the work of artists and others of superior abilities; that those who can use it properly and know it are closer to God, that those who cannot know it must be considered excluded from God and supreme knowledge and identified as the servants of those who know important things. These servants can know only what is needed to provide service.[41]

From elites the likes of Locke and Burke to dissenting radicals the likes of Thomas Paine to aliens/outsiders the likes of Equiano, the different even confounding responses to the ideologies and politics of language are evident. In the scene with the Musquitos, Equaino oddly depicts himself representing the same elitist agenda/interest in differentiating and hierarchializing people according to language. Insofar as the Musquitos do not speak and understand a European language, they are assumed by Equiano to be vulgar and not worthy of being heard. They are considered to be quite ignorant and manipulable. Over against what would be considered by readers to be their local babble, Equiano invokes what, according to the challenges of Locke, would be considered a language that is, if not totally "purified," at least, is imitative of the transcendent and universal. Such language carries with it authority and power. The great irony is that it is Equiano—a black stranger, by origins dramatically low on the chain, totally outside the socialization process imagined by Locke—who represents the authority figure, and the lordly universal language. It is Equiano who is the representative and wielder of such a language. He practices the same sort of politics and ideological and psychological games with language as does Columbus and Locke. The reader of Equiano's narrative can easily connect Equiano's depiction of himself in relationship to the Musquitos with his description of the offices of the Ah-affoe-way-cah, the Igbo priests/magicians, in the first chapter of his narrative. In the same way that Equiano described the Ah-affoe-way-cah as being the ones who know things, who could calculate time, who could explain things, presents himself as just such a figure before the Musquitos. Equiano became the front man not only for Locke's deprovincialization/universalization/globalization of language, but also the Igbo-like priest/magician in a larger world. In the same way in which the Igbo priests were said to calculate time, Equiano claims to know how to communicate with God and even to direct "him" to act in certain ways. This was an example of his "unbounded influence."

What certainly cannot go without comment is the use of scriptures by Equiano in his power play with the Musquitos. He makes clear that the symbol for knowledge/power are scriptures. There is no reference to any particular textual passage, no concern about any particular teaching or doctrine, nor any particular incident or wise saying; there is only the general reference to the "book." This is an important distinction: the focus is not on content but on phenomenon and phenomenology of the book, what it means. So it is the meaning of the book in the world that Equiano claims to represent in this incident.

For the world that Equiano claims to represent, the book stands as symbol for language—in fact, for the most powerful expression of language. It could easily be conjectured that the book referred to is the Bible.

Perhaps. But it is probably more accurate to suggest that it is the phenomenon of the book itself that is at issue for Equiano and for the world he represents. And it is the Bible—the scriptures understood as sacred text in the narrow sense of the term for that world—that is the baseline for the complex of issues that the book raises. But as Equiano's story line has it, the most critical issue seems to be that of the power of communication, the power of language, that turns in general around the mystification of the written. This, of course, assumes that the cultural assumption that it is the Bible as the scriptures that models the (general) scriptural.

Such phenomenon involves some very specific assumptions about how language can be used. In this case, language/writing in the form of a book is understood to convey mysterious power that has its origins in another realm—from God—and that can be employed to influence others.

This is in fact the dramatization and performance of scripturalization: not of this or that text but an order, a system of power based on the mystification of the written and, through such, the psychology of language. It presumes that the written and the ability to read it convey special knowledge and with it special power. The claim to special knowledge is the trick: with it many sins are committed and covered up. The strategy seems always to turn around convincing others that there is some knowledge that eludes them, that they could never possess on their own. This is power play. The ultimate power play has to do with writing or with the book.

It was Equiano's recognition of this power system—what I term scripturalization—in place in Britain that provided the opening for his depiction of his engagement of the Musquitos. His understanding that power turned around knowledge and claims about it inspired him to position himself as a person of knowledge, to construct his life story as one about the pursuit of knowledge, and in this important incident with the Musquitos, to depict himself as the exemplar of knowledge. In fact, he was the wielder of ultimate knowledge understood that was communicated through writing, through the Good Book that was the Bible.

Fully aware that in the minds of most of his readers possession of mystifying knowledge was associated—within European societies—with (elite) white men, Equiano nonetheless depicted himself with bravura and cleverness as the possessor of such knowledge. His self-depiction reflects his understanding of the means by which white men came to be and powerful; it also reflects his understanding that it was with possession of such that he could be transformed into a successful and powerful person. This understanding made his status as stranger and his racial identity "almost"—as in "almost an Englishman"—irrelevant. In terms of the logic of his narrative, it mattered only whether he was an able reader and wielder of the book.

This was the tight logical space into which Equiano lured his readers: in the wake of first contact between the West and the rest and the violence and rigid racialist hierarchialization that developed from it, the depiction of the nonwhite man actually performing the authority of the white man must have been and continues to be (not for white men alone) rather startling. In writing as he did, Equiano was clearly being provocative; he seems to have wanted readers to be shocked and disturbed; at the very least, he wanted them to reconsider the established hierarchy—the rigid and overdetermined identifications with parts of hierarchy, if not hierarchy itself. His entire life story, and the incident with the Musquitos in particular, threw into some confusion the traditional European perspective that associated face color with power and authority. What Equiano's story challenged readers to consider is that insofar as it was assumed that power was to be found in the knowledge that the book represents, it mattered not what may be the color of the face of the one who "speaks" to the book. Assumed to be, at least in historical terms, white men's magic, scripturalization was also viewed by Equiano as highly imitable and exploitable.

Beyond the shock value to his readers, Equiano's depiction of his performance also made clear something else: that scripturalization was about power. Long before Foucault lectured on the matter, Equiano seemed to recognize what is now termed power as a complex web of social-psychological relations. So what I term "scripturalization" was for Equiano recognition of the construction, projection, and persisting obfuscation of such power in social (political, institutional) relations. Clearly, there remain many issues to be addressed. But ultimately, what was of chief importance to Equiano was not so much the morality and ethics of the situation or his actions, but his recognition of how power works and his performing it. With such recognition and performance he established himself as a figure of power because he pointed to his understanding of how power works.

Of course, this was all a matter of limited even if strategic narrative depiction. The narrativized Equiano did not, perhaps could not in the context of the incident with the Musquitos, be declared to be a "white man," his wielding of the book notwithstanding. The actual historical circumstances in which the historical writerly Equiano lived with his readers would not allow this to happen. This incident dramatized the near possibility of Equiano's assumption of power. Equiano the writer would take strategic opportunity that was the narrative of his life as well as other communications in order to make this single incident a compelling and fraught one, pointing the reader to narrative moments that show how power was seized and used.

7

"I could read it for myself": Scripturalization, Slavery, and Agency

Now the Bible was my only companion and comfort; I prized it much, with many thanks to God that I could read it for myself, and was not left to be tossed about or led by man's devices and notions.

—OLAUDAH EQUIANO, *Interesting Narrative*, chapter 10

AFTER HAVING ESTABLISHED Equiano the stranger's critical grasp and clever depiction of the way of the white world and the way power works within it, especially in relationship to writing and the book—the regime that I call scripturalization—in this chapter I explore Equiano's complex messages regarding his standing in the white world. Having signified on white men's magic as scripturalization, having provided a dramatic high-point demonstration of his single-incident possession of white men's power, how does he position himself, and others like him, in ongoing relationship to it? What did he want to possess? What did he want to be? What did he want to take place? What does it mean in terms of his ongoing possession and exercise of power and agency? His narrative does not seem to be linear in development or direct and explicit in terms of argumentation on this matter; instead, it seems at different points to hint at what Equiano the writer already thinks he realizes or will soon realize in terms of power.

In the first chapter of his narrative Equiano dwells primarily on the social textures of the world from which he was violently torn as a child. He compares aspects of that world of his early childhood, especially some general cultural and religious traditions, to aspects of Christian Britain. He suggests the possibilities of a genetic relationship between "Eboan Africans" and (biblical-world) "Jews" (the latter a coopted group that was a stand-in for white Christians). And in this first chapter he first broaches the delicate subject of "colour of difference" and "prejudice" against "the natives of Africa." At the end of the chapter he makes a direct emotional appeal to his readers:

> Are there not causes enough to which the apparent inferiority of an African may be ascribed, without limiting the goodness of God, and supposing he forbore to stamp understanding on certainly his own image, because "carved in ebony"? Might it not be naturally ascribed to their situation? ... Does not slavery itself depress the mind, and extinguish all its fire, and every noble sentiment? ... Let the polished and haughty European recollect that *his* ancestors were once, like the Africans, uncivilized, and even barbarous. Did nature make *them* inferior to their sons? And should *they too* have been made slaves? Every rational mind answers, No. Let such reflections as these melt the pride of their superiority into sympathy for the wants and miseries of their sable brethren, and compel them to acknowledge that understanding is not confined to feature or colour. If, when they look round the world, they feel exultation, let it be tempered with benevolence to others, and gratitude to God, "who hath made of one blood all nations of men for to dwell on all the face of the earth; and whose wisdom is not our wisdom, neither are our ways his ways." (45)

At the end of his second chapter he describes his and his sister's kidnapping, their separation from each other, his traumatic experience of the middle passage, his arrival in Barbados, and his being sold into enslavement. And given such situations, he communicates his perception of all things as new, strange, and astonishing, many things appearing to be full of "bad spirits," or "magic." Equiano then reflects on a moving memory about fellow enslaved Africans. Several brothers were "sold in different lots" and were crying with full emotion at their separation from each other. There it was—the scene told the story of Africans' experiences in the Atlantic worlds: as Equiano remembers[1] this episode, it greatly moved him at the time of occurrence; and his remembrance of it stirred him again at the point of writing to address directly and with fierce emotion his white Christian readers:

> O, ye nominal Christians! Might not an African ask you, learned you this from your God? who says unto you, Do unto all men as you

> would men should do unto you? Is it not enough that we are torn from our country and friends to toil for your luxury and lust of gain? Must every tender feeling be likewise sacrificed to your avarice? Are the dearest friends and relations, now rendered more dear by their separation from their kindred, still to be parted from each other, and thus prevented from cheering the gloom of slavery with the small comfort of being together and mingling their sufferings and sorrows? Why are parents to lose their children, brothers their sisters, or husbands their wives? Surely this is a new refinement in cruelty, which . . . adds fresh horrors even to the wretchedness of slavery. (61)

Both sets of comments reveal much about Equiano, his sensibilities and sentiments, his politics and strategies. Most significant at this point are Equiano's explicit references to Africans. References to his and others' African-ness are very important in the passages quoted above and throughout his narrative. After having taken deliberate steps to reference his homeland as the land of "Ebos"/"Eboans" in much of chapter 1, it is almost startling to notice "Africa"/"African/s" used at the end of both chapters 1 and 2 and throughout the rest of the narrative. What accounts for this change in terminology, this change from designation of a specific self-named ethnic identification to the more general freighted initially forced designation intended to confuse and destroy continuing strong ethnic identity?[2] The change may reflect Equiano's interest in representing for the reader the nature and history of his character's dramatic transformation and change in self-consciousness. This transformation—from an Igbo to African—was the point of his story-telling.[3] According to the story he tells, this change in identity and consciousness was facilitated—forced?—by the challenges and pressures and new opportunities faced by him and others like him who were stolen from various tribes in western Africa and made slaves (in some cases again and again) in various places in the North Atlantic worlds. Before being stolen away from their various "African" homelands, they had been known by various tribal names and identities; but because of their new experiences of enslavement—including forced adoption of new names; general proscriptions against and contempt for using homeland languages, observances, traditions, and rituals—there was both necessity and opportunity for the forging of new identities and new orientations.[4]

The invention and widespread use of the name "African" by Europeans in reference to the black peoples of diverse ethnic origins and identities they had encountered in sub-Saharan, especially western Africa, advanced Europeans' economic and ideological interests in connection with their lucrative slave systems and their structures of domination. Dominance was much better maintained over blacks-made-slaves of various tribal and regional origins and their different languages and customs by adhering to a logic and ideology of power relations that undermined communications, solidarity, and resistance. Ethnic tribal identity and communications across such identities were at first facilitated to a limited degree by the forced promiscuous collectivities of plantation-style enslavement. These collectivities were regularly frustrated by white dominants but eventually became the most important situations out of which a new black *koine* language and identity was forged. This was done in spite of the logic of dominance that was reflected through the forcing of the appellation "African" that aimed to destroy the integrity and power of ethnic differences. But of course such a violent practice was actually only the surface sign of the intended enslavement.[5] The real point was to impose any appellation other than the ones that really mattered and thereby take away opportunities for slaves to recognize themselves as human agents. Again, Charles H. Long puts the matter most pointedly and poignantly:

> [M]y community... knew that... it was... signified by another community. This signification constituted a subordinate relationship of power expressed through custom and legal structures.... By signification I am pointing to one of the ways in which names are given to realities and peoples during this period of conquest; this naming is at the same time an objectification through categories and concepts of those realities which appear as novel and "other" to the cultures of conquest. There is of course the element of power in this process of naming objectification... the power is obscured and the political, economic, and military situation that forms the context of the confrontation is masked by the intellectual desire for knowledge of the other.[6]

From the point of view of the black peoples made slaves by the Europeans, identity formation in slave-trading North Atlantic worlds under traumatic and harsh conditions was, as it continues to be, like survival itself, enormously complicated and painful, fraught with irony, pathos, not a little humor along the way, and great ingenuity in resistance: "While aware of this fact [signification], the [subordinated] community undercut this legitimated signification with a signification upon this legitimated signifying."[7]

Equiano tells his story in a way that reflects this history of serious play with signs. In statements such as the ones quoted above, Equiano steps out of narratological time and inserts his mature, more self-reflective voice into the narrative. These insertions were made in order to speak directly to the particular issues raised in the immediate narrative contexts. They allowed Equiano to make clear to the readers the major framing point of his story: that he wrote as one who had been transformed—from (enslaved humiliated) Igbo to (freed Christian) African. What remained to be established was *how* this transformation had been accomplished and what it should *mean* to him and to his readers.

This chapter aims to open a wider window onto the nature of Equiano's transformation by focusing on another aspect of scripturalization—what it reveals about the writer (as opposed to the character) Equiano. Beyond the affiliations with confessional communities or participation in national (and nationalist) politics, it is important here to focus on what the transformation represented for Equiano the figure who left us the "interesting" narrative. "Beyond" is chosen here to convey something about Equiano's fullest understanding of scriptures that transcends the churches and nations and their politics. With the wide perspective on his narrative we are presented a picture of Equiano experimenting with this power. Of course, he is not presented here as fully developed ideologist of power; but there are strong implications for an understanding of power from his representations. His story provides a fascinating window onto the phenomenon of power as scripturalization. Equiano's participation in the regime of scripturalization provides a glimpse into his understanding of power and how it works, more specifically, how he can make it work for him (and others in solidarity with him).

The larger context of the quotation from Equiano that serves as epigraph for this chapter has already been addressed. As a part of the conversion narrative and the accompanying scriptural glosses, Equiano indicates not simply what happened to him but the meaning of what happened to him. Beyond the rhetorics of conversion found in conventional evangelicalism, especially eighteenth-century British evangelicalism, in his statements about the meaning of what happened to him the claim that he came to recognize that he could now "read [the book] for himself" is as stirring and profound as it is short and clipped. No reader should mistake

Equiano as a simple and straightforward writer here. His representation operates in several keys, on different planes. I am most interested in this chapter in what he claims for himself about free reading. Why was being able to read for himself important to Equiano? Inquiry into the matter, including some of the most basic and obvious issues and the relationship to the rhetoric about being "African," is in order.

On the basis of the facility he developed for reading and writing English, Equiano refracted his new identity as an African not exclusively but especially through his reading of the Bible. What doing so entailed was a creative and even bold use of the Bible that pressed it into service as an African/Africanized Bible, that is, as an instrument of his (and other blacks') identity as African Christian. Given the larger social, ideological, and power dynamics that obtained for him and his "countrymen" in Britain—a situation that might be termed, in the tradition of British understatement, somewhat difficult—and given the privileged relationship that Britain understood itself to have with the Bible, the fact that for Equiano and his black colleagues "even the Bible was made over to "suit [the African] imagination"[8] was evidence of Equiano's creative strategic abilities and his keen understanding of dominant cultural realities.

First, as I argued in chapter 4, Equiano recognized Britain as a biblical formation. Second, as chapters 1 and 2 above established, Equiano recognized that such formation is reflective of the work of invention. Third, he recognized the possibilities of strategic imitation of the practices that were part of such formation (above in my chapter 5).

It is his strategic mimetics of English scriptural practices, captured most dramatically in his conversion narrative (his chapter 11), that I think best characterizes and makes understandable Equiano's story and the politics that he and his fellow African Christians rather artfully practiced. Beyond merely pointing out the fact of his mimetic practices, what I will do in this chapter is excavate some of the views that subtend such practices and politics of the mature, converted, narrative-writing Equiano. More precisely, I will address how and why Equiano managed to make himself—on his own terms, apart from the gaze or dominance of white men—a reader of British-inflected scripturalization and a rather clever practitioner of signifying/mimetic scripturalizing. It seems important to recognize Equiano's dramatization of the way forward for himself and black peoples in the North Atlantic worlds, especially in Britain, as part of the attention he gives to his character's discovery of the "hidden meanin'" of the ways of the white world, the secret regarding what he regarded as the source of its power.

I begin with a passage that I understand to be key to Equiano's signifying and strategy of imitation, which was part of his dream—for all Afro-British Christians—of realizing free reading. In relating some of the different types of violence and other atrocities that had been perpetrated against blacks throughout the Atlantic systems of slavery, Equiano turns to one type of injustice he had witnessed that was "frequent in all the [Caribbean] islands":

> The wretched field slaves, after toiling all the day for an unfeeling owner, who gives them but little victuals, steal sometimes a few moments from rest or refreshment to gather some small portion of grass, according as their time will admit. This they commonly tie up in a parcel... and bring to town or to the market to sell. Nothing is more common than for the white people on this occasion to take the grass from them without paying for it; and... many others, at the same time, have committed acts of violence on the poor, wretched, and helpless females, whom I have seen for hours stand crying... and get no redress or pay of any kind. (108)

From this reporting Equiano rhetorically pivots to the raising of pointed emotional questions:

> Is not this one common and crying sin, enough to bring down God's judgment on the islands? He tells us, the oppressor and the oppressed are both in his hands; and if these are not the poor, the broken-hearted, the blind, the captive, the bruised, which our Saviour speaks of, who are they? (108)

This rhetoric is a fascinating conflation of contemporary evangelical religious sentiment that draws on many sources, and ultimately the English Bible. There is no doubt that the sentiment has its ultimate origins in the New Testament Gospel of Luke, a text known for the privileging of the poor and oppressed in its redaction of the tradition of stories about sayings of Jesus. "He tells us" is a reference to God as God "speaks" the "word" as contained in the (English) Bible. But the particular source from the Bible is not clear. The concept of "oppressor and "oppressed" may very well have come from several different parts of the Bible.

The expression "in his hands" is certainly resonant of biblical stories about God's sovereignty and care, but as rendered, its direct source was more likely a contemporary popular para-biblical source, perhaps some catechetical material or other popular religious literature.

The second part of the passage, beginning with "and if these," as part of a pointed question, should probably be understood as an effort to relate the passage to the immediate context of Equiano's story. I think the question actually draws more directly from the Bible, probably Luke 4: 18–19 as a reading of Isaiah 6:1–2. The full implications of this passage are made clear in this saying of Jesus turned into a rather disturbing question: "and if these are not the poor, the broken-hearted, the blind, the captive, the bruised, which our Saviour speaks of, who are they?"[9]

"These" in Equiano's context is reference to the "negroes" who have been enslaved. Equiano makes clear that they are the ones about whom Jesus speaks. So, according to Equiano, the Bible "says" the black poor are privileged; they are the focus of special divine attention. This switch may not appear to mean much to the typical reader of the twentieth-first century, situated for the most part on the gentler side of a long ideological war involving color symbolization that has done violence to black peoples. But under the circumstances of eighteenth-century black enslavement and humiliation, including the ratcheting up of the discourses of ideological-religious-theological-philosophical and scientific antiblack racism, this was no mean rhetorical and ideological trick. The *white* scriptures are taken up, in this case by a *black* stranger, and interpreted to mean that God is on the side of the oppressed *blacks*.

The white scriptures that in the British context had "spoken" only to and about (white) British destiny are made by Equiano and his (black) cohorts to speak exclusively to the black poor and oppressed. This switch represented a radical transvaluation, a creative ideology and politics of imitation. The imitation is evident first in Equiano's taking up scripturalizing itself, reading a text as though in it, through it, God now "spoke"—to him!, spoke about matters that "applied to me with great comfort."[10]

A bizarre phenomenon! God speaking through a book? Really?! Only a "stranger," like Equiano, as opposed to a "pagan," like the Chinese, who not knowing God made claims about knowing in respected forms, that is, in sacred scripts, would likely raise this issue in this manner.[11] The "stranger" (=nonwhite) was considered a "heathen," one who was outside the semiospheres of scriptural civilizations altogether. Unlike the "pagan," like the Chinese, who did not know God but whose sacred script was given grudging respect, the "stranger" as "heathen" was held in contempt. Orientation on the part of the stranger to the Christian way would become a test for white Christian sentiment. At any rate, only the curious and intelligent self-reflexive "stranger" who was also invested in negotiating that world would learn to imitate it and signify on it and thereby highlight and problematize the fundamental issues at stake in its structuring and operations and power relations.

As I have already argued, Equiano seemed very much aware of the phenomenon that I term scripturalization as an invention and veiling that operates in a way similar to traditional magic. It was understood as a structure of power, a regime, associated with—perhaps even understood as another aspect of—the dominant British culture. He showed that he understood how scripturalization worked and what were its effects. The use of the term "magic" as a description of the ways of the dominant white world was hardly accidental. Notwithstanding the orientation toward magic and the fetishism of the lower classes in early modern European societies, elite societies across Europe defined their worlds over against the fetish-believing and magic-practicing heathenish Other. The establishment of such difference turned around claims about language and a certain epistemology. In using the term "magic," Equiano was positioning himself in that world, identifying himself—even if only strategically and for the sake of narratalogical effect—with the assumptions and biases of the elites, the sort that thought of nonelites, women, and outsiders as the "swinish multitude."[12]

Having associated black slaves with the "poor" and "oppressed" (101–112), there can be little doubt that what Equiano was doing was defining black slaves as the true focus and legitimate legatees of Jesus' mission. With the use of the Ethiopian figure in his conversion story in his chapter 10 (discussed above in my chapter 5) every black diaspora convert is represented as being the primary exemplar of the pious poor, the poor pious, for whom salvation was intended. This was indeed powerful cooptation as imitation.

Equiano's larger agenda seems to have been to contribute to the building of an African Christian diaspora. Such an effort had as part of its strategy, no doubt complex and multipronged, the practices of a reading formation, a community of readers of the Bible. This strategy was not unlike what Britain on a much larger scale had already become: a society that was a reading formation, particularly a Bible-reading formation.

Of course, the formation of which Equiano was principal if not founding figure was differently oriented. The "sons of Africa," as he and associates sometimes called themselves,[13] read both similarly to and differently from white Britain. They read themselves in (and into) the same Bible in (and into) which the British read themselves. They wanted and sometimes claimed to be British in some specific ways—beginning with political freedom and rights and economic opportunities. They wanted to be free and British in a different respect, on a different order: they wanted to be African *and* British. This also meant that they wanted Britain to be different. It is a simplistic and ungenerous and dangerous reading of their reading to assume that Equiano and associates wanted only to be like the British, as in the stereotypic and flat understanding of aping, even if not in terms of the nuances of Kafka's ape.[14] Through their self-reflexive uses of the Bible, "the sons of Africa" registered that they wanted mainly—and worked aggressively and courageously for—Britain to imitate *them*, that is, to reflect their ideology of an Africanist view of modern pluralism.[15] This goal would seem to me to qualify as "read[ing] for myself," "appl[ying]" texts to (the African) self "with great comfort."

Near the end of his conversion story Equiano makes a reference that is critical to the formation and understanding of his Africanist consciousness. It is the reference to the Ethiopian figure in the book of Acts (8:26–39) who is converted to the Christian way. This reference to the figure must now be discussed in more detail. As was already discussed above, this figure represents for Equiano the integration of the archetypal stranger into Western Christian society and culture. But I should like in this chapter to make the point that the figure serves a different but complementary function. Given the reference later in Equiano's conversion story to "my spots"—a collapsed allusion to Ethiopians/Nubians and their skin color, and to leopards and their characteristic defining spots in the book of the prophet Jeremiah[16]—Equiano seemed to have identified with the Ethiopian, in terms of both his skin color and his positionality in relationship to the center of social consciousness and structure. This identification is decisive: it is the key to Equiano's self-consciousness and self-understanding as mature writer. The Ethiopian was not merely one with dark skin who had been enslaved; he was now an African Christian who could without qualification represent "God's children." The "spots" link the Ethiopian and Equiano and all black peoples across time spans. The spots were transformed from being, in the original context, a reference to a simple physical marker to a unique sign in the context of first contact in the early modern era of humiliation for blacks to Equiano's view in which it refers to a physical marker or accident of human existence throughout the world that also makes it carry the freight of special symbolization. Equiano is the Christianized Ethiopian. Through this interpretive prism, the reader can see the whole point of Equiano's story-telling: to chart the "interesting" life journey of one who had been a stranger to one who had become African-British-Christian—ultimately simply British, in a different and challenging way.

Of course, given the enslavement of black peoples, it was tricky business to play with the representation of sinful human existence in terms of the symbolization of blackness. Equiano showed sensitivity to this matter. His rhetorical treading was rather careful. But let's be clear here: the nexus of blackness and sinfulness or humiliation had already been overdetermined: ancient and medieval Jewish and Christian writers had already constructed, with devastating long-term effect, certain Jewish and Christian identities at the expense of black peoples. And the troping continued and was even extended in theological-doctrinal arguments and tomes as well as popular discourses throughout Europe well into the modern era.[17]

Like all black peoples dragged into the North Atlantic worlds, Equiano had little choice but to engage this tradition of troping the black. How otherwise could he negotiate such a world and argue for his integration into it? What he did was not merely to turn the trope on its head, he manipulated it to the point of making it work for him and his associates. He appropriated Luke's construction of the Ethiopian as the outsider as highly symbolic convert to the Jesus movement. But he radicalizes the construction by making it clear that he does not mean—as nonblacks over the centuries meant and most modern-era white Christians still mean—to make of the Ethiopian only a symbol of the universal reach of the Christian faith, for the sake of missionary apologetics. He surely was such for Equiano and his comrades. But for them he was also their physical ancestor. And as such they were in a special relationship with him. He afforded them the opportunity in their own time to embody the Ethiopian, to be the black outsider whom the scriptures depicted as belonging to God's family. This meant, of course, that the troping/metaphorizing/spiritualizing practices that long marked Christian traditions, from the ancient and late ancient Mediterranean worlds to medieval and modern era shifts in Europe, would be put to the test: what to do with *real* Ethiopians—up close? What to do with the challenge they present to shift the focus of time from the constructed and firmly controlled ancient world to the pressing modern one in which the savage other may speak and be spoken to?

The logics, psychology, and politics of identification associated with the Ethiopian and applied by Equiano—the Ethiopian as the symbol of the universality of Christian faith; all converts are Ethiopian, having come with "spots"; all oppressed blacks are Ethiopians in spiritual and physical terms—were indeed powerful. Through them not only was Equiano positioned to make claims for himself and his associates about being included in the Christian nation. This reading reflects critical political reflection and self-awareness as well as a sense of solidarity with other blacks. Scriptures were understood and used as a force for deformation—of the humiliation that was enslavement—and for formation of blacks as African Christians. Scriptures were a site of formation; scripture reading thereby represented part of an identifiable psycho-social-political agenda.

Equiano's scriptural readings are evidence that his interest had to do with more than merely being included into British Christendom; it had to do also with finding a vehicle for articulating the cries, challenges, and hopes of black peoples finding themselves in the North Atlantic worlds. The scriptures were understood as an instrument or wedge. They were the site on which to facilitate a particular reading formation, that is, a set of rhetorical gestures in relationship to a set of issues and concerns, a particular way of understanding and addressing the world. I think of Equiano's reading strategy as Africanist, insofar as it threads the Ethiopian figure through all readings as an African Christian. The scriptures were activated and read as Africanized scriptures. Apart from such activation—this is always the case with all peoples—there are only texts. But with the perspective, the consciousness that is Africanist, these texts were made by Equiano and his circle to be their "scriptures."[18]

The activated Africanist reading strategy, I want to suggest, is the most powerful determinant of and the most important interpretive key to Equiano's story as a complex and layered story. It is the single most important point of inspiration for the conceptualization and writing of the narrative, notwithstanding unsurprising clear evidence for his sensitivity to the need to perform in certain ways, that is, to dissemble, deflect, obfuscate, or otherwise encode as an art of resistance.[19] The writing of the narrative as a type of performance represents Equiano's creative, even playful but critical and serious engagement of different cultural texts and traditions as well as his facing of the more obvious immediate social-psychological, economic, and political pressures. Given that he understood himself to be writing in relationship to scriptures and scripturalization, he really was in a "tight" discursive "space." How should he address at once the challenge of showing himself to be a reader of scriptures—that sign of being an Englishman (= Christian)—but also a reader of scripturalization, the sign that his reading was metalexical,,befitting the metadiscursive regime that was in place and his status as stranger (= African)?

Yet Equiano maneuvers quite well. He not only makes the case for his and other blacks' inclusion in British society, he establishes Christian faith on a different basis altogether. That basis was Africanist. With the indirection or subtlety that was required Equiano seemed to argue that special insights and experiences were to be associated with the Ethiopians, the people singled out as having visible "spots." Special or privileged insights are seen in the narrative in connection with the Ethiopian insofar as he is made to stand for the profound mystery of God's logic of building God's "family." All groups are invited into the family. The surety of such inclusion is seen in the Ethiopian figure and in his family, his progeny, among whom are Equiano and the black peoples brought into the North Atlantic worlds. But not very many people get it: not many can understand what God has wrought and what it means. Not many understand that, according to Equiano, it is through the Ethiopian, representing all dark-skinned peoples, that God designs the future of the world. This is now the manner in which God's "family" is constituted.

This seems to be the point of Equiano's pointed but veiled references, his wink and nod, to readers' understanding—or lack of such—in connection with his narrativization of his conversion. Immediately following his comment that the "worth of a soul cannot be told," he directs himself to the reader: "May the Lord give the reader an understanding in this" (191). In chapter 5 above I made the point about what is at issue with the winks and nods to the reader in general connection with the conversion narrative; but as part of the after-discourse, the discourse about the implications of the conversion experience in connection with the development of the figure of the Ethiopian, this gesture is even more compelling. Equiano had already referenced the Ethiopian; so in an attempt to comment on his significance, he took rhetorical flight: "Oh! The amazing things of that hour can never be told" (190). Here the most important connection is made: what the Ethiopian represents inspires thinking about the "worth" of a soul—that is, a human being. What Equiano did was to make the Ethiopian stand for every black person faced with the threat of tribal betrayal and enslavement in the white world, the world in which the black "soul" was reduced to economic "worth." The world is confused and ignorant: it accommodates a situation in which there is, on the one hand, trafficking in slavery, in which human beings are made slaves, reduced to the physical domain and their worth or value assessed in purely monetary terms, and, on the other, the world of spirit, in which worth is equated with the condition of the soul. Only a few get it that these dark people are the ones through whom God teaches and challenges the world. It is a paradox, hidden from most. So most people will need to be clued in, taught how to read the scriptures in a way that will allow them to see the truth.

The side nod to the reader occurs again, at his end of the chapter (10) that includes the conversion experience. After having alluded to Acts 4:12 twice already in this section of the chapter, the verse is actually quoted in full (192). And immediately following the quotation there is another nod to the reader: "May God give the reader a right understanding in these facts!" On the rhetorical heels of the Acts passage around which the theme of the entire narrative may be said to cohere—namely, regarding the terms and scope of salvation—and occurring most explicitly within the narrative section in which the Ethiopian is featured and in which reference to the "spots" occurs, Equiano seems here to make the somewhat traditional point about the universal scope of salvation. But the wink and nod to the reader reflect the special knowledge, shared by a limited few, that black peoples are included in God's family and that no force on earth can undo this situation.

The epexegetical use of the somewhat elliptical verse, "To him that believeth, all things are possible, but to them that are unbelieving, nothing is pure" (Titus 1:15), that follows the wink and nod to the reader after the quotation of the Acts passage, also reflects what is at stake for Equiano in his use of the Ethiopian as figure. In this context—that is, according to Equiano's reading formation or in his Africanized Bible—a few questions are begged: who are among those who "believeth"? Would they not be those who are convinced that black peoples are among those who are saved? And who are the "unbelieving"? Would they not be those who do not believe that black peoples are worthy of being saved? Within the former group the reigning sentiment must be that "all things are possible," that is, the inclusion of blacks in God's economy of salvation means that God can do all things, that seemingly odd, impossible, nonsensical things are possible. Within the latter group the sentiment must be that "nothing is pure," that is, the prospect of blacks in the economy of God's salvation means that the traditional systems and beliefs—black as other and as inferior—no longer apply; chaos and fear must then be assumed to follow. Equiano would seem with this passage—as part of an offensive against those who would deny him and black folks generally membership in God's family, those whose sentiment is expressed in the statement "nothing is pure," that black peoples as spotted peoples are not pure and not acceptable—to be communicating a bit of hard-hitting sarcasm that aims to level the discursive playing field. This "leveling," this turning of the world upside down, is unsettling. What is at stake here in using the Ethiopian figure is not merely Equiano's conversion; it also involves an inversion: from black peoples as strangers to black peoples as major figures of the political economy of salvation, figures who stand to radically reshape that economy. Now the issue is really about God's wisdom and power, and belief in God's wisdom and power.

Who did Equiano have in mind to pick up on his wink and nod? White evangelicals? But it would take a radical conversion—not merely from "sin" in the conventional moralizing sense, but from the "sin" of a racialized and racist society, a tall task indeed—for such folk to understand the point being made. Should we imagine that all Equiano wanted to do was to address, perform for, and ingratiate himself with white sympathizers? It should be obvious by now that I think the complexity of Equiano's writing, especially his identification of and use of what I term scripturalization as analytical thread, suggests something different.

Winking and nodding as rhetorical strategy would seem to imply the need for secrecy or the recognition that the matter addressed has been keep secret. But from whom is the secret being kept? And by whom is the secret kept? The nature of the argumentation in Equiano's conversion story—with the intense exegetics—does not suggest that the ones to be won over are those outside the circle of converts. Why should not Equiano's winking and nodding have been intended for written in behalf of the real or imagined black convert who, like Equiano himself, comes to a "right understanding" of God's plan having to do with salvation and slavery? Equiano's coded language and his gestures toward his fellows and their common understanding of the world constituted the "right understanding" about the worth of every human soul and at the same time represented the wedge principle by which the Bible was to be interpreted. Given its consistent if subtle play around the Ethiopian, why should we not read Equiano's narrative as a work that is itself carrier of "hidden meanin'" that nonetheless shows it to be performative of an Africanized Bible that expresses an Africanized worldview that reshapes the world?

Equiano's black comrades were in evidence both within and outside his narrative. He indicates clearly that he was often found expressing his solidarity with enslaved Africans in the new world. They were, he argued, among those who, although not learned in European letters, nonetheless possessed understanding. The conviction that "understanding is not confined to feature or colour" (45) was in an era of slavocracy and humiliation of black peoples quite assertive. As his quotation of Acts 17:26 fused with rhetorical intimations of Paul's first letter to the Corinthians[20] indicates, God, "who hath made of one blood all nations of men for to dwell on all the face of the earth; and whose wisdom is not our wisdom, neither are our ways his ways," had inverted the normal worldly scheme of valuation and hierarchy (45). Again, in Equiano's Africanized Bible this means that the "rude and uncultivated" Africans are privileged. Who could miss the point here? Who in the setting of the late eighteenth century is in mind here? Notwithstanding the official and public rhetorical gestures of address in the narrative, who is really being engaged, challenged, provoked?

There is more evidence or at least hints in the narrative that for Equiano black peoples transforming themselves into Africans are the primary interest. In the spring of 1785 Equiano found himself in Philadelphia, ready to take to the sea again, this time as steward aboard a ship called the *London*. But before departing, he visited a community of Quakers. He took great joy in how they treated "my oppressed African brethren." He made it clear that he was especially pleased to see that the Quakers had started there a "free-school" for "every denomination of black people."[21] The impact of the school on the black peoples in the area was expressed by the Quakers in terms of cultivation of mind and virtue—toward making such folk "useful members of the community" (224).

The scriptural quotation at the end of Equiano's discussion about the Quaker school was included in the disturbing question addressed to readers about Caribbean planters: "Does not the success of this practice say loudly to the planters, in the language of scripture: 'Go ye, and do likewise'?" The source of the quotation is Luke 10:37, part of the famous Good Samaritan story. Here Equiano identifies contemporary planters (Christian owners of colonial slave plantations) with powerful insider (Jewish) officials in the biblical story who pass by those in need without offering aid. The Quakers would seem to be identified in Equiano's mind with the good outsiders (Samaritans) helping those in need.

But I think more was at issue for Equiano, more than he thought himself allowed to express openly. Why was this particular example of Quaker altruism so important to Equiano? Why the direct biblical exhortation to slave-holding planters to imitate the Quakers? Did he really think such planters would be moved by biblical exhortations? Did he think planters as a group would really think it reasonable or wise to found schools for those they enslaved and depended on for their livelihood? Did he assume planters would think that a black mind was a terrible thing to waste? That the cultivation of the minds of black slaves would in some way preserve the planter-slavers' economic and power advantages?

Immediately following the narrative about the Philadelphia school, Equiano includes information that provides a clue to the possibility of some other reading. He makes mention of and actually records a letter (225) "presented" to Quakers in England by "some of the Africans." The letter is important both as an event and in terms of content: it reflects the existence of a group of literate, articulate, and politically active blacks in solidarity, and it reflects their aggressive advocacy for "the poor, oppressed, needy, and much degraded negroes." It reflects their invention and cultivation/acceptance of themselves as "Africans"—on their own terms, turning slavocracy's policy of scrambling and undermining if not erasing their different ethnic and tribal differences into an opportunity for coalition building. It reflects their social intelligence, their activism, agency, and social power, no matter how limited and circumscribed. And it suggests that the activism demonstrated by their literacy was in turn facilitated by some sort of association or "school," possibly inspired by the Philadelphia free school.

The letter leads me to suspect double levels of meaning in the narrative: on the plain surface of the scriptural text (the ancient world as symbol of the normally unmarked or unnamed white evangelical modern world) the readers were made to be the addressees of the exhortation to "go and do likewise." But just below the surface of the text, at the level of Equiano's exegetical application the (more self-conscious evangelical or modern world) readers are made to be a substitute for the (physically distant modern world) planters. Even further below the surface of the scriptural text and aside from Equiano's exegetical glosses—as though in secret or with "hidden meanin'"—both reader and planter are made to stand in for contemporary conscientized black peoples, such as those in the circle of activists who called themselves "sons of Africa." They are indirectly exhorted to "go and do likewise," that is, to school themselves for the sake of achieving results inspired by, if not exactly those Equiano noted regarding, the Philadelphia situation.

The letter written by "some of the Africans" as part of an effort to solicit aid to improve the lot of "the poor, oppressed, needy, and much degraded negroes" suggests the validity of this interpretation. My suspicion that Equiano was throughout his narrative actually interested in winking and nodding to fellow blacks, or in representing them in some way, is heightened by the difference I detect in the language used to reflect the interests of general readers and planters, on the one hand, and the actual agency and activism in the letter written by the Africans, on the other: The general readers of Equiano's story, like the Quakers of Philadelphia and England and the distant planters, are assumed to be interested in the cultivation of minds and virtue and "useful" existence of black peoples. But the letter presented by Equiano and seven others on October 21, 1785, to "the gentlemen called Friends or Quakers, in Whitehart-court, Lombard Street" in London reflected a different orientation and set of interests. This difference is not radical; Equiano does not find great fault in what the Quakers in Philadelphia did. No, it is precisely the overlap and subtle difference in sentiment and in interest that raises the flag. For example, the letter from the Africans reflects individuals less interested in demonstrating themselves to be "useful members of the community" than in coming into speech on their own terms, including arrogating to themselves the power of self-ascription ("We, part of the poor," "we, as a part of those captivated, oppressed"), advocating on behalf of the oppressed, and asserting their worth as human beings as part of divine will. It seems that with regard to the schooling of black peoples, the writers of the letter had in mind something other than the agenda of the white Quakers. Schooling for slaves and ex-slaves seemed to carry special meaning, special burden and opportunity.[22]

More background for the letter is in order. It was written as a group response to the "book" or antislavery tract that had by formal ascription been written by a collaborative, but in actuality primarily by Anthony Benezet. Entitled "A Caution and Warning to Great Britain and Her Colonies in a Short Representation of the Calamitous State of the Enslaved Negroes," it was originally published in Philadelphia in 1766, reprinted and retitled in London in 1767. It was printed and distributed by the Quakers throughout England, especially to clerics and government officials, so it was likely a fairly well-known publication in the 1780s, thought of as something of a primer on the subject.

In the first paragraph of the letter written by the Africans there is praise for Benezet's tract because of the attention it turns to the plight of their "brethren." It repeats the language of the tract in referring to blacks as "poor, oppressed . . . negroes" and "heavy burthened negroes." The use of "negroes" for self-description is especially noteworthy. But in the second paragraph, in which the writers pivot to their specific request, the language of self-description changes—from the overdetermined "negroes" to "the afflicted," "[God's] creatures," "the oppressed," "those captivated, oppressed, and afflicted people." Beyond the discursive straitjacket placed on them by whites, including the sympathetic Quakers, the black writers view themselves differently and in terms that they deem more appropriate, terms that open up possibilities for more complex and layered self-interpretation.

The very fact of the letter writing by the Africans and the comments in the letter about the tract written by Benezet establishes Equiano and his co-writers as critical and self-possessed readers and writers. For the times and the situations in which most black peoples found themselves, this fact was astounding enough. The phenomenon and the language suggest something more: that Equiano and the other writers already constituted something like a reading formation, perhaps, even a "school," of blacks who self-consciously used a complex of expressions in much the same way in order to advance the same agenda. Certainly, the way Equiano refers throughout his story to blacks as "oppressed Africans" is significant.[23] The same description of black peoples occurs again and again in the preserved correspondence with which Equiano is associated. The use of certain terms suggests that Equiano and his circle were trained by a common teacher/tutor or in a common setting and/or trained or socialized themselves to read and comment with common voice on what was going on in the North Atlantic worlds.

The fruits of such training can be seen most dramatically in the correspondence associated with Equiano. Some of the pertinent letters Equiano authored alone; some other letters have joint/committee/school/circle authorship. Equiano was certainly one of the leading figures of such.

In a letter dated December 15, 1787,[24] and addressed to Granville Sharp as an expression of thanks for his advocacy of black people, Equiano (aka Gustavus Vassa) was among the signatories. The writers styled themselves "Sons of Africa"—"descendants of the much wronged people of Africa." They understood themselves as spokespersons and advocates for "our brethren and countrymen unlawfully held in slavery."

On July 15, 1788, a letter[25] was addressed to William Dolben, leader of the successful fight in Parliament in 1788 to pass a law regulating the overcrowding of slave ships. Signed by some of those who were signatories to the letter sent to Sharp—no doubt understanding themselves as "Sons of Africa"—this letter was sent to *The Morning Chronicle* and *London Advertiser.* It was an expression of gratitude to Dolben for his motion to alleviate the miseries of "our unhappy brethren on the coast of Africa." It also expressed hope that the small community of "persons of colour . . . [might be] providentially released from the common calamity" that they experienced and indicated that all in the community intended to return Dolben's gesture by behaving "with sobriety, fidelity, and diligence in our different stations," whether remaining in England or returning to Africa or to the "West India islands." The larger and concluding point was that in "feeling for their kind," they were "not ignorant" of the importance of an assumed pact that "our whole race" pledged in covenant with Dolben and his kind—to "merit, by dutiful behavior" their support and advocacy.

Letters of the same type were sent also on July 15, 1788, to the Right Honourable William Pitt and the Right Honourable Charles James Fox via the newspapers.[26] These were also signed by the group—six men, "ourselves and Brethren"—that had sent the letter to Dolben. Not much more was added to the expression of thanks for support of "our unhappy race," "our kind," the themes that had been struck in the letter to Dolben.

On April 25, 1789, a letter was published in *The Diary; Or Woodfall's Register.*[27] It was addressed to William Dickson, "formerly Private Secretary to the Hon. Edward Hay, Governor of the Island of Barbados." Dickson was a subscriber to Equiano's book. And he was author of *Letters on Slavery . . . To Which Are Added, Addresses to Whites, and to the Free Negroes of Barbadoes . . .* (1789). This letter, also written by a group of black males in solidarity, was of the same genre as the others: it was an expression of thanks to Dickson for the light his book cast on slavery and the regard shown in it "for the poor and much oppressed sable people."

This letter also offered brief opinion on Dickson's book. The writers stated that they thought the book had provided "too just a picture of the Slave Trade, and the horrid cruelties practiced on the poor sable people in the West Indies, to the disgrace of Christianity." They expressed hope that the book would lend support to ongoing efforts to pass legislation to stop the trade.

It is worth taking note of the letters Equiano wrote by himself during this period. They reflect exactly the same expressions, sentiments, and politics as the letters signed by the "sons of Africa." In reading all of his extant single-authored correspondence, one should have little doubt that Equiano was prime mover of the circle and its politics.

One of the most fascinating letters Equiano wrote was addressed to Raymund Harris and published in the *Public Advertiser* on April 28, 1788.[28] The occasion was the recent publication (1788) of Harris's controversial book entitled *Scripture Researches on the Licitness of the Slave Trade, Shewing Its Conformity with the Principles of Natural and Revealed Religion, Delineated in the Sacred Writings of the Word of God.* Harris was an ideological hired gun for the slave traders in and around Liverpool and was paid 100 pounds for his pro-slavery work. He was a Jesuit of Spanish background whose real name was Hormasa. Dedicated to the mayor, recorder, aldermen, bailiffs, members of the Common Council of the borough of the slave port that was Liverpool, the bold apologia for the slave trade immediately provoked heated responses from a number of quarters.[29]

Harris indicated that he wrote in order to examine whether the slave trade has the "sanction of divine authority," more precisely, to "try the merits of the present controversy by the Sacred Canons of the Written Word of God."[30] He divides his long dissertation of "Scriptural Researches" into three parts corresponding to the "three Religious Dispensations" of world history: the Law of Nature; the Mosaic Dispensation; and the Christian Law—all, as he claims, evidenced in the "Sacred Writings of the Word of God." In order to make his case compelling, he cleverly indicates that the relevant scriptural passages that he researched were taken from the (English) "Protestant Vulgar Translation of the Bible," "most generally received in these Kingdoms."

Harris's conclusions are made clear in his "corollaries," the most important of which are the first and the last ones. His "researches" led him to conclude that the Bible gives legitimacy to the slave trade, notwithstanding infractions and cruelties here and there:

> **I**
>
> Since the Sacred Writings of the Holy Bible contain the unerring Decisions of the Word of God, the Authority of which in both the Testaments is founded on the essential veracity of God, who is Truth itself; it follows necessarily, that, as there can be no prescription against that Authority, which, in the several scriptural passages quoted in the series of the foregoing Researches, has positively declared, that the Slave-Trade is intrinsically good and

> licit, this, by a necessary consequence, must be essentially so in its nature, however contrary such declaration may be to the received opinion of some men for any length of time...
>
> VI
>
> Since no abuses or malpractices whatever, though of the greatest magnitude, committed in former times in the prosecution of the Slave-Trade (a), ever induced the Almighty to prohibit or abolish that Trade, but only to check by wholesome and coercive Laws the violence or unnatural Masters (b), and to punish the transgressors with the greatest severity (c); there appears no reason whatever, why the abuses and malpractices said to be perpetrated in our days in the prosecution of the same Trade, evidently subject to the control of the Legislature, should be deemed a powerful indictment to proceed to the abolition of it.[31]

Equiano's letter was a full-throated critical review of the book. It seems likely that he wrote, if not in direct response to the prompting or request of others—fellow "sons of Africa," or, perhaps, white evangelicals and other types of abolitionists—at least with their emotional encouragement and support and political and ideological-religious agreement. In other words, this letter, like so many others associated with Equiano during the same period, was likely written out of the conversations and emotional textures that marked the other letters identified as having been produced by a circle or "school."

At the end of this letter, in response to Harris's book, Equiano signed his name as "Gustavus Vassa, The African." Clearly, he intended to write, and he intended that his readers understand, that he wrote as an African Christian, as one who was capable of participating on the basis of his literacy in the British Protestant Christian culture's discourses. His stance within such a culture—of readers of the Bible—further identified him with a particular orientation and set of assumptions, that is, as one who reads and understands texts that make it clear to him that God's work in the world now includes, even privileges, poor oppressed black peoples. Being an African Christian meant for Equiano that he was empowered along with other Christians to engage important public issues on the basis of argumentation through the Bible. So he addresses Harris's arguments, using the Bible in support of the slave trade with his own arguments using the Bible against the trade. The Bible provided the matrix and framework for discourse in general, this issue in particular.

But Equiano does not simply counter Harris's biblical exegetics with his own biblical exegetics. He does indeed do some of that, arguing again and again that Harris had, for example, "wrested St. Paul's words" out of context. The Bible in Protestant Britain was still one of the most important sites of ideological contestation, so it was very important to make it support one's position on the important issues. But precisely because of Equiano's understanding of the work that the British people made the Bible do for them, his strongest offensive tactic was to establish Harris's interests in relation to one or more characters of the Bible. Because Harris had made Paul's writings on slavery the most important site in the Bible for addressing the issue of slavery, Equiano also made them so for his rhetorical argument. In Harris's reading of the New Testament letter to Philemon, in which Paul appealed to Philemon (a Christian who was also a slave master) to receive Onesimus (a believer who was also a slave who had run away from Philemon) as "brother," Equiano challenged Harris regarding the lens through which Harris read the letter. He questioned the cogency and truthfulness of Harris's reading not on the basis of the historical background, about ancient world slavery and so forth, or on strict exegetical-philological analysis—what the historical Paul really meant—but in terms of his identification with a narrative-character and what such identification suggests.

In Equiano's view Onesimus is the character in Paul's letter to Philemon that the reader should identify with in the present. As the runaway slave, Onesimus is seen as the Christian figure. Just as the Ethiopian figured the expansion of Christian hope, so Onesimus figured the radical nature of Christian freedom: freedom from all forms of worldly oppression, humiliation, and enslavement. Harris's misreading, according to Equiano, was his failure to read Paul's text with and through Onesimus as the figure of radical Christian freedom; reading in that way should have led Harris to understand that as Onesimus the Christian must be free in every respect so slavery in any form in any era going forward must be rejected and seen as anti-Christian.

Equiano's reading implied that the Ethiopian was Onesimus and Onesimus was the Ethiopian, that black peoples were indeed part of God's family, even the poster-tribe for God's family, the belatedly privileged if not originary constitutive group among believers. Black peoples were privileged insofar as they had represented the "strangers" of the world. Who otherwise signified so dramatically the stranger than the slave?[32] Equiano clearly identified himself as stranger, outside the dominant culture. His status as stranger is overcome only as he defines himself as an African Christian. And he showed his African Christian status and self-understanding most dramatically through his reading of the Bible as an African Christian.

In his response to Harris's pro-slavery tract Equiano's reading of the Bible reflects his critical participation in, even leadership of, the sons of Africa "school." This role can be seen most clearly in comparison between the writings of Equiano and Quobna Ottobah Cugoano, baptized as John Stuart. Cugoano and Equiano were known to have collaborated on letter writing and other projects, challenging slavery, the slave trade, and the general humiliation of Africans; working with resettlement projects; and encouraging commerce with Africans.[33]

It is speculated that Equiano assisted Cugoano with the writing of his manifesto *Thoughts and Sentiments on the Evil and Wicked Traffic of the Slavery and Commerce of the Human Species*. Published first in 1787, with a shorter version appearing in 1791, this jeremiad was a fierce assault on slavery and the slave trade and all those who participate in and profit from them. It is worth noting that the shorter version of the manifesto was addressed "to the Sons of Africa."[34] So in ways that were quite different from those of Equiano, at least in the writing of what might be considered his "narrative," he made his interests and agenda quite clear. Among his commitments, included in the later version of his document and likely shared with Equiano and others, was the founding of a school (in the narrow institutional sense) for Africans in Britain.

> The Author...proposes to open a School, for all such of his Complexion as are desirous of being acquainted with the Knowledge of the Christian Religion and the Laws of Civilization. His sole Motive for these Undertakings, are, that he finds several of his Countrymen, here in England, who have not only been in an unlawful Manner brought away from their peaceable Habitations, but also deprived of every Blessing of the Christian Knowledge, by their Masters and Mistresses, either through the motives of Avarice, or the want of the Knowledge of their own Religion, which must be a Dishonour to Christianity.

> Nothing engages my desire so much as the Descendants of my Countrymen, so as to have them educated in the Duties and Knowledge of that Religion which all good Christian People enjoy; these Blessings cannot be well conveyed without Learning... my Design, therefore, is to open a Place for the Instruction of such who can attend.[35]

There is no record of such a school actually having been established. And after 1791 there is no evidence of the existence of Cugoano. Might there be a relationship between the two situations? The collaborations between Cugoano and Equiano beg many questions: Did Equiano share, if not in fact suggest, the idea of the school? Was there ever a "school" in other respects, viz. without ever existing in a "Place" but nonetheless operating among the sons of Africa, insofar as they taught one another to engage in discourse on certain terms? And as for Cugoano's manifesto, whatever may have been Equiano's offices in connection with it, did Equiano learn from it something about how to write a "manifesto"?

In Cugoano's manifesto one can easily see the uses of certain biblical texts and tropes that he shared with Equiano. Emphasis is placed throughout on the concepts and images that are found in Equiano's work: the "stranger," the "poor" "African," the troping of the Ethiopian, symbolization of darkness, the play with the leopard spots from the Jeremiah passage. These similarities point to shared symbology and discursivitiy, a particular way of thinking and talking and writing about the world, a similar use of a common source. The sharing reflects membership in the same discursive circle, participation in a sustained and mutually beneficial conversation. I think it not inappropriate or far-fetched to conclude that the situation between Cugoano and Equiano (and others) was much like a "school" insofar as "school" is imagined not so much in terms of a formal institutional reality and structure but in terms of an ongoing likely semiprivate conversation, participation in a type of discourse as part of an ideological-rhetorical reading and social formation.

Cugoano and Equiano and some others were likely part of a school in which they cultivated strategies regarding the plight of black peoples in Britain. Making use of public forums—including letters to newspapers, book reviews, debating clubs—their argumentation heavily and creatively used the Bible. Identifying themselves as evangelical Christians, they essentially wrote themselves, their private piety, and their public interests and commitments into mythic biblical history. So Cugoano, without a doubt representing the sentiments of the "Sons of Africa":

> [S]o far as I have been able to consult the law written by Moses, concerning that kind of servitude admitted by it, I can find nothing imported thereby, in the least degree, to warrant the modern practice of slavery. But, on the contrary, and what was principally intended thereby, and in the most particular manner, as respecting Christians, that it contains the strongest prohibition against it. And every Christian man, that can read his Bible, may find that which is of the greatest importance for himself to know, implied even under the very institution of bond-servants; and that the state of bondage which the law denounces and describes, was thereby so intended to point out something necessary, as well as similar to all the other ritual and ceremonial services; and that the whole is set forth in such a manner, as containing the very essence and foundation of the Christian religion.[36]

Here Cugoano was exegeting blackness, as well as black interests. Given the larger society in which he and Equiano were located and which they struggled to negotiate, why would they not—as they noted others did—play with the Bible? Why would they not attempt to determine where black peoples fit into the long biblical story of humankind and into the present? And since there were plenty of contemporary public speakers and writers who justified the enslavement and selling and buying of blacks through their readings of the Bible, why would Cugoano, as part of the agenda of the "school" to which he belonged, not want to found a school as an institution located in a place—emphasizing Christian traditions and morality and practices, including biblical exegesis—through which he and others would seek to improve the lives of black peoples?

Equiano's fascination with the Quaker school in Philadelphia and Cugoano's more direct statement of intention to found a school (in London?) point to the existence of a sort of "school" that likely tutored and socialized students to use language in order to empower themselves even as they would fend off others' uses of language that humiliated them. Such school practices involved making words from a traditional alienating context serve a different context. The envisioned school, seemingly concerned only about conventional Christian evangelical indoctrination, would facilitate subversive (re)socialization. The very idea of a school for "Africans," having become the essential Other/"strangers" in the British social-cultural economy, obviously provides a different perspective, including the very meaning of basic categories. Representing what might be termed in an ideological analysis of language a specific sort of "contextualization," the discursive work that was biblical interpretation of the already operative "school" for Africans provides perspective on the socio-psychological implications and social-political ramifications of differences of perspective in relationship to different contexts:

> [U]sing the text itself as point of departure, and allowing it to index dimensions of context as the narrator... forges links of contextualization to give shape and meaning... moving us closer to a balanced understanding of that most fundamental of all anthropological problems, the dynamic interplay of the social and the individual, the ready-made and the emergent, in human life... the process... in which individuals situate what they do in networks of interrelationship and association in the act of expressive production.[37]

Equiano and the "school" to which he belonged and which I posit here seemed, on the simple surface of word usage, to mimic European, a specifically British-inflected mix of culturalist establishment traditional-nationalist and somewhat evangelical disestablishment biblical interpretation. Yet more was at issue. I suggest the more had to do with recontextualizing scriptures so that they were made to do special duty for him and his colleagues who were becoming Africans on their own terms.

Here I return to the statement quoted at the beginning of this chapter that is found in Equiano's narration of his conversion experience, including his glosses on its meanings. That narration has already been addressed in chapter 5. In this chapter I need to return to the conversion narrative, but will focus for the sake of advancing a different argument (having to do not with conversion as orientation, but agency) on only one of the glosses made and the other statements throughout the narrative that are related to it. In his chapter 10 Equiano remarks that after the "Lord was pleased to break in upon my soul," the Bible became his "only companion and comfort." What he seemed to prize more than anything at that point—"many thanks to God"—was that "I could read it for myself." It seems to me that in such a statement is a key to the construction and meaning of Equaino's narrative: insofar as his narrative is about and was in fact an enactment of his self-authorization, his speaking/writing back, it communicated simply and powerfully the resolution of the narrative logic and structure and goal of his life—and how to read them both. Everything should be read, in other words, in relationship to the realization of his goal of becoming a scripture-reader, one to whom the book now speaks, and more important, one to whom the book now belongs—not in the strict sense of ownership, but in terms of power and authority, the capacity to manipulate, to use, for one's own interest. From a position of profound insecurity and humiliation this was quite a feat. Equiano himself indicates that this ownership meant he could "appl[y] many things to [himself] with great comfort." Given his agenda of highlighting scripturalization in the ideological and power structuring in England, and given the outsider status of the black figure in such a structuring, the statement has to be understood as rather assertive.

That the statement is key can be seen first in the most immediate context: here Equiano connects the importance of his being able to read the Bible for himself to his avoiding being exploited and abused—"not left to be tossed about or led by man's devices and notions." Clearly, the backdrop here can be assumed to be a religious-doctrinal market of competition. With the assertion that "The worth of a soul cannot be told," Equiano seems to broaden and layer the backdrop quite a bit. The soul is his own and those of other blacks. And, yes, to be sure, religious partisans might argue in the heat of polemics about unenlightened souls being "tossed about" by the other groups' "devices and notions." But that Equiano had something more in mind, something that belongs to a different discourse, is hinted at with the first of his rhetorical winks and nods to the reader: "May the Lord give the reader an understanding of this." These words, as I have already argued in chapter 5, seem to call for and then actually achieve the recontextualization of the foregoing assertions so that they might mean differently. Behind the recontextualization is knowledge to which Equiano seems privy. (About this "knowledge," more below.) Whatever the words actually mean has to do with Equiano's sure knowledge that he is no longer an insecure stranger but a "saved" soul that is part of a formation or community. This point is made clear by the appearance of the second rhetorical wink and nod at the end of the same paragraph, thereby providing a framing for this important section of the conversion narrative:

> Thus I was, by the teaching of that all glorious Deity . . . confirmed in the truths of the Bible; those oracles of everlasting truth, on which

> every soul living must stand or fall eternally, agreeably to Acts iv.12. "Neither is there salvation in any other, for there is no other name under heaven given among men whereby we must be saved, but only Jesus Christ." May God give the reader a right understanding in these facts! (192)

Sandwiched between the two rhetorical winks and nods is Equiano's assertion that he has been enlightened and "saved" and that this means that he—even he, especially he, a black stranger—is placed on an equal footing with all other believers and is now authorized to read the "oracles" on his own. This consciousness and arrogation—of psychic and social power and status—on the part of one whose profile in the white scripture-reading world that was England seems so startling that Equaino realizes he must account for it by referencing a special source of knowledge and insight, beyond even the Bible.

This source is unnamed; it is from "God"/"the Lord" and is another form of revelation that provides deeper insight into the meaning of the Bible and the mystery of Equiano's consciousness and his social and spiritual power and status. Several terms are used by Equiano as equivalent for "God"/"Lord" as source of the powerful insight: "Sure I was that the Spirit which indited the word opened my heart to receive the truth"; "the same Spirit enabled me to act with faith upon the promises"; "By free grace I was persuaded that I had a part and lot in the first resurrection"; "I was, by the teaching of that all glorious Deity, confirmed in the truths" (191–192). "Spirit," "grace," and "teaching"—these three terms, with the first appearing to be favored, are attempts to point to the needed special alternate source that confirms Equiano's authority as scripture-reading Englishman.

The narrative in all its parts points backward and forward to this powerful moment and the assertion that marks it. At the beginning of the story and at many points leading up to the moment of assertion, Equiano betrays his creative scripture-reading capabilities: for one thing, as was already pointed out, the famous frontispiece depicts him as something of a Protestant scripture-reading gentleman evangelical, looking directly ahead, with open Bible in hand. Such a depiction was heavy with meaning.[38] Second, the title page contains a scriptural quotation (from Isa 12:2, 4) that is full of meaning, both asserting confidence in his salvation and the knowledge that reflects it and announcing what will be the creative prophetic biblical exegetical nature of his narrative:

> Behold, God is my salvation: I will trust, and not be afraid, for the Lord Jehovah is my strength and my song; he also is become my salvation.
>
> And in that day shall ye say, Praise the Lord, call upon his name, declare his doings among the people.

Third, he tended to end chapters by quoting at least some part of scriptures as part of a homiletical-exegetical summation. Fourth, he includes several poems that reek of intimate acquaintance with scriptures, even if not with great poets and poetry. Fifth, his unwavering defense of Protestant England over against Roman Catholic nations shows not merely his (unsurprising) acceptance of the one over the other, but his understanding of what the difference means in terms of discursive play and resistance.

What these instances indicate is Equiano's intention to structure his story around his progress toward—and the challenges in the way of-his becoming an adept reader of scripture. The assumed white reader is made to confront the truth about Equiano's progress. It is assumed that this truth is very hard to grasp; it is an event that he understands to be deeply mysterious and puzzling, thus, quite paradoxically, requiring the puzzling and mysterious Bible to explain it.

At the end of the section in which the second wink and nod occurs and in which another assertion is made Equiano quotes Acts 4:12: "Neither is there salvation in any other, for there is no other name under heaven given among men whereby we must be saved, but only Jesus Christ." He had mentioned his reading of this passage at the beginning of the conversion narrative (189), so this verse frames the larger conversion narration. It is fascinating to find an attempt on Equiano's part to explain the import of the Acts passage by misquoting/"misreading"[39] another passage, Titus 1:15: "To him that believeth, all things are possible, but to them that are unbelieving nothing is pure." The misreading points to Equiano's understanding of what is at stake for him in terms of the inclusion that is salvation, but also, I want to stress, in line with the focus of this chapter, the strategy around which he stakes his ground, claims his voice and agency. He certainly demonstrates that he understands that the claims of scripturalization allow the manipulation, the recontextualization, of texts. And notwithstanding the constraining effects of writing and textuality, he seems to know that he, like so many others, can be creative and reflect a type of exegetical ingenuity. He does so, with a flourish.

So with the paraphrasing of Titus1:15a, Equiano is showing not only that he is saved, but that he knows that he is saved and therewith knows other things about the world. As I indicated in discussing this passage in chapter 5, in the biblical text the contrast that is set up is between the attitudes and presumptions of the "pure" and the "corrupt" and "unbelieving" persons. Here I want to stress a slightly different aspect or implication of the contrast that is set up. In chapter 5 I saw Equiano as reader/exegete, seeking participation, inclusion, seeking/reflecting orientation to the world of believers. Here I stress Equiano as reader/excavator, engaging the same texts, but also asserting power for himself, making words do what he wants and needs them to do for him. What he also sees in this text is an explosion of possibilities beyond the authorized textual field (on which at the highest level of authority facility with Greek may be assumed) and the dominant naturalized social-cultural-political domain (in which Edmund Burke's politics of language may be presumed): the "pure" consider all (earthly) things, like themselves, to be pure (Gk: *kathara tois katharois*); the "corrupt," "unbelieving" ones consistent with their attitude, so the writer opines, consider nothing in the world to be pure (Gk: *memiammenois kai apistois)*. But according to Equiano's rendering, the contrast is made to be between "him that believeth" and "them that are unbelieving." The former believes that "all things are possible," while for the latter, "nothing is pure." Equiano changed the focus of the original text from *judgment* regarding purity of things of the world made by God to *belief* in God's wisdom and power in making "pure," in saving, even a "poor wretched" one, even the black stranger. The manipulation was made in order to reflect the different context of reading, to show his reader the truth—that "all things are possible" or that "nothing [no one] is pure"—that had been specially revealed to him, as he was able to divine from the scriptures. So the believers in this case are those who believe that God has saved Ethiopians, all black peoples, and therefore all peoples; the unbelievers are now those who cannot believe that God can save *all*, without exception, and so do not believe God can save at all.

Only special revelation, special knowing, makes such exegesis possible. It is in fact not so much exegesis as it is excavation, the excavation that is divination, in which the reading is complexly self-referential. Equiano demonstrates his reading ingenuity, his self-authorization and knowledge, his "methods," his skill in "calculating" the times, his "unbounded influence" that recalls (from his chapter 1) the wise men, priest, and magicians, the "Ah-affoe-way-cah". Equiano is not merely, flatly, a saved person;

he makes and declares himself through means other than learned scribal exegesis or through cultivation of enlightened sentiment and sensibilities a *knowing* person.

This pointed assertion about special knowing—about the inclusion of himself and black peoples generally in God's scheme of world salvation—is all the more intriguing given what appears to be the veiling of such knowing throughout Equiano's story. Clearly, among Equiano's interests in writing his "interesting story" was addressing, even if not always directly or at length, the situation faced by blacks in England and other parts of the North Atlantic world. Notwithstanding Equiano's impressive skills and capacity for expressing himself, and his opportunities to do so, he was, as he very poignantly reminded his (white) readers, in the context of the slave trade and the antiblack racialism that it increasingly reflected and induced, was nonetheless very much limited in what he could do and say in public, even what space he could occupy. The reader could hardly ignore the picture painted by Equiano of blacks living under constant duress and threats and humiliations of all kinds, including that of being forced into (re)enslavement. As much as his story registered the exceptional experience of a black man in the North Atlantic world of the mid to late eighteenth century, it probably would not have gotten the weight of the printer's press and it certainly would not have become a best seller and a powerful expression had it been explicitly about a possible black diaspora abolitionist agenda going forward. In other words, had it been more like Cugoano's manifesto—an excoriation of the perfidy of white Christians.

No, what is compelling about Equiano's story is that it is so complexly arranged and layered: it is the exceptional interpreter who, having read the story, thinks it simple and straightforward. Especially as regards Equiano's interest in and sentiments having to do with black peoples, the story is expressed in veiled terms. It reflects the phenomenon of what African diaspora folklorist Zora Neale Hurston dubbed "hittin' a lick with a crooked stick"[40]—with deflection or indirect, coded speech. Equiano's story registers, among other things, sentiment about black peoples in England (and other locations in the North Atlantic world) that was likely either part of advanced discussions within a circle/"school" of blacks—"sons of Africa"—about the present and the future, or Equiano's contributions intended to advance such discussions. Given the general power arrangements that obtained, the veiling of the sentiment was understandably necessary even if, as will be discussed below, somewhat worrisome in terms of the enduring effects on those who structure the veiling. Equiano's sentiments about and communications to his immediate circle of black fellows and all black peoples made to undergo the Atlantic worlds was accomplished with rhetorical winks and nods—special insider language such as one would find in a "school" tradition—that represented a thinking and speaking beyond the perspective of white readers in general.

Yet there is the question that can hardly be avoided: Was there no purpose behind the veiling of the radical assertion other than tricking white readers? How should the rhetorical strategies and tricks that characterize the story be understood? Was there not more at stake than trickery? Did signifying have no social-political significance?[41]

There was more at stake here than realizing safety from the white gaze or simply registering evangelical sentiments: the winking and nodding was, to be sure, strategically and necessarily veiled, but it did not render totally silent the registration of what were some of Equiano's deepest and hard-to-articulate, hard-to-fathom sentiments. Using the "other words" that were the veiled terms and concepts and images of the English Bible, Equiano's communication in the form of narrative was strategic, even necessary, for facilitating the articulation of "hard things," mysterious things with a "hidden meanin'" about the condition of black folks.[42]

So what makes Equiano's veiling possible and compelling and perhaps paradoxical is that it was advanced within the structure of scripturalization and thereby makes use of scriptures. The uses of scriptures may suggest something not only about the social historical situation in which scripturalization is found (early modern England and North Atlantic worlds in general), not only about the rhetorical-linguistic field on which it is played out,[43] but also the power relations and dynamics that it represents, the nature of the social-psychological-economic situation and challenges faced by the black stranger/exile/slave in the North Atlantic.

Critical perspective on what work Equiano (and his circle) made the English Bible as scriptures do for them can be gained from analysis of how black North Atlantic writers engaged the North Atlantic worlds. What scriptures seem to represent in the most basic terms is another language, a deflecting, veiling, if not necessarily hidden discourse. Whether out of considerable concerns about vulnerabilities in a hostile society or out of several mixed motives and other factors, veiling is part of the performances and political strategic gestures in evidence throughout African diaspora history.[44] Equiano's engagement of the Bible should be briefly analyzed in relationship to a history of African diaspora sentiments, arguments and practices having to do with memory, knowledge, consciousness, power. A brief detour and summary discussion of selected writers who have been self-reflexive in their engagement of these issues is in order.

Because of his prescience and sharp sensitivity to issues of interpretation and/as consciousness, I find still challenging and useful as expansive perspective on the existence and challenges of persons of African descent in the United States W.E.B. Du Bois's argumentation found in his classic collection of essays *Souls of Black Folk,* originally published in 1903.[45] As part of his attempt to name the major challenges faced by the "folk"—or perhaps more accurately, faced by the type of black person he knew himself to be, thereby speaking in complicated ways for so many others—Du Bois refers again and again to the "veil."[46] Notwithstanding their internal differentiations and infrapolitics, about which he as historian and social scientist was very much aware, all black folks, Du Bois argued, had been placed, no, forced, behind the "veil." Referred to (by my count) more than thirty times, the metaphor of the veil in *Souls of Black Folk* is Du Bois's attempt to define black folks in the United States as those marked, in the terms now more famous and more often quoted than understood, by "divided consciousness." Thus, the poignant meaning of the plural term "souls": not as reference to the many souls as in many persons, but as reference to the two "souls," two orientations, in the one representative body, divided, warring against each other. This division was for Du Bois the deep internal psychologically felt reflection of the external social-political existence of black folks as the chronic persistent other, as the subaltern, as the enslaved/colonized living next to, and reduced to looking at themselves through the gaze of, the enslaver/colonizer.

> Then it dawned upon me with a certain suddenness that I was different from the others...shut out from their world by a vast veil....
>
> After the Egyptian and Indian, the Greek and Roman, the Teuton and Mongolian, the Negro is a sort of seventh son, born with a veil. [47]

Modified variously in terms of the "veil of Race,"[48] "Veil of Color,"[49] as that which imprisons,[50] as that within which black folks are born and in which they grow up,[51] as that which casts a shadow,[52] as that against-over and beyond, which the black self strives to live,[53] as that world beyond which white folks live,[54] as the haunting which the black self overcomes only in death,[55] and that which, based on hope, is to be rent.[56]

Scholars of Du Bois have argued that in the metaphorization of the veil, Du Bois drew most directly from (Plato via) Hegel, indirectly from Emerson and other late nineteenth-, early twentieth-century persons of letters; from nascent psychology; and from the Bible.[57] They suggest that he took from Hegel the idea of the veil and its effects on consciousness and wedded them to the Bible's stories regarding transformation. Because he needed language and concepts through which he could articulate what he understood to be the profundity of the crisis of divided consciousness as well as the ascetics and performativity of transformed consciousness, he drew upon Hegel.[58] The Bible was mined for pertinent references to the veil that have to do with enlightenment and transformation.[59]

A great part of the purpose of *Souls of Black Folk* was to celebrate the social power and contributions of the people forced behind the veil. The way of doing this was through emphasis on the forms of black expressivity—music, literature, religion. To be sure, Du Bois understood the veil itself, and black folks' forced positioning behind it, as problematic, to be gotten rid of. He and others during his long life constantly challenged black folks to strive to rend the veil. He seemed to have concluded that he would not likely see in the United States the progress in social relations and political and economic empowerment for black peoples that he had desired and long fought for. So he departed for Ghana.[60]

Yet even as the matter of the amelioration of social-economic position among black folks of the North Atlantic diaspora continues to be debated, it is clear that the concept of the veil itself has proved to be rather elastic, communicating more than one message, used in more than one kind of discursive operation. At the end of *Souls*, after having consistently and dramatically used the term "veil" to describe and provoke strong emotions about the separation of black folks from "the kingdom of culture," Du Bois used it in a different, more positive sense, as the language of the slave songs that encodes the most profound and sensitive sentiments:

> In these songs...the slave spoke to the world. Such a message is *naturally veiled and half articulate.* Words and music have lost each other and new cant phrases of a dimly understood theology have displaced the older sentiment...the music is distinctly sorrowful.

> [They] tell in word and music of trouble and exile, of strife and hiding; they grope toward some unseen power and sigh for rest in the End.
>
> The words...cleared of evident dross...conceal much of real poetry and meaning beneath conventional theology and unmeaning rhapsody.
>
> ...Over the inner thoughts of the slaves and their relations one with another the shadow of fear ever hung, so that we get but glimpses here and there, and also with them, eloquent omissions and silences.
>
> ...The things evidently borrowed from the surrounding world undergo characteristic change when they enter the mouth of the slave. Especially is this true of *Bible phrases*.[61]

These songs seemed to have been for Du Bois evidence of a serious grappling with the "veil" of the other valence—the "veil" that was not so much to be overcome, but to be understood as complex communication. Here Du Bois was pointing to a certain type of veiling as a critical layered interpretive strategy and form of expression. So paradoxically, veiling (of deep sentiment) he seemed to assume was needed by those forced behind the veil (of white dominance and violence). Du Bois seemed to understand that beyond the basic and perhaps original issue of keeping oneself safe in a hostile antiblack world, black folk had come to express their deepest sentiments in veiled terms, "in other words," for other reasons. They had begun to "hide" the meaning of their hard, deepest sentiments—hide from the (white) public gaze and ears, not so much in terms of being always out of view and out of earshot, but in terms of clear and straightforward articulation that would facilitate apprehension. Their expressions were deemed "naturally veiled and half articulate." This was another knowing, another epistemological system, another form of expressivity. To be sure, this other knowing was cloaked in "conventional theology," but it went underneath such framing and cloaking with the strategy of "eloquent omissions and silences." The meanings of the "conventional" changes radically in the different context of usages—in the mouths of those singing about "trouble and exile, of strife and hiding."

And then Du Bois indicates, almost as a throwaway assertion—as the lack of any explicit elaboration seems to suggest—that what he had argued about black slaves' power of expressivity was "especially" true with respect to "Bible phrases." Now it seems clearer that "conventional theology"

Du Bois understood to be interpretive frameworks associated with Western Christendom, determined by and reflective of the Bible. He understood that black folk understood that the "Bible phrases" were "especially" strategic for their articulations, allowing them to "hide" or protect the integrity of their true selves, as they felt they must.

Referred to already in this and in several contexts of discussion above, Zora Neale Hurston here again comes immediately to mind as a provocative scholar, artist, and critic of folklore who documented and narrativized the veiling aspect of folklore and other forms of black expressivities. And most interesting for me, although she did not elaborate on what it meant, she also noted the uses of the Bible (and other sacred texts) in the folkways, the language forms, of black folk. That veiling, indirection, encoding, signifying were prominent in the forms of expressions of the folk is powerfully indicated in that favorite saying, already quoted several times in this book, that Hurston picked up on in her field work and offered as a handle for "reading" the world and the self—"hitting a lick with a crooked stick." In the manner in which she picked up on the lore, myths, and rhythms, the textures and gestures of black folk, and in the connection she made between the use of the Bible and free liquid self-authorized interpretations among them "...even the Bible was made over to suit our vivid imagination."[62] Hurston named some of the critical issues involved in self-reflexive interpretation about and among black folks. Her reading of black "readings" of the world highlights the mysterious, the fantastic, the elusive, the uncanny that constituted the (re-)constructed worlds of the black Atlantic:

> "Now all y'all heard what Ah said...
> Dat's just an old time by-word...."
> "I done heard my gran'paw say dem very words many and many a time...There's a whole heap of them kinda by-words...They all got *a hidden meanin', jus' like de Bible.* Everybody can't understand what they mean. Most people is thin-brained. They's born wid they feet under the moon. Some folks is born wid they feet on de sun and they kin seek out de inside meanin' of words."[63]

That the Bible and certain black traditions of communication were associated with "hidden meanin'" is important: their conjuncture is rather powerful: not only can one read the Bible to find in it veiled meanings, one could also use it as key to unlocking the meaning of veiled communication, the key to "untying the knots" of life's puzzles.[64] But important, in the assertion of the folk claim about veiled meaning as it is compared to the Bible is the arrogation of nothing less than authority of, and, most important, authority in relationship to, scriptures. In other words, not only were black folk claiming to understand the Bible as container of esoteric knowledge, but also they were themselves inventors of scriptures—of esoteric knowledge. That such claims have been downplayed or rejected within the culture of black folk or explained away by critical interpreters is very much evident and also very astounding.[65]

Very much related to both Du Bois's insight about the sorrow songs and the Bible and Hurston's representation of the Bible as a depository of the uncanny, the mysterious, the "hidden meanin'," is Toni Morrison's focus, and challenge regarding memory and self-revelation within the African diaspora. Her focus brings us back to Equiano and the meaning of his story.

Albeit without directly referring to them, Morrison picks up on the connection between the Du Boisian metaphorical use of the veil and the folk/vernacular uses of the Bible illuminated by Hurston, in order to problematize black existence and interpretation. Regarding the veil in the history of black diaspora writing, she deepens and widens Du Bois's metaphorical application. Historically the veil had to do, she argued, not (merely) with the needed response to antiblack segregation, "other-ing," and violence. She expands the Du Boisian notion of divided consciousness into an argument about a type of shutting off, occlusion, and silencing—of the interior life/self. This was done, she seems to argue, out of respect for larger cultural sensibilities. In an essay entitled "The Site of Memory," published in 1987 in a book of multiauthored essays edited by William Zinsser that is hauntingly entitled *Inventing the Truth*,[66] Morrison addresses the veiling of the interior life of the black self—the muting of deeply felt sentiments, pain, stresses, trauma. With special attention to what were among the first of African American literary works written in English—the autobiographical slave narratives of the eighteenth and nineteenth centuries—she identifies what is for black folk the perduring problem of uniting the divided consciousness and probing and articulating the movements of the interior life:

> [N]o slave society in the history of the world wrote more . . . about its own enslavement. The milieu, however, dictated the purpose and the style . . . popular taste discouraged the writers from dwelling too

> long or too carefully on the more sordid details of their experience. Whenever there was an unusually violent incident, or a scatological one, or something "excessive," one finds the writer taking refuge in the literary conventions of the day. "I was left in a state of distraction not to be described" (Equiano). "But let us now leave the rough usage of the field...and turn our attention to the less repulsive slave life as it existed in the house of my childhood" (Douglass). "I am not about to harrow the feelings of my readers by a terrific representation of the untold horrors of that fearful system of oppression....It is not my purpose to descend deeply into the dark and noisome caverns of the hell of slavery" (Henry Box Brown).
>
> Over and over, the writers pull the narrative up short with a phrase such as, "But let us drop a veil over these proceedings too terrible to relate." In shaping the experience to make it palatable to those who were in a position to alleviate it they were silent about many things, and they "forgot" many other things.[67]

Morrison's perspective seems diametrically opposed to those I have associated with Du Bois and Hurston. According to Morrison, the slave narratives represent more than anything else the phenomenon of the too long practiced silencing and forgetting of, the hiding and receding from, the self. Her quotations of selected slave narratives above do not actually include the specific term "veil" itself. She did not make the argument turn around the use of the term as euphemistic allusion to the phenomenon about which she argues. Yet there is no doubting the examples' support of what seems to be her general argument. She used the pointed metaphor of the veil as a way to make the point about what she seems to consider the great occlusion.

The one selection from which she quotes which includes actual reference to the term comes from Lydia Maria Child's introduction to Linda Brent's "tale" of sexual abuse. It seems to be the reference that for Morrison makes clear the problem faced and suggests the language with which a solution can be found:

> I am well aware that many will accuse me of indecorum for presenting these pages to the public; for the experiences of this intelligent and much-injured woman belong to a class which some call delicate subjects, and others indelicate. This peculiar phase of Slavery has generally been kept veiled; but the public ought to be made

acquainted with its monstrous features, and I am willing to take the responsibility of presenting them with the veil drawn [aside].[68]

Morrison goes on to make her most important point—that it was striking to her that in the narratives there was "no mention of their [the slaves'] interior life." As a writer thriving "not much more than a hundred years after Emancipation, a writer who is black and a woman," she saw her responsibility to be to instruct persons "how to *rip that veil* drawn over 'proceedings too terrible to relate.'" She argued that this project was "critical" for all who belong to the "marginalized category" in society, because "we were seldom invited to participate in the discourse even when we were its topic."[69]

Morrison's research into the slave narratives surely did allow her both to problematize and to provoke more thinking about the occlusion that is effected by what is understood as divided black consciousness. But it seems to me that notwithstanding her lack of acknowledgment of it—at least in "Site of Memory"—Morrison was surely aware of Du Bois's uses of the "veil." If she did not use him as starting point, she eventually came to be in conversation with Du Bois. Here I have in mind in particular her conversation with him about his intimation of what the "sorrow songs" signify, what they hold out as possibilities in helping contemporaries to "rend the veil," to unite a divided consciousness, to articulate powerful and difficult sentiments and yearnings. As I have already pointed out, it is ironic that the term Du Bois used for the solution to the problem of dividedness is another construal of the "veil." That is, he thought that one powerful response on the part of black folks to the dividedness of the black soul was the music—especially, but not exclusively, the "sorrow songs." The music was understood to be evocative, powerful; Du Bois found himself undone by it; he first experienced and then understood it as powerful carrier of veiled sentiment. The music, then, should be compared to the slave narratives as expressive form, with respect for the obvious differences and shared possibilities and limitations of each form.

From her different social historical vantage point, Morrison saw more sharply the limitations of both the music (but going beyond the sorrow songs) and the literature (but going beyond the slave narrative). Regarding music, she argued in an interview that it "kept us alive, but it's not enough anymore."[70] It is, of course, no surprise that she favors literature: she has made it clear that she thinks that fiction, the novel in particular, can now speak most directly and powerfully to and for the people having migrated to the cities.[71]

Morrison seemed to see music, including the music that profoundly moved Du Bois, as a continuing part of the veiling, understood as a problem, needing to be ripped. The veiling here is what keeps black folks from probing their interiority, on their own terms. Such a problematic and the way outward seem to be precisely what Morrison addresses in most of her novels, most profoundly in the novel *Beloved*. But it is precisely the texture of this novel that implicates Morrison in the very culture work the relevance and power of which she denied. It is also the work of this novel that opens a larger window onto the work Equiano may have been doing. Only a summary sketch and argument can be offered here.

There is still raging debate about many issues around the character Beloved: whence she comes, who or what she represents; the meaning or import of this or that statement or action attributed to her/it, whither it/she goes. But all interpreters generally agree that *Beloved* is a story about a haunting. The haunting of those who are survivor-heirs of the "sixty million and more" made to undergo the Middle Passage (and to whom the book is dedicated). It is a story about the failure on the part of all black peoples to remember those who died in such an experience and thereby remember who black people are. It is about the refusal of those who died to go away and remain forgotten; it is about the haunting of the memory of those who died. It is about why and how the memory of those who died is held back, made difficult or impossible to embrace. Why the memory persists. Why it hurts, traumatizes. It is about consciousness, the impact that the haunting has upon the black soul and consciousness. It is about the impact of the loss of memory, the prevention and refusal of memory upon the black soul. It is also ultimately about how the black soul may be reconstituted, healed, united. So it is, then, about consciousness, interpretation, and articulation, about the terms on which, the framework within which, the black self, the one who is survivor-heir of the middle passage, may now look back, remember, see/interpret, and speak to the world about what it thinks, how it feels, what it knows, how it travels and experiences. More specifically, the book is made to be about "ripping the veil" that prevents the black self from remembering and healing itself. It is a pointing in the direction in which the psycho-social-cultural stitching and weaving work can be carried out.

Although it is clear what character in the book does the haunting, not entirely clear in every part of the book is the matter of how the haunting is to be understood, that is, how it works, why it persists. It should occasion little surprise that I would notice and want to exploit—as very few other interpreters have—Morrison's epigraph, which is taken from Paul's letter to the Romans (9:25), and which also supplies the name of the character for whom the book is entitled:

> I will call them my people,
> Which were not my people;
> and her beloved,
> which was not beloved.

No argument need be made here about the importance of epigraphs in summing up a writer's agenda. But what I want to stress here is the importance of the epigraph in naming the deeper issue behind the surface narrative issue. In order for this is to be made clear, it is important that the larger discursive context of Paul's statement[72] be established.

The larger context of Paul's letter to the Romans is his effort to address the believers at Rome, who were of mixed cultural-religious background, viz., Jews and Gentiles (with subdivisions in each of these categories), regarding what appears to be, in light of the success of the Pauline mission, an ironic and even paradoxical twist of fate and circumstance: the phenomenon of the turning to God in great numbers on the part of Gentiles. Since the promise of God's favor was given first to the Jews, how has it come about that the non-Jews, the Gentiles, are turning in what seems to be great numbers and so many Jews in comparison seem not to be accepting God's "call"?

Paul tries his best to clarify matters, but his arguments are contradictory and confusing. It is worth reciting a part of the larger rhetorical context—at least from 9:22 to 9:26—that includes the passages Morrison used in her epigraph:

> Yet what if God, wishing to display his wrath and make known [God's] power, has endured with much long-suffering those vases of wrath, fashioned for destruction? This was done to make known the riches of [God's] glory for the vases of mercy, which [God] had fashioned beforehand for such glory. Even for us [believers], whom [God] called, not only from among the Jews, but also from among the Gentiles, as indeed [God] says in Hosea,

Those who were not my people
I shall call "my people";
And her who was not loved
I shall call "my beloved"
And
In the very place where it was said to them,
"You are not my people,"
there they shall be called "children of the living God." (NRSV)

Take note that at the end of the even larger rhetorical section, chapters 9–11, in which is found the prophetic statement that Morrison used for her epigraph, Paul sums up how he thinks the matter of turning to God/God's work of election should be understood: "I do not want you to be ignorant of this *mystery*."[73] In this section Paul engages in wonderful play, specifically on the words "call" (*kaleo*) and "mystery" (*musterion*). These words and Paul's play with them—that is, signifying on them as markers of "hidden meanin'," of paradox—draw Morrison's attention and inspire her to play with the passage.

Morrison seems to have applied the Pauline "mystery" that equated "the call" (as election) and being called "beloved" to black existence: she renders the historical and perduring exclusion and marginalization, the historical enslavement, the otherness, and the subjugation and hoped-for elevation and self-possession among black peoples mysterious. Paul's "beloved" is recontextualized and translated by Morrison as black folks' coming to be loved and loving themselves. So it seems that what for her is most mysterious is the matter of *why* black peoples were first enslaved and *how* they can or may come to be healed, elevated. In Morrison's thinking, drawing on the socio-logical categories of the world that Paul knew, black peoples are the "Gentiles," the ones thought at first to be outsiders, marginals, strangers, slaves. And just as a mysterious thing happened with the Gentiles of Paul's day, as even they were brought into the fold, into the family of God, so black folks, according to Morrison, are destined to be "called," to be loved.

Morrison argues for addressing black existence—how it evolved, the survival strategies, and the terms of self-acceptance, healing, and empowerment—as a mystery. But what is first required, her essays and novels (especially the book *Beloved*) seem to suggest, is the work of identifying and "ripping the veil." With *Beloved* Morrison makes narratological, thus, more complex and layered, the identification of both the problem and the direction of the healing for the characters. No matter how one interprets the book, it is very clear that it is not a "straight stick that hits a clean lick." Whatever *Beloved* means, it means not in a straightforward manner. So Morrison's criticism of some of the all too veiled, all too indirect expressions of folk culture notwithstanding, her story *Beloved* is also a "crooked stick"; it is also a type of veiling, even as it may be considered an effort to address the historical problem of veiling in the African diaspora. (This veiling ironically remains one of the points of criticism of Morrison's works.)

The characters of the story force readers into a scrambling of any kind of simple narrative line. Instead of a line, circles come to mind; the characters tell versions or aspects of the same story; or they tell multiple stories, which are varied and overlapping. For all of the characters, but especially for the main character Sethe, the "symbolic order" that the language of the master represents cannot translate her experience. For example, Sethe's killing of her baby girl cannot be told simply or directly, that is, not through the language of the master. It was to prevent her from having to undergo the humiliation of slavery that Sethe killed her baby girl. This experience was deemed by Sethe and by all observers to be horrible. But it was as a horrible representative act, resonant of classic apotropaic[74] tradition; it was traumatic, "unspeakable": there were no words that could carry the meaning of the act, the depth of the impulses and feelings involved.

It is the master language, the "symbolic order" that Morrison stresses must be ripped in order for black folks to come to be called beloved. Not just the slave narrative and its formal and rhetorical elements, but dominant Western discourse itself, with its need and tendency, as Pierre Bourdieu puts it, to "occult the aphasia,"[75] to veil the veiling, as Morrison might put it. This phenomenon must be ripped. This ripping is signaled in the book by the multiple repetitive and varied tellings by the characters about their horrible experiences and hauntings. But the matter was brought to a head by Sethe's effort finally to come to speech about what happened to her. It is Morrison's description of Sethe's movements as she comes into speech that is important to notice here: she was found "spinning. Round and round the room . . . turning like a slow steady wheel. . . . Circling [Paul D] the way she was circling the subject."[76] This spinning seems to reveal Morrison's understanding of knowledge, self-awareness, critical interpretation in terms of indirection and fragmentation, perhaps, functioning in terms of therapy. Her actions seem to represent for Morrison some sort of critique—of the master narrative and its fixed views about her existence and self. It also seemed to point toward reconstitution and healing. The circling/spinning suggests critique of and resistance to linear discursivity and politics. Might this not especially include scripturalization? It also reflects an effort to reconstitute the self. This difference in orientation suggests that the ripping of the veil is accomplished not so much by a refusal to engage language as a refusal to accord it the power to carry meaning in the same way, in uncritical naturalized terms, as though it were part of what Bourdieu termed the realm of *doxa*, the domain of the taken for granted, the undiscussable.[77]

Sethe's circling/spinning critiques and explodes this structuring. It is functionally much like the "silence" that Houston Baker discussed in his *Afro-American Poetics*, in particular the essay on "Lowground and Inaudible Valleys: Reflections on Afro-American Spirit Work." He argues that the interpretive orientation of black folk culture is to be understood as silence, that is, as holding back from traditional uses of language, in order to express critique and healing. Drawing upon Susan Sontag's essay on silence, Baker calls for a "criticism of silence" in order to "match the depths of a magnificently enhancing black sounding of experience."[78] Here is the radicalism and power of the interpretive stance shared by Morrison and Du Bois and Hurston and so many others registered by Baker: that for black and subaltern critical consciousness there is no meaning in any narrative, any text, unless such is first ripped, broken and then "entranced," blackened, made usable for weaving meaning. "Merely arranged in a traditional... problematic... words are ineffectual. Only when they enter into entranced performance... do they give birth to sounds of a new order."[79] The entranced performance about which Baker speaks is realized only when there is an addressing of the lowground and inaudible valleys of black experiences. Then the canonical arrangements and structures are exploded, the veil is ripped.

John Coltrane's version of Rodger's "My Favorite Things" is a splendid example of this addressing of the lowground and inaudible valleys and veil ripping. According to literary critic K. Benston, Coltrane's performance

> suggested that unchecked expressive inquiry—the articulation of the moment's disposition, desire, and intuition—was the "favorite thing" of Coltrane's New Thang.... Interpretation thus serves not

> as either assassination or acknowledgment of the prior but as an agitative intervention that propels a dazzling movement of substitutions.... By...exploring a tune in order to thematize the plurivocality of its enunciation, Coltrane signaled that his project was not just that of producing new meanings but of reopening the question of meaning's production.[80]

Such a performance as a reopening really means allowing memories to flow out of and through the collective self, to find sites of memory of the sort discussed by Pierre Nora in his provocative essay "Between Memory and History: Les Lieux de Mèmoire":

> [W]hat makes...lieux de mèmoire is precisely that by which they escape from history. The lieu de mèmoire is...a site of excess closed upon itself, concentrated in its own name, but also forever open to the full range of possible significations.[81]

Morrison's argument is that for African Americans, for whom there is so much loss, what is particularly important is the recovery of images for the flow of memory. In her view this means beginning with images—images especially of ancestors or something in association with them:

> [They] are my access to me; they are my entrance into my own interior life. Which is why the images that float around them—the remains, so to speak, at the archaeological site—surface first....
>
> [T]he act of imagination is bound up with memory....
>
> You know, they straightened out the Mississippi River in places, to make room for houses and livable acreage. Occasionally the river floods these places. "Flooding" is the word they use, but in fact it is not flooding; it is remembering. Remembering where it used to be. All water has a perfect memory and is forever trying to get back to where it was. Writers [= readers/interpreters] are like that: remembering where we were, what valley we ran through, what the banks were like, the light that was there and the route back to our original place. It is emotional memory—what the nerves and the skin remember as well as how it appeared. And a rush of imagination is our "flooding"...like water, I remember where I was before I was "straightened out."[82]

"Ripping the veil" for Morrison means not allowing the self to be "straightened out," which means refusing to veil the self, refusing to think according to and live within the realm of *doxa*, the realm of the canonical. It means, as was the case with Du Bois and Hurston, like Coltrane and Morrison, interpreters all, accessing the sites of memory and then from such sites allowing the waters of the memories to flow, to flow in relationship to—over, under, through—the received (master, canonical) scripts/texts so that they might flow outside the artificially established banks of dominant discursivity, the most important instantiation of which we have historically called and may for sake of argument and analysis continue to call "scriptures." Only when these memories on their own terms, carrying their own significance, not behind the veil of script/ure/s as texts or as canon, only when these are woven together or are (re-)textualized and re-contextualized in critical/signifying relationship to scripturalization can some sort of social therapy of the sort that Morrison and others hoped for truly begin.

Now a basic pointed issue regarding Equiano is in order: wanting to avoid interpreting Equiano as singular phenomenon in the history of the black Atlantic, having been provoked by some of the gestures and strategies and silences—including, but going beyond the formal literary and rhetorical features—of his narrative into an admittedly limited foray into what seem to be similar sentiments around consciousness in other black Atlantic writings that developed in the United States, I must ask: does Equiano's effort that is his narrative fit into the long history of the wide range of sentiments, projects, strategies, institutional starts and orientations, only some of which are focused on above, that were intended to represent and save the black Atlantic? His narrative reflects little or no familiarity with the slave songs about which Du Bois wrote. It does not reflect the vernacularisms of the black folk about which Hurston wrote. And it does not represent Morrison's critical unveiling discourse that she understands to be the purpose of the novel. So where, with whom, and how does Equiano fit? We know that he, like so many writers and activists, worked tirelessly to ameliorate the plight of the black poor. We know also that he knew himself to be in solidarity with—perhaps, even the principal leader of—the "sons of Africa." But how does this strange narrative fit that profile? What work does his narrative do?

Let me be clear: Equiano's story was not intended as a blueprint for black nation-building or a program for black solidarity in eighteenth-century England or within the black Atlantic more generally. It is too complex and multidirectional to be useful in these respects. Most important and to the point, the demographic of the story's hoped-for readers would not have been a logical match for such an agenda. Black peoples, en masse, were hardly presumed to be the readers of his story. He seemed clear that his story was not a manifesto in the way that Cugoano understood his work to be (or in the way it would come to be understood by others). Nevertheless, we all know by now that his story is anything but simple. No issue is simple in Equiano's story. Yet in the face of the very powerful ideological and structural power arrangements as impediment, about which he creatively wrote, the story does contain hints about what work he was making it do for him and for others.

Michael Taussig provides an interpretive framework that may also help here to explain some of what Equiano's story is made to do. He does not refer to Equiano at all, but in his conviction that all of us must seek to understand ourselves in relationship to the fallout from the first contact between the West and the Others he places those who have become white and those who have become black African in sharp analytical relief. I take the step of applying Equiano to Taussig's interpretive schema.

I have already referred to Taussig's book *Mimesis and Alterity: A Particular History of the Senses* in an effort to understand Equiano's imitation of white men's magic (chapter 6). I have also drawn attention to his poignant reflection on the disturbing image of an Igbo mbari shrine that he discovered in Julia Blackburn's book *The White Man: First Responses of Aboriginal Peoples to the White Man.* I quoted Taussig's full reaction to the shrine, in the context of discussion about Equiano's imitation of British scriptural practices. But now I should like to focus on Taussig's last lines that are, again, without direct reference to Equiano, yet have much to do with the work the latter tried to do in solidarity with Du Bois and other leaders of the black diaspora. I am here forcing Taussig to read Equiano:

> The white man as viewer is here virtually forced to interrogate himself, to interrogate the Other in and partially constitutive of his many and conflicting selves.... Such face-to- faceness no doubt brings its quotient of self-congratulation. "They think we are gods." But being a god is okay as long as it isn't excessive. After all, who knows—in imaging us as gods, might they not take our power?[83]

Power—this is what Equiano aimed to possess. His story conveys his quest for power—for himself and his "countrymen." His story is a type of mimetics in the vein of the image of the mbari shrine. It represents "mimetic excess" as it represents Equiano's heightened self-awareness of his status in the white world turned back upon itself and the "colonial endowment." His is a complex story that shows the reader his understanding of how the white world is structured around scripturalization and how he negotiated such a structure. Equiano the character and Equiano the writer are our window, our way out, our way forward: having constructed/performed a mirror for the critical observation and perspective on scripturalization as the epistemological-ideological structural center-arrangement of the white world, and having forced the reader into defamiliarization of this world, he presents to the readers a picture of an ex-centric and of an ex-centric's modes of knowing.

But we must take caution here: not all ex-centrics can read in this way. Not all flip their readings back in mimetic excess. The lack of such flipping is mimetics of the fundamentalist sort, of which there is disturbing evidence among blacks of the diaspora (and in Africa).[84] Not all know how to read themselves reading the larger worlds that surround them and dominate them. Ex-centric knowing is through its positionality—if not always and necessarily, certainly normally expected to be—a straining toward decentering, the provincialization, self-reflexivity, defamiliarization, and the fractional, all in relationship to the center and to regimes.[85] So ex-centric knowing means reading the center reading itself. Since centers always contain scriptures and some centers frame scriptures by scripturalization, such knowing requires attempts to engage not merely in historical criticism but critical history.[86] Through such history it can reconnect with things that are basic, things forgotten, things hidden and submerged. It means coming to terms with the serious psycho-social-cultural play—and violence—involved in claiming to know. And it means coming to terms with the self-authorization to pursue a system of knowing that excavates hidden meanings, unveils truths, and remembers where and how waters of refreshment flow.

Equiano's story shows that insofar as he was aware that he could "read" (for) himself he could also try to build in relationship to- in imitation of- the structure of scripturalization an "almost" alternate ideological-rhetorical structure in order to address the plight of black peoples in the Atlantic worlds. What he faced—and what he thought all black diaspora peoples faced—was the challenge of constructing an identities beyond slavery and away from home. On what basis was formation and solidarity—among the many differences that obtained among black diaspora peoples—to be achieved and sustained? What name should black peoples call themselves? What should be the main agenda of such peoples? In addressing these issues, he did not so much exegete and perform the texts called scriptures as he excavated and analyzed the regime that is scripturalization. Such work had enormous potential as it facilitated the necessary step toward agency and freedom—identifying that which is of "unbounded influence," that which enslaves. Identifying that which enslaves does not guarantee but it facilitates salvation.

Epilogue

I don't read such small stuff as letters, I read men and nations.

—SOJOURNER TRUTH

SEVERAL YEARS AGO I taught a special course that had a close reading of Equiano's narrative as its focus. As I recall, there were nine or ten students in the class. They were all intelligent, mature, and well traveled with successful careers, in ministry and other domains. They happened to be African Americans all. What stayed with me was the negative reaction to Equiano on the part of almost all of them, with one or two exceptions. To my astonishment, most students fought him throughout the course. They consistently commented that in their view he was "not really black," that he did not act, did not signify, "black," and so forth. It was clear to me that these students were not uninformed about the history of black peoples or black literatures. They were in fact translating and representing a long and thick cultural-ideological, discursive, and rhetorical orientation that bordered on a type of essentialism of or cultural-political correctness around blackness. This orientation often assumes and argues that "blackness" can and should be registered—across time and space—in particular ways, in the rhythms of one's gait, in speech and so forth. One can either "talk that talk" and "walk that walk"—or not. The operating assumption among the students, reflecting this long and strongly held view, was that "black is. . . . ," and "black ain't," Ellison be damned.

I fought hard to show that I thought Equiano was in fact questioning if not undermining such assumptions he understood to be held by white folks, that he was playing with their unchecked and unmarked ideas and assumptions about themselves as well as black peoples as he worked to invent himself. His story tells us that we make up identities as we go along. The period in which he lived he was aware was a rich period of identity formation and invention. It was a complex and fascinating period—of working through the meaning of first contact with difference—in which identities for white folks were being forged. Indeed, whiteness was being invented over against black folk. So Equiano's story confounds the expectations—for the slave narrative, the conversion narrative, the travel narrative, for blackness and for whiteness, as he shows readers how white men made up their world.

There are no white men. There is no magic. There are no books that talk. There are no scriptures. Except—as Equiano's story helps us understand—to speak of. That is the point: what is real is the politics and uses of language, the work of the metadiscursive regimes that enslave, that control language use and the effects of such. The discovered regime that was scripturalization afforded Equiano opportunity and space to perform a self—not a fixed one for all time, but for what each moment requires for his survival and thriving. This was the hidden meaning that his story conveys. A rich and layered and fluid identity was forged in relation to the framework or regime that was scripturalization.

What I found compelling about Equiano is precisely what disturbed my students and has always confounded many of his readers: that getting to the truth about things requires first getting to the truth not about "blackness" or "Eboes or "Africans," or.... These were inventions for the sake of the successful project of the formation of the modern white world. What is required is uncovering the hidden truth about "white men," about "white men's magic," the system of slavery that would control seeing and knowing itself. Here Equiano's crafty narrative discloses (too?) much—about scripture-reading British (and by extension Euro-American) civilization as a regime whose main feature is its self-enclosure, its enslavement to its tight self-referential reading, its "unbounded influence." That is the meaning of "white men's magic." Herein certainly is the pre-condition for modern world fundamentalisms. The latter, Equiano shows his readers, is not tangential to, an exaggeration of, Euro-American civilization; it is its core.

Equiano named for me what my early stumbling around was about or could be about. He shows the reader who is willing to read him up close, approaching his subtlety and ludics, with a view to examining the hidden things of the world, that he would reward with an "interesting" narrative, a rich narrative that would reveal much more than what was expected about either a slave narrative or conversion narrative. The reading—of scripturalization, not merely scriptures—that his narrative represents remains a compelling performance of the critical imagination. It provides a powerful challenge for the defamiliarization and provincialization of Euro-American civilization, as well as the formation of the "Ethiopian" as "African" as "black," less as an essential but as *not*-white, that is, a nonfixed presence that has the potential for stumbling onto the modern complexly human, as much as, if not far beyond, what Shakespeare, notwithstanding Bloom's claims, can be said to have had in mind.[1]

Equiano was aware of the need not so much to find in scriptures lexical meanings that buttress tribal gestures, but to position himself in relationship to scripturalization as regime so that might maximize his agency if not freedom, his economic survival if not thriving. His claim to have seen "things new," to read "for myself," to "appl[y] with great comfort" the scriptures was less about textual exegesis or even textual therapy and more about the politics of the textual as the politics of knowing and its correlative economic ramifications.[2] For such interests, Equiano made himself the figure of the Ethiopian who was "willing to be saved." But in the larger context of Equiano's discursive play the Ethiopian is *not* in the end of his story figured as the model Christian but as a type of psycho-socio-cultural and ideological *maroon*, the one who, like Equiano, comes to read and understand "white men's magic" as a system of "unbounded influence," the enslaving box, Plato's cave of shadows, that is scripturalization. He then seeks to escape from it—or, certainly, more realistically, learns what it entails, and so learns to negotiate it.

Equiano's story seems to suggest that white men's magic/scripturalization is a type of "unbounded influence" that is ultimately about the politics of language, with universal and ongoing ramifications. Such politics subtly but profoundly enslaves, controlling our thinking about thinking, our language about our language. We are trapped, made anxious because, according to psychologist Steven Pinker, language is "a window into human nature."[3] "The view from language shows us the cave we inhabit, and also the best way out of it."[4] As he reads Plato's allegory of the cave, he understands it to be about the language-using humans who are by language politics, "emotions infusing our language,"[5] made captives, shackled in a grotto, with heads and bodies chained and able to look only at the rear wall. The cave is somewhat like "a movie theatre out of the *Flintstones*" in which master "projectionists" (= religious, political, academic, financial, military magicians/wizards/scribes/exegetes) "hold up cutouts and puppets," which cast shadows onto the wall. The imprisoned know only the reality of that projected world. Departure from such reality will be dizzying, perhaps, painful.[6] But remaining in a state of slavery is disastrous and deadly:

> The automatic punch of emotionally laced words can fool us into thinking that the words have magical powers rather than being arbitrary conventions. And the taboos on thinking and speaking that shield our personal relationships from the mutual knowledge that might break their spell can leave us incapacitated as we try to deal with problems at the unprecedented scale of a modern society.[7]

Equiano dramatized his understanding of what was for his age and remains for our own the ultimate politics of language—scripturalization. He could only hint at the depth of the problem and depth of response to it that was required. In the end he posited the (necessity of the) invention of the figure of the Ethiopian. He did not, perhaps, could not, elaborate, could not fully depict what could be the work of such a figure. We might paradoxically and poignantly speculate that had the politics—about language!—in Equiano's own time been right or simply expansive enough for him, such a figure may have been developed more fully—as a figure of marronage, as one who shows all the escape route from the (language) cave. The history of attempts at such ideological and psycho-social-cultural marronage, and of continued enslavement, to which all of us are subject, remains to be charted.

Scripturalizaton.

Slavery.

Marronage.

I am now beginning to figure out what for many years was haunting me. I am beginning to figure out how and what to read—and to what ends. There are no texts that speak. There are no white men. There is no white men's magic. Except—to speak of, in the way of Equiano's story. Equiano's story makes clear that in order to escape enslavement and orient oneself to freedom the slavery that is scripturalization, that is, "white men's magic," must be "read," must be fathomed, critiqued, resisted. Another track-layer of the black Atlantic, Sojourner Truth, made the case for the agenda going forward when she reportedly indicated that she "read[s] men and nations."[8] Heir of Equiano's and Truth's track-laying for the black Atlantic, contemporary griot Stevie Wonder in his 1970s top of the chart song "Superstition"[9] seems to have understood and conveyed in other words and through another medium and in his inimitable key the truth about this matter: "If you believe in things you don't understand, then you suffer…"

Notes

PROLOGUE

1. Zora Neale Hurston, *Mules and Men* (New York: Harper Perennial Library, 1990 [1935]), 125. This interest in knowing I would later learn to take into larger cross-cultural quests for knowledge such as those analyzed in Philip M. Peek, ed., *African Divination Systems: Ways of Knowing* (Bloomington and Indianapolis: Indiana University Press, 1991); and Galit Hasan-Rokem and David Shulman, eds., *Untying the Knot: On Riddles and Other Enigmas* (New York: Oxford University Press, 1996).
2. See the remarks by Kimberly W. Benston, *Performing Blackness: Enactments of African American Modernism* (New York: Routledge, 2000), 13, regarding Amiri Baraka's understanding of the term as a "moving through the text to the truth of blackness beyond it." I have also come to see Baraka's concept and my youthful play in larger cross-cultural historical and theoretical terms, such as those included in Johan Huizinga, *Homo Ludens: A Study of the Play Element in Culture* (Boston: Beacon Press, 1955 [1950]).
3. Here I am drawing on Michael Taussig's discussion regarding mimesis in his fascinating book *Mimesis and Alterity: A Particular History of the Senses* (New York: Routledge, 1993). What he calls the "mimetic faculty" is "the nature that culture uses to create second nature, the faculty to copy, imitate, make models, explore difference, yield into, and become Other" (xiii).
4. Mr. Redmond and Ms. Doll in grammar school; the male leader of the BECS program and Ms. Hill in middle school; Ms. Penn through high school; Mrs. Isabella Tobin, high school guidance counselor and her initiative and good offices and support in directing my way to college; professors Anibal Bueno and Melvin Watson in college; professors James Washington, Nils Dahl, Carl Holladay, and Krister Stendahl through graduate school years.
5. Hurston, *Mules and Men*, 125.

6. The late Paul Holmer, philosopher of religion at Yale Divinity School, saw in me a gift for philosophical work and encouraged me to look into further study in the field. Re: ministry and ministry studies, the late James M. Washington, then instructor of church history, friend-mentor, and committed churchman, as he proudly preferred to think of and call himself, had encouraged me to pursue the M.Div. degree program and to seek ordination—just in case... that is, for strategic professional reasons. Although I had my doubts about the wisdom and appropriateness of the advice from both men, I made gestures in both directions. A few more courses in Philosophy/Philosophy of Religion as I had to experience it—with its principled a-historical bent and blindness to the legitimacy of the wisdom of my folk—convinced me that it was not for me. And, ironically, two good church internship experiences convinced me that the way of the church was not for me. I realized I had made others' general assumptions about me and about different domains overdetermine my decision-making. Slowly I began to make some decisions—some wise, some not so—based on my gut check, put differently, on the offices of the "little me" as it communicated with the "big me." (See Mechal Sobel, *Trabelin' On: The Slave Journey to an Afro-Baptist Faith* (Princeton: Princeton University Press, [1975] 1988), xix, 71, 108).
7. I think at that point and thereafter it often occurred to me—in very low-level degrees of awareness—that the arena of knowledge of scriptures, after all, was where the larger world seemed to make its claims about things that mattered and that such an arena was where I ought to stake my claim. This ongoing low-wattage hunch I now understand to have haunted me over the years. I have wrestled with it and understand this book to be a representation of its maturation. And, of course, it was likely no mistake that my chosen sub-field was "New Testament and Christian Origins." Given the orientation of my scholarship in the last two decades, reflected in the nature of this book, this appellation of my chosen field of study is of course suffused with irony, if not paradox. It must be so: no one had spoken to me about what was at issue in making such a selection. The decision not to pursue ministry was by now clear. It would seem I had in mind the importance of gaining command of the academic discourse that claimed to get at the roots of something that would explain things—how things in the Christianized world came to be and developed as they did, and how things now must or could mean, and so forth. With such knowledge I would really know. That this thinking took place in a Protestant subculture in a historically predominantly Christian nation is clear enough—and to the point of my story, Equiano's story, and this book.
8. See Warren's poem "Pondy Woods," in *New and Selected Poems: 1923–1985* (New York: Random House, 1985), 319–321. His buzzard was by no means alone in holding and registering such sentiment. See discussion of the matter

in Henry Louis Gates, Jr., *Signifying Monkey: A Theory of African-American Literary Criticism* (New York: Oxford University Press, 1988) chap. 4; Gates, ed., *"Race," Writing, and Difference* (Chicago: University of Chicago Press, 1986); and Emmanuel Chukwudi Eze, ed., *Race and Enlightenment: A Reader* (Oxford: Blackwell Publishers, 1997). And of course, as any person of color at least fifty years of age will testify, and as the paucity of black and other non-white scholars in the guild indicates, biblical studies was clearly part of the critical discourse that the buzzard thought was beyond the ken of the "nigger" Big Jim.

9. The few exceptions—a course I took as part of my minor concentration in History of Religions from historian of religion Wilfred Cantwell Smith gave me opportunity to read about (his) theorizing of scriptures, and encouragement from advisor Krister Stendahl to write a short essay for the Yale Divinity School alumni organ and to make it about African Americans—proved to be island experiences of refreshment and hope as well as plaintive signs of the issues I sorely wanted to engage.
10. The use of this term is quite intentional as an expression of the general history of the violence laden in Western notions about acquiring knowledge. And it accurately reflects my feelings about, not the actual circumstances around which, I came into possession of the degree.
11. Here I riff on the conceptualization and critique of scholarly practices involving textual interpretation as discussed in J. Z. Smith, *Drudgery Divine: On the Comparison of Early Christianities and the Religions of Late Antiquity* (Chicago: University of Chicago Press, 1990).
12. I was for years very much drawn to, almost haunted by, Rilke's concept of the "thrown" ball and what it may have to do with knowing and the development of consciousness. See his poem, "Solange du Selbstgeworfnes faengst," in: *Uncollected Poems: Rainer Maria Rilke*, ed. and tr. Edward Snow (New York: North Point Press; Farrar, Straus and Giroux, 1996), 138–139. I think I had some hunch that my wanting to know had to do with more than accumulating data. Rilke seemed to help me begin to grasp that I wanted and needed to "catch" that "ball," that "I"—an historicized and collective "I"—had thrown up and forgotten that I had done so.
13. For critical cross-cultural perspective on ways of knowing see Philip M. Peek, ed., *African Divination Systems: Ways of Knowing;* and Galit Hasan-Rokem and David Shulman, eds., *Untying the Knot: On Riddles and Other Enigmas*; re ludics and knowing, see John Huizinga, *Homo Ludens: A Study of the Play Element in Culture.*
14. An expression used and unpacked in a fascinating way by writer Richard Rodriguez as part of his plenary address given to a conference ("Reading America, Reading Scriptures") I conceived and convened in Claremont, California in 2010 as director of the Institute for Signifying Scriptures.

15. See Pierre Nora's reflections ("Between Memory and History: Les Lieux de Memoire") on how *lieux de mèmoire* transform historical criticism into critical history. In Genevieve Fabre and Robert O'Meally, eds., *History and Memory in African-American Culture* (New York: Oxford University Press, 1994), 300.
16. "It's the economy, stupid!" would become Bill Clinton's 1992 election campaign mantra.
17. The project involved transdisciplinary conversation over a period of two years (1997–1998) and resulted in an international conference in 1999 and a book (*African Americans and the Bible: Sacred Texts and Social Textures*, ed. Vincent L. Wimbush, with the assistance of Rosamond C. Rodman [New York: Continuum International, 2000, 2001]).
18. I had already experimented a bit with an essay contributed in response to what is now considered the first call for a research agenda on the history of African American readings of the Bible as a baseline for an interpretive history ("The Bible and African Americans: An Outline of an Interpretative History") to the now historic collection of essays entitled *Stony the Road We Trod: African American Biblical Interpretation*, ed. Cain H. Felder (Minneapolis: Fortress, 1991), 81–97. Building on this essay and on the conversations that were part of the African Americans and the Bible project, I wrote what I considered the next level of conceptualization of such a historical schema in an extended essay that was published as *The Bible and African Americans: A Brief History* (Minneapolis: Fortress, 2003).
19. The international conference that formally marked the beginning of the ISS also resulted in a collection of essays that I edited (*Theorizing Scriptures: New Critical Orientations to a Cultural Phenomenon* [New Brunswick, NJ: Rutgers University Press, 2008]). This collection reflected the type of conversation that I thought should characterize the ongoing project on critical studies of scriptures. It also provided me opportunity to deepen and expand my thinking about my own thoughts and the shape of the major projects. During this period (from the mid-1990s to the present) also I continued to write various essays and articles, including some that directed me to the present book. Such projects include: "African American Traditions and the Bible," *Oxford Companion to the Bible*, ed. Bruce M. Metzger and Michael D. Coogan (New York: Oxford University Press, 1993), 12–15; "Reading Texts as Reading Ourselves: A Chapter in the History of African American Biblical Interpretation," in *Reading from This Place: Social Location and Biblical Interpretation*, ed. Fernando F. Segovia and Mary Ann Tolbert (Philadelphia: Fortress Press, 1995), 95–108; "The Influence of the Bible in African American Culture," in *The Encyclopedia of African American Culture and History*, ed. J. Salzman et al. (Macmillan Library Reference USA; Macmillan, 1995); "Interrupting the Spin: What Would Happen Were African Americans to Become the Starting Point for Biblical Studies," *Union Seminary Quarterly Review* 52, nos. 1–2 (1998): 61–76; "Introduction: Reading Darkness, Reading

Scriptures," in *African Americans and the Bible*; "Signifying on Scriptures: An African Diaspora Proposal for Radical Readings," in *Feminist New Testament Studies: Global and Future Perspectives*, ed. Kathleen O. Wicker et al. (New York: Palgrave MacMillan, 2005); "We Will Make Our Own Future Text: A Proposal for an Alternate Interpretive Orientation," in *True to our Native Land: African American New Testament Commentary*, ed. Brian Blount et al. (Philadelphia: Fortress, 2007), 43–53; "'Naturally Veiled and Half Articulate': Scriptures, Modernity, and the Formation of African America," in *Still at the Margins*, ed. R. S. Sugirtharajah (Maryknoll, NY: Orbis Books, 2008); "Scriptures for Strangers: The Making of an Africanized Bible," in *Postcolonial Interventions: Essays in Honor of R. S. Sugirtharajah*, ed. Tat-siong Benny Liew (Sheffield: Sheffield Phoenix Press, 2009).

20. See discussion regarding the phenomenon in Harold Bloom's *A Map of Misreading* (New York: Oxford University Press, [1975] 2003).
21. See Wesley A. Kort, *"Take, Read": Scripture, Textuality, and Cultural Practice* (University Park: Pennsylvania State University Press, 1996), for a fascinating discussion regarding the themes and issues that are raised by scriptures as phenomena in culture.
22. Equiano was known most of his life not by the name I use throughout this book but by another given to him as a slave. That his story, beginning with the title page, intentionally juxataposes the two different names goes to the heart of the issue to be addressed in the story: identity formation.
23. There were a few other black writers around the same time or just before Equiano, to be sure, but no other writer had the success that Equiano enjoyed. See Vincent Carretta's discussion in chap. 12 of his *Equiano the African: Biography of a Self-Made Man* (Athens: University of Georgia Press, 2005); and James Sidbury, *Becoming African in America: Race and Nation in the Early Black Atlantic* (New York: Oxford University Press, 2007), chaps. 1–2.
24. On this point see Toni Morrison's argument regarding veiling of sentiments among the writers of slave narratives, in her provocative essay "The Site of Memory," in William Zinsser, ed., *Inventing the Truth: The Art and Craft of Memoir* (Boston: Houghton Mifflin, 1995), 109–110.
25. Charles H. Long, *Significations: Signs, Symbols, and Images in the Interpretation of Religion* (Philadelphia: Fortress, 1986), 4–5.
26. Taussig, *Mimesis*, xv.
27. Ibid., xiii. Taussig is here quoting from Franz Kafka's "A Report to an Academy": "To put it plainly, much as I like expressing myself in images, to put it plainly: your life as apes, gentlemen, insofar as something of that kind lies behind you, cannot be farther removed from you than mine is from me. Yet everyone on earth feels a tickling at the heels; the small chimpanzee and the great Achilles alike."
28. See Srinivas Aravamudan, *Tropicopolitans: Colonialism and Agency, 1688–1804* (Durham and London: Duke University Press, 1999), 271–283; and essays

by William Pietz, "The Problem of the Fetish, I: *Res: Anthropology and Aesthetics* 9 (Spring 1985), 5–17; "The Problem of the Fetish, II: The Origins of the Fetish," *Res: Anthropology and Aesthetics* 13 (Spring 1987): 23–45; "The Problem of the Fetish, IIIa: Bosman's Guinea and the Enlightenment Theory of Fetishism," *Res: Anthropology and Aesthetics* 16 (Autumn 1988), 105–123; and "Fetishism and Materialism: The Limits of Theory in Marx," in *Fetishism as Cultural Discourse*, ed. Emily Apter and William Pietz (Ithaca, NY: Cornell University Press, 1993), 152–185. See also Henry Krips, *Fetish: an Erotics of Culture* (Ithaca, NY; Cornell University Press, 1999).

29. Webb Keane, *Christian Moderns: Freedom and Fetish in the Missionary Encounter* (Berkeley: University of California Press, 2007), 27.

30. Aravamudan, *Tropicopolitans*, 274.

31. *Tropicopolitans*, 274; and 399, note #80. See Bruno Latour, *Petite reflexion sur le culte moderne des dieux faitiches* (Paris: Synthelabo, 1996), 26, 31. 44.

32. I follow throughout this book the single-volume text included in *Olaudah Equiano: The Interesting Narrative and Other Writings*, ed. and intro Vincent Carretta (New York: Penguin Books, 2003).

33. See Aravamudan's sketchy discussion of history of interpretation, in *Tropicopolitans*, 233–288. The literature is voluminous. Among the most important arguments about what and whose side Equiano is on are found in the following works: Houston Baker, *Blues, Ideology, and Afro-American Literature: A Vernacular Theory* (Chicago: University of Chicago Press, 1984); Wilfred D. Samuels, "Disguised Voice in the Interesting Narrative of Olaudah Equiano, or Gustavus Vassa the African," *Black American Literature Forum* 19 (1985), 64–69; Valerie Smith, *Self-Discovery and Authority in Afro-American Literature* (Cambridge: Harvard University Press, 1987); Keith Sandiford, *Measuring the Moment: Strategies of Protest in Eighteenth-Century Afro-English Writing* (Selinsgrove, PA: Susquehanna University Press, 1988); Susan Warren, "Between Slavery and Freedom: The Transgressive Self in Olaudah Equiano's Autobiography," *PMLA* 108.1 (January 1993): 94–105; Joseph Fichtelberg, "Word Between Worlds: The Economy of Equiano's Narrative," *American Literary History* 5.3 (Fall 1993); Geraldine Murphy, "Olaudah Equiano, Accidental Tourist," *Eighteenth-Century Studies* 27.4 (Summer 1994): 551–568; and Sylvester Johnson, "Colonialism, Biblical World-Making, and Temporalities in Olaudah Equiano's *Interesting Narrative*," Church History 77 (2008): 1003–1024.

34. There are many differences in perspective, argument, and conclusion about where Equiano should be located and how he should be used. But the fiercest battle has ensued especially between Aravamudan and Adam Potkay, along with Potkay's colleague Sandra Burr. See Adam Potkay and Sandra Burr, eds., *Black Atlantic Writers of the Eighteenth Century: Living the New Exodus in England and the Americas* (New York: St. Martin's Press, 1995). Aravamudan

thinks Potkay and Burr's interpretation of Equiano's religious conviction to be too simple and flat; they challenge Aravamudan and others to take Equiano's religious convictions seriously and argue that such conviction pretty much determines interpretation of his orientation. Aravamudan represents the critical position I find most persuasive and defensible.

35. I am mindful that Gates's *Signifying Monkey* has been enormously influential in scholarship on Equiano and other early black Atlantic writers—and deservedly so. Such work has focused on what Equiano represents in the history of the black literary tradition. This book does not so much contradict Gates's and others' readings as it represents a challenge to them to be open to a deeper reading of Equiano's play with the categories and problematics that we have come to term "religion."

CHAPTER 1

1. This concept appears in Toni Morrison's novel *Beloved*. But her essay "Site of Memory" also anticipated development of this concept. "Re-memory" entails much more than a recall of the facts; it has to do with allowing difficult things to surface and be dealt with.
2. See the now widely known and well-regarded analysis of such a concept in Dipesh Chakrabarty, *Provincializing Europe: Postcolonial Thought and Historical Difference* (Princeton, NJ: Princeton University Press, 2000).
3. See Susan Buck-Morss's arguments in *Hegel, Haiti, and Universal History* (Pittsburgh: University of Pittsburgh Press, 2009). Using Hegel and the Haitian revolution as backdrop, she provides compelling analysis of how historical social ruptures may cast light on the struggle to realize the universal. Also, see on these issues, with focus on Britian, Roxann Wheeler, *Complexion of Race: Categories of Difference in Eighteenth Century British Culture* (Philadelphia: University of Pennsylvania Press, 2000).
4. All known letters to date are collected as appendices in Caretta's Penguin (2003) of the narrative.
5. Re: conceptualization of the center, see Rudolf Arnheim, *Power of the Center: A Study of Composition in the Visual Arts* (Berkeley: University of California Press, 2009 [1982]).
6. See Linda Colley, *Britons: Forging the Nation, 1707–1837* (New Haven: Yale University Press, 1992); and Olivia Smith, *The Politics of Language, 1791–1819* (Oxford: Clarendon Press, 1984), for historical backgrounds.
7. See Srinivas Aravamudan's discussion in *Tropicopolitans* (Durham and London: Duke University Press, 1999), 275–283.
8. The matter of Equiano's change in consciousness is of course a key issue. It will continue to be raised throughout this book. It is enough for now simply to raise the issue as an important one, not to draw a conclusion.

9. See here Aravamudan, *Tropicopolitans*; Michael Taussig, *Mimesis and Alterity* and Pietz articles on the fetish, all cited in the notes to the Prologue, re: complexities of imitation but with a difference. See also Homi K. Bhabha, *Location of Culture* (New York: Routledge, 1994), especially. chap. 4, for what has become the touchstone in critical thinking about such matters. Re: sources likely used by Equiano, see Henry Louis Gates, Jr., *Signifying Monkey* (New York: Oxford University Press, 1988), 152–158; Aravamudan, *Tropicopolitans*, chap 6; and Vincent Carretta, *Equiano the African* (Athens: University of Georgia Press, 2005), chap. 13.
10. What should be considered in making an argument about Equiano's leadership and stature is the fact of his involvement in so many correspondences advanced by a collective; his friendship and collaboration with Cugoano; his advocacy of the "black poor," and of course his selection to lead the Sierra Leone resettlement project. See Carretta, *Equiano the African*, chaps. 10, 14; and James Sidbury, *Becoming African in America* (New York: Oxford University Press, 2007), 41–42, 45–47, 50–58, 64–65; and collected letters in appendices to Carretta's edited volume of Equiano's narrative.
11. A point eloquently made by Gates, *Signifying Monkey*, chap. 4.
12. On this point, see François Furstenberg, *In the Name of the Father: Washington's Legacy, Slavery, and the Making of a Nation* (New York: Penguin Press, 2006), 168–186, with focus on the United States. See also Smith, *Politics of Language*, chap. VI, with focus on rustics, peasants, and plough-boys in Britain. That blacks are hardly mentioned in this context makes the point about the situation to which Equiano needed to respond.
13. Gates, *Signifying Monkey*, chap. 2.
14. What this entails I address in the final chapter (chap. 7) of this book.
15. See on these matters Catherine Catherine Obianju Acholonu, "The Home of Olaudah Equiano—a Linguistic and Anthropological Search," in *The Journal of Commonwealth Literature* 22 (1987): 5–16. She argues that there are hints of an effort on the part of Equiano to approximate—with all allowances for the considerable challenges in spelling and orthography—some types of persons and aspects of traditions among the Igbo. But only through considerable force and stretching can his terminology be accorded with the terminology and meaning from anywhere near the area of modern Nigeria that can be identified with the home Equiano claims to remember. Far more important is recognition of what Equiano may be doing with such terminology, what work he may be attempting to make it do for the shaping of his story.
16. See James W. Fernandez, "Afterword," 217–218, and Philip M. Peek, Introduction, 2, in Peek, ed., *African Divination Systems*..
17. This qualification is important because below (chap. 7) I offer an argument that Equiano also winked and nodded at blacks with whom he was in solidarity.

18. See Taussig, *Mimesis*, re: mimetic surplus/excess, 207–08, 254–55.
19. See Carretta, *Olaudah Equiano*, his note #38, re: providence. As good a summary statement as can be found on the topic, without a fall into hopeless theological thickets.
20. Precisely what Thomas Jefferson, in his *Notes on the State of Virginia*, ed. with an Introduction and Notes by Frank Shuffelton (New York: Penguin Books, 1999 [1785]) (Query 14), and so many other white dominants had argued or assumed blacks could not share. The assumption about such a difference was, among others, advanced as explanation or justification for the plight of blacks. See also Eze, ed., *Race and Enlightenment*,, especially. re: views of Hume, Kant, Hegel.
21. Although one should remain open to the possibility that during his travels Equiano had met figures in Britain or elsewhere who may have functioned similarly to the figures he describes in his story. The latter may be a fusion of images from several sources—contemporary human or textual.
22. See re: ludics and culture-making, in Huizinga, *Homo Ludens*.
23. It is very much worth the reader's effort to refer to the works of J. Z. Smith in *Drudgery Divine: On the Comparison of Early Christianities and the Religions of Late Antiquity* (Chicago: University of Chicago Press, 1990), chaps. I, II; David Chidester, *Savage Systems: Colonialism and Comparative Religion in Southern Africa* (Charlottesville: University of Virginia Press, 1996), chaps 5, 6; and Jean and John Comaroff, *Of Revolution and Revolution: Christianity, Colonialism, and Consciousness in South Africa, Vol. 1* (Chicago: University of Chicago Press, 1991), chap 6, on matters having to do with presumptions and politics of comparison in connection with religion.
24. See Galit Hasan-Rokem and David Shulman, eds., *Untying the Knot* (New York: Oxford University Press, 1996), esp. General and Theoretical section.
25. See Jack Goody, *The Power of the Written Tradition* (Washington, DC: Smithsonian Institution Press, 2000), a summary of much of his research and arguments; *A History of Reading in the West*, ed. Guglielmo Cavallo and Roger Chartier (Amherst: University of Massachusetts Press, 1999 [1995]) for broad view of Western European and North American history; Jonathan Boyarin, ed., *Ethnography of Reading* (Berkeley: University of California Press, 1993), for cross-cultural collection of essays; Karin Littau, *Theories of Reading: Books, Bodies and Bibliomania* (Malden, MA: Polity Press, 2006), for a provocative critical analytical discussion; Cathy N. Davidson, ed., *Reading in America: Literature and Social History* (Baltimore: Johns Hopkins University Press, 1989), for collection of essays with good critical focus on the United States; Smith, *Politics of Language*, with focus on late eighteenth- and early nineteenth-century Britain; John Locke, *Some Thoughts Concerning Education*, ed. with an Introduction, Notes, and Critical Apparatus by John W. and Jean S. Yolton (Oxford: Clarendon Press, 1989), as classic and enormously influential text,

setting the tone and orientation in Anglo-American educational politics and politics; Janet Duitsman Cornelius, "*When I Can Read My Title Clear*": *Literacy, Slavery, and Religion in the Antebellum South* (Charleston: University of South Carolina Press, 1991); and Alan Cole, *Text as Father: Paternal Seductions in Early Mahayana Buddhist Literature* (Berkeley: University of California Press, 2005), for history of religions/culture perspective, with focus on Indian and Chinese Buddhist traditions.

26. On the matter of nationalization and religious statements, see William R. Hutchison and Hartmut Lehrmann, eds., *Many are Chosen: Divine Election and Western Nationalism*, Harvard Theological Studies, (Minneapolis: Fortress Press, 1994); and Heniz Schilling, *Early Modern European Civilization and Its Political and Cultural Dynamism* (Hanover and London: University Press of New England, 2008).

27. This phenomenon of cooptation is obviously a part of the entire span of the history of Western Christianity. The point here is the need to make such a phenomenon less obvious and natural. See, re: early modern Britain in particular, Linda Colley, *Britons: Forging the Nation, 1707–1837* (New Haven: Yale University Press, 1992), chap. 1; re: pan-European practices see Colin Kidd, *The Forging of Races: Race and Scripture in the Protestant Atlantic World, 1600–2000* (Cambridge: Cambridge University Press, 2006), chaps. 3 and 4; and re: how the patterns and practices continued in European empires, see Chidester, *Savage Systems*, chap. 2; J. and J. Comaroff, *Of Revelation and Revolution*, vol. 1, chap. 2 ("British Beginnings").

28. I think the most useful distinction here is that between the sensibilities and politics of the civilizations of the transcendental/"world religions" and that of local traditions. See re: the transcendental religions as civilizations: Tomoko Matsuzawa, *The Invention of World Religions*, Or, How European Universalism Was Preserved in the Language of Pluralism (Chicago: University of Chicago Press, 2005); Jennifer I. M. Reid, ed., *Religion and Global Culture: New Terrain in the Study of Religion and the Work of Charles H. Long* (Lanham, MD: Lexington Books, 2003); Mark Juergensmeyer, ed., *Global Religions: An Introduction* (New York: Oxford University Press, 2003); Sheldon Pollock, *The Language of the Gods in the World of Men: Sanskrit, Culture, and Power in Premodern India* (Berkeley: University of California Press, 2006); S. N. Eisenstadt, ed., *Origins and Diversity of Axial Age Civilizations* (Albany: SUNY Press, 1986); S. N. Eisenstadt and B. Wittrock, eds., *Axial Civilizations and World History* (Leiden/Boston: Brill, 2005); and with a slightly different (more apologetic) perspective, Karen Armstrong, *The Great Transformation: The Beginning of our Religious Traditions* (New York: Alfred A. Knopf, 2006). For perspective on the nonglobal traditions, see Jacob Olupona, ed., *Beyond Primitivism: Indigenous Religious Tradition and Modernity* (New York: Routledge, 2004); *Indigenous Knowledges in Global Contexts: Multiple Readings of Our World,*

ed. George J. Sefa Dei, et al. (Toronto: University of Toronto Press, 2000); *Modes of Thought: Explorations in Culture and Cognition*, ed. David R. Olson and Nancy Torrance (Cambridge: Cambridge University Press, 1996); and Michael Taussig, *Shamanism, Colonialism, and the Wild Man: A Study in Terror and Healing* (Chicago: University of Chicago Press, 1987), among many others.

29. See discussion in Smith, *Politics of Language*; also a fascinating and very compelling argument is in Richard Bauman and Charles L. Briggs, *Voices of Modernity: Language Ideologies and the Politics of Inequality* (Cambridge: Cambridge University Press, 2003).
30. Pierre Levy, *Collective Intelligence: Mankind's Emerging World in Cyberspace*, trans. Robert Bonino (Cambridge, MA: Perseus Books, 1997).
31. Levy, Collective Intelligence, 49–50.
32. Yuri M. Lotman, *Universe of the Mind: A Semiotic Theory of Culture* (London/New York: I. B. Taurus Publishers, 2001), 3.
33. Lotman, *Universe*, 2.
34. Ibid.
35. The expansion of the concept of the semiosphere, with attention to the politics of language, will be taken up in later chapters.
36. See Bauman and Briggs, *Voices of Modernity*, for historical-cultural background and critical analytical discussion re: the politics of language use.
37. See Mary Louise Pratt, *Imperial Eyes: Travel Writing and Transculturation* (New York: Routledge, 2008 [1992]); and *Apocalypse in the Andes: Contact Zones and the Struggle for Interpretive Power* (Washington, DC: IDB Cultural Center, 1996); and Taussig, *Mimesis*, re: white/colonial travel, seeing, recording, and interpreting others.
38. Note that this expression occurs in the context of the talking book story, with emphasis on the practice that characterized true membership in the British world. The quest for origins reflected here is fully implicated in the turn to the modern.
39. The term that occurs in this context is "magicians," another label, along with "doctors," "physicians," and "priests," to refer to those figures of power in the homeland culture. The term "magic," it is important to understand, occurs in subsequent chapters and is used there to refer *only* to "white men" and their practices. The point here is that the Igbo and British worlds are in Equiano's mind collapsed: they share practices and orientation—"superstition" (Igbo) and "magic" (British). More about this subject in later chapters.
40. Perhaps, at the level of comparative cultures, it can be said that he held somewhat romantic if not nostalgic views about his homeland. But his story was clearly not focused on this imagined situation. He made use of such for narratological purposes.
41. Sidbury, *Becoming African in America*, 44–54.

42. On the concept of reading formation, see Tony Bennett, "Texts, Readers, Reading Formations, *MMLA* 16.1 (Spring 1983), 1–17; and "Texts in History: The Determinations of Readings and Their Texts," *MMLA* 18.1 (Fall 1985), 1–16.

CHAPTER 2

1. See Matsuzawa, *The Invention of World Religions* David Chidester, *Savage Systems* Charles H. Long, *Significations* Jean and John Comaroff, *Of Revolution and Revolution* for some of the most theoretically sophisticated and provocative discussions re: the historical permutations and problematics of the category "religion" in the modern world.
2. See Sheldon Pollock, *The Language of the Gods in the World of Men: Sanskrit, Culture, and Power in Premodern India* (Berkeley: University of California Press, 2006); and John F. Sawyer, *Sacred Languages and Sacred Texts* (New York: Routledge, 1999).
3. See John K.Thornton, *Africa and Africans in the Making of the Atlantic World, 1400–1800* (Cambridge: Cambridge University Press, 1996), Pt. I, esp. chaps. 3 and 4.
4. See William R. Hutchison and Hartmut Lehrmann, eds., *Many Are Chosen: Divine Election and Western Nationalism,* Harvard Theological Studies (Minneapolis: Fortress Press, 1994); Heniz Schilling, *Early Modern European Civilization and Its Political and Cultural Dynamism* (Hanover and London: University Press of New England, 2008); and *Konfessionalisierung und Staatsinteressen: internantionale Beziehungen, 1559–1660* (Paderborn: Schoeningh, 2007).
5. Schilling, *Early Modern European Civilization,* chap II.
6. See references to Pietz and others, above (chapter 1, note #28). See Aravamudan, *Tropicopolitans,* 271–283, with Equiano as part of the theorizing.
7. See Pollock, *Language of the Gods,* Part 2, re: general patterns in South Asia.
8. I note here the fascinating argument offered by Helen Thomas, *Romanticism and Slave Narratives: Transatlantic Testimonies* (Cambridge: Cambridge University Press, 2000 [2001]), re: the romantic sensibilities of Equiano and other ex-slaves that are reflected in their writings as the "discourse of the spirit." According to Thomas this focus, "initiated" (?) by dissenting Protestant traditions, "facilitated the slaves' entry into the dominant literary order... otherwise obstructed... [it] identified the role of the slave in the black diaspora as sanctioned by a spiritual entity whose power was considered both impregnable and absolute.... [It] also enabled a form of cultural exchange between Christian and African belief systems.... "(7)

   There is some complementarity between Thomas's argument and the arguments associated with some other scholars—notably Mechal Sobel,

Trabelin' On and Jerome Murphy, *Working the Spirit: Ceremonies of the African Diaspora* (Boston: Beacon Press, 1994); and Thornton, *African and Africans*, chap 9.

As compelling as is this focus on the spirit in analyzing the African diaspora, I am skeptical about whether it has been made sufficiently complex and tensive as a concept to help explain what Equiano and other persons of the black Atlantic world thought and practiced. As provocative as it appears to be—especially insofar as it, at least in Thomas's work, ties subjectivity to language use—the argument falls too quickly into the recourse to spirit as vague explanation, without the deconstructive and self-reflexive thinking required to handle such a freighted concept, and threatens to explain away or not account enough for black agency and its ascetics. No one has done this work to my satisfaction, but I do like what Houston A. Baker was trying to do in his works: *Workings of the Spirit: The Poetics of Afro-American Women's Writing* (Chicago: University of Chicago Press, 1991); *Afro-American Poetics: Revisions of Harlem and the Black Aesthetic* (Madison: University of Wisconsin Press, 1988); *Modernism and the Harlem Renaisssance* (Chicago: University of Chicago Press, 1987); and *Blues, Ideology*.

9. About the general concept of the center, see Rudolf Arnheim, *Power of the Center: A Study of Composition in the Visual Arts* (Berkeley: University of California Press, 2009 [1982]); and with specific reference to early modern Europe, see Anthony Grafton, *New Worlds, Ancient Texts: The Power of Tradition and the Shock of Discovery* (Cambridge: Harvard University Press, 1992). About Grafton's arguments, more below in chapter 3.
10. See comprehensive but also rather thrilling and compelling narration—openly and honestly in solidarity with nonelites—of the history of events and characters, racialist arguments and sentiments of the period, forms of violence and resistance in this period in Peter Linebaugh and Marcus Rediker, *The Many-Headed Hydra: Sailors, Slaves, Commoners, and the Hidden History of the Revolutionary Atlantic* (Boston: Beacon Press, 2000) The book includes discussion about the development of this biblical concept and others like it and what they mean in the discourses of the dominant Europeans.
11. Linebaugh and Rediker, *Many-Headed Hydra*, 4.
12. In the discussion about these matters I am following Linebaugh and Rediker, esp. chaps. 2 and 3.
13. See Burke's *Reflections on the Revolution in France* (1790), para. 133. And see Thomas Paine's response in his *The Rights of Man* (1791).
14. There is much literature on color symbolization. I highly recommend Michael Pastoreau, *Black: History of a Color* (Princeton: Princeton University Press, 1999), a wide-ranging, very creative, multidisciplinary discussion.
15. Linebaugh and Rediker, 99. *Pilgrim's Progress*, Part One, Sect. IX.

16. Linebaugh and Rediker, 99. *Pilgrim's Progress*, Part Two, Sect. IX.
17. Ibid.
18. Ibid.
19. Linebaugh and Rediker on Bunyan: "[He] associates the African with the activities of the Ranters, or of his own youth...here Bunyan blames the victim". (99).
20. See edition by Roger Hayden, 3d ed. (Bristol: Bristol Record Society, 1974). According to Linebaugh and Rediker, the records were published first by E. D. Underhill in 1847. A second edition was published in 1865 by Nathaniel Haycroft, who, it is important to note, preserved much of the original orthography, paragraph divisions, capitalizations, and emphases. The preservation of the latter is especially important for interpretation. Linebaugh and Rediker include the entire passage that concerns sister Francis on pp. 73–74.
21. See the moving novel by Sherley Anne Williams, *Dessa Rose* (New York: Harper Perennial, 1999 [1986]), re: similar situation faced by black female. The protagonist, a fiercely courageous slave woman who had been part of a slave revolt that resulted in the killing of several white men, escapes but is captured. Her execution is delayed on account of her pregnancy. While waiting, she is interviewed by (the significantly named) Adam Nehemiah. Much poignancy turns around Nehemiah's interview questions and writing of a "record" of her testimony. Ultimately, who inscribes whom?
22. Linebaugh and Rediker, 74. Bold emphasis in text source.
23. Linebaugh and Rediker, 73. It is thought that founder Dorothy Hazzard was an oral source.
24. And perhaps in a strange ironic twist also, if not more so, within this self-styled radical evangelical circle, striving in Terrill's time to become somewhat "mainline."
25. This interest in the use of scriptures among the likes of Francis is of course what explains my focus on Equiano. It is the historical development of that use that has led me to commit to the writing of a second volume.
26. See Peter Fryer, *Staying Power: Black People in Britain since 1504* (Atlantic Highlands, NJ: Humanities Press, 1984), for a comprehensive treatment.
27. See Hume, in Eze, ed., *Race and Enlightenment*, 33.
28. See Kant, in Eze, ed., *Race and Enlightenment*, 39–48.
29. See his *Notes on the State of Virginia*, ed. with an introduction and notes by Frank Shuffelton (New York: Penguin Books, 1999 [1785]), "Query IV," 146–151.
30. Gates Jr., *Signifying Monkey* (New York: Oxford University Press, 1988), is still considered the most definitive literary-critical study of the use of the "talking book" story among the earliest black Atlantic writers. See chap. 4, esp. the useful table on p. 168.

31. Perhaps, with the assistance of Equiano. Equiano seems to be the better and more confident writer. The two may have discussed their two projects as different genre types, different strategies with similar purposes.
32. Quobna Ottobah Cugoano, *Thoughts and Sentiments on the Evil of Slavery*, ed. with Intro. and Notes by Vincent Carretta (New York: Penguin Books, [1787] 1999) 63–64.
33. (London: Miles Flesher, 1688). Spanish edition is El Ynca Gracilasso de la Vega, *Historia General del Peru* (Cordoba, 1617).
34. Gates, *Signifying Monkey*, 150–152.
35. So according to Sterling Lacater Bland, *Voices of the Fugitives: Runaway Slave Stories and Their Fictions of Self-Creation* (Westport, CT: Praeger Publishers, 2000).
36. See Carretta, *Equiano*, chap. 12, esp. pp. 28–94, regarding the phenomenon of the stranger as Equiano understood and made use of the concept. And, of course, Julia Kristeva's masterful work, *Stranger to Ourselves*, trans. Leon S. Roudiez (New York: Columbia University Press, 1991), provides wider critical and historical perspective. Although Kristeva does not reference Equiano's work, she does address the phenomenon in a broad sweep—from ancient Greek and Roman history through modern Europe.
37. See on this matter the ferocious and compelling argument about the wider, more complex world of black diaspora discourse and communications in Grey Gundaker, *Signs of Diaspora, Diaspora of Signs: Literacies, Creolization, and Vernacular Practice in African America*. The Commonwealth Center Studies in American Culture (New York: Oxford University Press, 1998), chap 1.
38. No matter—the point is that white men's magic is found in books of all kinds; the Bible has become what it is—in culture—literally on account of the fact that it is scriptural, words constituting a book.
39. See Gates's comparative discussion, *Signifying Monkey*, chap. 4, esp. pp 129–169.
40. This perspective notwithstanding, questions are now being raised—most notably by V. Carretta, *Equiano the African*, chap. 1—regarding Equiano's birthplace. That Equiano may not have been born in Africa does not affect the argument I make in this book.
41. See Jack Goody, *The Power of the Written Tradition* (Washington, DC: Smithsonian Institution Press, 2000); Walter Ong, *Interfaces of the Word: Studies in the Evolution of Consciousness and Culture* (Ithaca, NY: Cornell University Press, 1977); and Ong, *Orality and Literacy: the Technologizing of the Word* (London and New York: Methuen, 1982), for critical perspectives.
42. See here the literature on the interactions among blacks and whites in the eighteenth- century abolitionist-reform movements: Linebaugh and Rediker, *Many-Headed Hydra*; Adam Hochschild, *Bury the Chains: Prophets and Rebels in the Fight to Free an Empire's Slaves* (New York: Houghton Mifflin Company/

Mariner Books, 2005); Simon Schama, *Rough Crossings: Britain, the Slaves and the American Revolution* (New York: HarperCollins, 2006); and Iain McCalman, *Radical Underworld: Prophets, Revolutionaries and Pornographers in London, 1795–1840* (Cambridge: Cambridge University Press, 1988).

43. So Gates, *Signifying Monkey*, 129–132. But on this point see Grey Gundaker's more nuanced and convincing argument, *Signs of Diaspora*, 102–109, regarding the tradition of nonreading, even when there was evidence of "conventional" literacy skills among peoples of the African diaspora.
44. Throughout most of the narrative the young Equiano is really narratologically bracketed, backgrounded; the reader clearly gets the voice of the mature Equiano. But in the story about talking books the sentiments of the youthful and mature Equiano are curiously both evident. I think there was more at issue here than the nature of the source, about which see Gates, *Signifying Monkey*, 152–158. At any rate, I suspect the confusion reflects the import of the story as lynchpin for the narrative.
45. Note again Gundaker, *Signs of Diaspora*, chaps. 1, 4, and 6, regarding the truth about different types of literacies. I think this may help explain the several different construals of the talking book story within and beyond the African diaspora.
46. In addition to the non-talking-book story in his chap. 3, the reader should note the instances in which Equiano depicts other peoples as "strangers" to whom the book is silent, in his chap. 11. Of course, in these episodes he depicts himself as one to whom the books speak, indeed, as one who is in command. About this more in later chapters.
47. See Gates, *Signifying Monkey*, 130, 167; Jefferson, *Notes on Virginia*, Q#14.
48. See Long's discussion re: "hardness of life," "oppugnancy," "lithic existence," in *Significations*, 177–178, 197, in particular reference to blacks in North Atlantic diaspora, but as usual with Long, with wide reverberations and implications.

CHAPTER 3

1. With April Shelford and Nancy Sirasi (Cambridge: Belknap Press of Harvard University Press, 1992). The book was commissioned by the New York Public Library in connection with an exhibition intended, according to president Timothy Healy, to "trace the transforming effects of the voyages of exploration upon European scholarship, learning, and culture from 1450 to 1700" (Foreword, vii). It was also a celebration of the magnificent holdings of the NYPL—as conservator and fierce upholder of such a legacy. About such matters in general more below.
2. Grafton, *New Worlds*, Introd., esp. p 2, chap. 1, and Epilogue.
3. Grafton, *New Worlds*, 2–3.
4. Grafton, *New Worlds*,, 7.
5. Ibid.

6. Ibid., 10.
7. Ibid., 16.
8. Ibid., 28–35, 197–205, 212–217; see also Grafton's *Bring Out Your Dead: The Past as Revelation* (Cambridge: Harvard University Press, 2001), especially II: 5, 6, for more detailed analysis re: humanism.
9. Grafton, *New Worlds*, 58.
10. See Michael T. Ryan, "Assimilating New Worlds in the Sixteenth and Seventeenth Centuries," in *Comparative Studies in Society and History*, vol. 23, no. 4 (October 1981): 519–538. See esp. pp. 530, 532, 536.
11. Ryan, "Assimilating," 536. Really? No other possibility?
12. Ryan, "Assimilating," 524; cf. Charles Webster, *The Great Instauration: Science, Medicine, and Reform*, 1626–1660 (New York: Holmes & Meier Publishers, 1976), for background information.
13. Ryan, "Assimilating," 525.
14. Yet I am not sure I could detect a sense of the paradox in Ryan's work. Note pp. 526–529, 532, 536. See his reference, p. 526, note #18, to Peter Martyr, __*De novo orbe*, or the Histories of the West Indies (1612), as example.
15. Ryan, "Assimilating," 534.
16. Ryan, "Assimilating," 535–36. See the interest in making the British heirs of Noah in John Bale, *Scriptorium illustrium Brtyannie quam nun & Scotiam vocant* (Basel, 1557).
17. The exceptions being those—Chinese and Indians—who had what was perceived to be noble literary traditions, scripts, books that could be seen as comparable to western classic texts and scriptures. The new peoples in the modern era were sometimes seen as exotics whose traditions, especially any literary or book traditions, were canonized, made to assume the status of European literary traditions. Ryan, "Assimilating," 533.
18. This was the case also with the works of travelers and missionaries. See Ryan, "Assimilating," and Mary Louise Pratt, *Imperial Eyes*, for critical pertinent discussion of sources.
19. Ryan, "Assimilating," 536–537.
20. Of course, Protestants and Catholics have been known to hurl the charge of pagan as weapon against each other. Cf. here J. Z. Smith about how such politics and sentiments have worked themselves into the operations—with focus on Protestants—of modern biblical scholarship. Also note the work of Susanna Heschel, *Aryan Jesus: Christian Theologies and the Bible in Nazi Germany* (Princeton: Princeton University Press, 2008), re: biblical scholarship and ramifications for relations with Jews.
21. Ryan, "Assimilating," 538.
22. His chapter 1 is not surprisingly more heavily footnoted than any other chapter. But throughout the narrative it is clear that Equiano is in conversation with popular and elite writers.

23. See Vincent Carretta, *Equiano the African*, 325–327, re some specific sources Equiano drew on.
24. See James Sidbury, *Becoming African in America*, chaps. 1 and 2, esp..pp. 44–65.
25. Again, this view of one of the practices of dominance, like Sherley Williams's *Dessa Rose* is poignant and instructive: Equiano depicts himself in writing, and writing the way he did, in imitation of whites, doing what white dominants did as a matter of course. He facilitated their confrontation with themselves by setting up the possibility of a kind of therapeutic defamiliarization.
26. Getting at this judgment seems to me to have been what Krister Stendahl was probing in his essay "The Bible as a Classic," *JBL* 103, no.1 (1984): 3–10". I do not think he resolved matters, but he opened a larger window for ongoing critical analysis.
27. See Joshua 9:23 (King James Version).
28. Christopher Hill, *The English Bible and the Seventeenth Century Revolution* (New York: Allen Lane/The Penguin Press, 1993), 413–435.
29. See discussion earlier in chapter 2.
30. See a fascinating discussion about the movements in Iain McCalman, *Radical Underground*, esp. the "Millenarian Spenceans" in I.3. Also note specific reference to Equiano, "the black," on p. 69, in the context of discussion about Robert Wedderburn as (half-) black West Indian "millenarian radical." The illustration (#22) on p. 212, with its depiction of undergrounds of (mis-)-readers, signifies on the bounded world that Grafton describes. The illustration is taken from H. S. Ashbee, Index *librorum prohibitorum* (1877). See also the Jacobin W. H. Reid, *Rise and Dissolution of the Infidel Societies in this Metropolis* (1800), who depicted the dynamisms of the tavern debating clubs.
31. See Miichael Taussig's fierce defense of constructionism in *Mimesis and Alterity: A Particular History of the Senses* (New York: Routledge, 1993), xii-xv, xvii, 70–71, 252, 255.
32. I am here playing with originary meaning of text, from Latin *textus*, "tissue"; *texere*, "to weave." Cf. *Oxford English Dictionary; Merriam-Webster Dictionary*.
33. This story, like all layered stories, can be used to illustrate more than one point or moral. It will discussed again in the next chapter.
34. Here he is quoting John 5:39.
35. Cf. 2 Corinthians 6:17.
36. I want to stress here that although Equiano was aptly reading and translating the sentiments and prejudices of the British, it is important that we not accept those views: a Catholic country should not be assumed to be uninfluenced by scriptures or, more important, for my argument in this book, scripturalization, more than a Protestant one. In point of fact, the former may represent a deeper strain of the phenomenon. The authority that priests arrogate to themselves to interpret the Bible for the laity does not suggest that

the Bible is less important among Catholics than it is in Protestant land. Also, that Protestants claim—with mixed success, everyone knows—that all can read the Bible for themselves does not mean it is therefore taken more seriously. What we are confronted with is differences in orientation to the actual engagement of the text. At any rate, what is most important is that, in regard to the power structure and relationship that is scripturalization, there is no difference. Both types of societies were built around the structure of relations of scripturalization.

37. The categories changed throughout Equiano's story and as much as if not more so throughout history going forward from Equiano's time, from the point of contact to the present moment, in which the 2010 U.S. census form includes a puzzling number of options—including "Negro"!—for persons of African descent to check off. This situation indicates the continuation of the challenges of the self-creation, self-naming project that burdens black peoples in the North Atlantic worlds.
38. Benedict Anderson, *Imagined Communities: Reflections on the Origin and Spread of Nationalism* (London: Verso, 1983).
39. Sheldon Pollock, *The Language of the Gods in the World of Men: Sanskrit, Culture, and Power in Premodern India* (Berkeley: University of California Press, 2006), Introduction.
40. Pierre Levy, *Collective Intelligence: Mankind's Emerging World in Cyberspace*, trans. Robert Bonino (Cambridge, MA: Perseus Books, 1997), 209–220.
41. This is the assumption or argument of almost all histories of the period. Cf. B. Anderson, *Imagined Communities*, on this point. He feels no need to argue the point.
42. Bhabha, *Location of Culture*, 236–256. From a different perspective—anthropology—on difference in perspective, see Faye E. Harrison, *Outsider Within: Reworking Anthropology in the Global Age* (Urbana and Chicago: University of Illinois Press, 2008).
43. See Levy's *Cyberculture*, trans. Robert Bonino (Minneapolis: University of Minnesota Press, 2001), chap. 6, for critical perspective on concepts of totality—or universal without such.
44. "Musquito" here being a corruption of "Miskito"/"Mosquito," a people located in the region of what is presently eastern Nicaragua and northeastern Honduras. The area was a British protectorate from 1655 to 1860; later it became known as Mosquito Kingdom. Nicaragua appropriated the kingdom in 1894. The northern part of the kingdom was awarded by the International Court of Justice to Honduras. The area had had a complex relationship to Jamaica as part of the slave trade. But note also the all too easy but poignant use of term "Indian." Why are there "Indians" in that part of the world? The history of the violence of renaming as part of the history of dominance tells the story.

45. See the comparative critical collection of essays, *Asceticism*, ed. Vincent L.Wimbush and Richard Valantasis (New York: Oxford University Press, 1995), about ascetic piety as cross-cultural dimension of religious life.
46. From earlier eds. 1–8. See Carretta, ed. *Olaudah Equiano*, note #578.
47. See my discussion above in chapter 1.
48. Of course, in this complex situation it was ironically the "Indians" who were made to represent the basic carriers of magic.
49. Re: Hurston, the expression is found in her *Mules and Men*, 218; and re: Marrouchi, the expression is from the title of his book, *Signifying with a Vengeance: Theories, Literatures, Storytellers* (Albany: SUNY Press, 2002).
50. Here I think of John Thornton's argument in *Africa and Africans in the Making of the Atlantic World, 1400–1800*, chap. 9, re: the provocative argument and challenge that continuities between African and European sensibilities in relationship to revelation is worth exploring.
51. Luke has historically been read as the story that privileges the poor, women, and the outcast of society.
52. That the issue of slavery in this context is not taken on directly by Equiano is a sign of his cleverness and sense of the strategic moment.
53. Note Houston Baker's argument in *Blues, Ideology, and Afro-American Literature*, 31, 35, re: Equiano's economic interest and strategy.
54. This term would seem to refer to ethnic background or (past and present) status in terms of enslavement/freedom.
55. See Cugoano's reference, at the end of his *Thoughts and Sentiments on the Evil of Slavery*, ed. with Intro. and Notes by Vincent Carretta (New York: Penguin Books, [1787] 1999), regarding plans to found a school for Africans.
56. Luke 10:37.
57. Might he not have thought, as Frederick Douglass thought and reported, that his paranoid master thought that "if you give a nigger an inch, he will take an ell"? See *Narrative of the Life of Frederick Douglass, An American Slave* in *Oxford Frederick Douglass Reader*, ed. William A. Andrews (New York: Oxford University Press, 1996), 48.
58. The first story is in Equiano's chap. 3, the second is the incident regarding the Musquito Indians, in Equinao's chap. 11.
59. See Carretta, ed. *Olaudah Equiano*, appendices, for the letters. I am in this chapter doing no more than making the case for the importance of the existence of Equiano's correspondence as a reflection of the recognition of his participation and influence in contemporary debates. Discussion of some substantive themes will follow in subsequent chapters.

CHAPTER 4

1. Linda Colley, *Britons: Forging the Nation, 1707–1837* (New Haven: Yale University Press, 1992). See also Carla Gardina Pestana, *Protestant Empire: Religion and the*

Making of the British Atlantic World (Philadelphia: University of Pennsylvania Press, 2009).

2. See again William R. Hutchison and Hartmut Lehrmann, eds., *Many are Chosen*. See Introduction and chap. 1, by A. F. Walls, with response by W. R. Ward, re: Great Britain for discussion of issues most pertinent to Equiano's world.
3. Here I have in mind new vernacular translations. See on this point Sheldon Pollock, *The Language of the Gods in the World of Men*, re: Europe, for a comprehensive discussion of many of the relevant issues.
4. The concept was introduced above in chapter 2.
5. Heinz Schilling, *Early Modern European Civilization and Its Political and Cultural Dynamism* (Hanover and London: University Press of New England, 2008), 17–22. Different but not pure types of nationalizations have been isolated and made the focus of nationalist histories and histories of nationalization. Schilling's bibliography is worth consulting.
6. Literature by and on Foucault is voluminous, and there is no single place where power is discussed. I recommend beginning with Colin Gordon, ed., and trans., *Power/Knowledge: Selected Interviews and Other Writings, 1972–1977/ Michel Foucault* (New York: Pantheon Books, 1980), a basis for going forward with Foucault and other theorists. And now, of course, as cited earlier, Michael Mann, *Sources of Social Power*. Vol. 1 (New York: Cambridge University Press, 1986), chaps. 9 and 10.
7. For comprehensive historical background, see Keith Thomas, *Religion and the Decline of Magic* (New York: Scribner, 1971).
8. See S. N. Eisenstadt, ed., *Origins and Diversity of Axial Age Civilizations* (SUNY Series in Near Eastern Studies. Albany: SUNY Press, 1986); also Stephen Sharot, *A Comparative Sociology of World Religions: Virtuosos, Priests, and Popular Religion* (New York: New York University Press, 2001), chap. 3.
9. In broad and narrow terms—that is, in terms of sign-ificant/signifying "texts," or in terms of classic and sacred texts.
10. Mann, *Sources of Social Power*, vol 1, chaps. 9 and 10.
11. This concept was introduced above, in chap 1, p.46, note #42.
12. There were radical dissenters (even dissenters from the dissenters), to be sure, but I mean here only to make the argument that the scripture-inflected-confessionalized new nations were not open fields for free interpretation. They were leaner, more efficient ideological regimes in relation to what the late medieval world had come to represent. There was intentionality about making and controlling official and nationalist interpretation of the scriptures—now available in vernacular language—held to be the mirror reflection and defender of the nation. The Protestant mentality is misunderstood if it is assumed to mean that anyone's reading is acceptable. Perhaps to a degree this was true, but it

also meant that there were more readers who could potentially be fitted into and controlled by a reading formation.

13. See on this point Olivia Smith, *The Politics of Language, 1791–1819* esp. chaps. III, VI, especially re: language formation of those that Burke first called the "swinish multitude," but who subsequently—as the journals entitled *Politics for the People or a Salmagundy for Swine* and *Pig's Meat: Lessons for the Swinish Multitude* indicate—took up the moniker with pride and as part of cultural-ideological struggle.
14. See here Christopher Hill, *The English Bible and the Seventeenth Century Revolution*, esp. III. 10, 11.
15. Schilling, *Early Modern European Civilization*, 21–22, 74.
16. The actual passage, already identified above, is in John 5:39: "Search the scriptures; for in them ye think ye have eternal life: and they are they which testify of me." These are recorded as the words of Jesus; they were not, as is obvious, originally directed to the British people, of the eighteenth or any other century. Nevertheless, a nationalist orientation would make possible, if not necessary, a reading that identifies addressees as British. Equiano arrogates to himself the right to exegete the scriptures on British nationalist terms.
17. Cf. 2 Tim 4:14–15. Most interesting here is Equiano's effort to compare himself to the apostle Paul, at least that Paul imaged in the part of the tradition that includes the source from which the allusion to Alexander the coppersmith was taken, one of the pastoral letters of Timothy. According to early Christian tradition, Paul was indeed hounded and persecuted by many, including fellow Jews and Jesus-believers who would from a distance be seen to have much affinity with him. The source to which Equiano points for evidence of this part of tradition is very poignant if not somewhat ironic, because that part of the Pauline tradition whence the passage comes represents for many interpreters a reflection of an ancient world form of petit bourgeoise conservatism or certainly gestures toward accommodation to empire—in this case, the Roman empire. That late ancient Mediterranean and medieval and early modern societies in Europe would draw upon these texts to consolidate and legitimize traditional power arrangements should not surprise. It has been argued and firmly held by many that "Paul" (a creation to voice the sentiments of the wings of the Pauline "school") taught that in light of the last days of the world and in order to win converts, the authorities were to be accommodated or tolerated and an ethical code of urban bourgeoise respectability was enjoined. Long after the expectation of the imminence of the end had receded, the orientation to accommodation obtained and in fact in each era was reinscribed even more intensely.
18. See Carretta, ed., *Olaudah Equiano*, note #660 re: the act of 1788; and The Consolidated Slave Act of Jamaica, March 2, 1792.
19. For helpful and challenging perspectives, see Elisabeth Schuessler Fiorenza, *Bread Not Stone: The Challege of Feminist Biblical Interpretation* (Boston:

Beacon Press, 1995); *In Memory of Her: A Feminist Theological Reconstruction of Christian Origins* (New York: Crossroads, 1983); and *Rhetoric and Ethic: The Politics of Biblical Studies* (Minneapolis: Fortress, 1999). Also Elizabeth Castelli, ed., with the assistance of Rosamond C. Rodman, *Women, Gender, and Religion: a Reader* (New York: Palgrave, 2001); and Littau, *Theories of Reading.*

20. But note that even within socially radical dissenting communities there is evidence that the male prerogatives and power roles reemerge. This can be seen in the example of Edward Terrill's gendered revisionist history of the radical congregation to which he belonged. See discussion earlier in chapter 2.
21. For a helpful perspective, see Pierre Bourdieu, trans. Richard Nice, *Outline of a Theory of Practice* (Cambridge: Cambridge University Press, 1977), esp. pp. 159–171. And the missiological and anthropological literatures—beyond Equiano's own narrative—provide plenty of evidence regarding cultural outsiders. See Thornton, *Africa and Africans in the Making of the Atlantic World, 1400–1800*; Jean and John Comaroff, *Of Revolution and Revolution* and Chidester, *Savage Systems,* re: the clash of epistemologies on the European mission field. And note listing and discussion of pertinent primary sources.
22. This would square with the early modern development of confessionalization and nationalization: the agreement among European nations no longer to war against each other over religious differences was at the same time an agreement to banish religious life and sentiment to the private, nonpolitical sphere.

CHAPTER 5

1. For a sense of the wide-ranging overlapping discourses, fields, methods, orientations, and approaches among publications of the last twenty years or so that are pertinent see: Eileen Razzari Elrod, *Piety and Dissent: Race, Gender, and Biblical Rhetoric in Early American Autobiography* (Amherst, MA: University of Massachusetts Press, 2008); Christine Levecq, *Slavery and Sentiment: the Politics of Feeling in Black Atlantic Antislavery Writing, 1770–1850* (Lebanon: University of New Hampshire Press, 2008); Adetayo Alabi, *Telling Our Stories: Continuities and Divergences in Black Autobiographies* (New York: Palgrave MacMillan, 2005); Helena Woodward, *African-British Writings in the Eighteenth Century: The Politics of Race and Reason* (Westport, CT: Greenwood Press, 1999); Gauri Viswanathan, *Outside the Fold: Conversion, Modernity, and Belief* (Princeton: Princeton University Press, 1998); Henry Louis Gates, Jr., and William L. Andrews, eds., *Pioneers of the Black Atlantic: Five Slave Narratives from the Enlightenment, 1772–1815* (Washington, DC: Civitas, 1998); Adam Potkay and Sandra Burr, eds., *Black Atlantic Writers of the Eighteenth Century: Living the New Exodus in England and the Americas* (New York: St. Martin's Press, 1995). But the reader should take

note of the reliable perspective and arguments (and bibliography) found in the older publication: G. A. Starr, *Defoe and Spiritual Autobiography* (Princeton: Princeton University Press, 1965); and J. Paul Hunter, *The Reluctant Pilgrim: Defoe's Emblematic Method and Quest for Form in Robinson Crusoe* (Baltimore: The Johns Hopkins University Press, 1966).

2. Peter Fryer, *Staying Power,* chaps, 6–8, provides helpful perspective on history of formation and self-help efforts.

3. See Acts 8:26–39.

4. Specifically, black *male* existence in the diaspora. There can be no denial of Equiano's gendered perspective. But we should be reminded of Equiano's registration of sensitivity to the special plight and vulnerability of black females in his story, including his sister. See Francis Smith Foster, *Written By Herself: Literary Production by African American Women, 1746–1892* (Bloomington: Indiana University Press, 1993); Chanta M. Haywood, *Prophesying Daughter: Black Women Preachers and the Word, 1823–1913* (Columbia and London: University of Missouri Press, 2003); and Bettye Collier-Thomas, *Daughters of Thunder: Black Women preachers and their Sermons, 1850–1879* (San Francisco: Jossey-Bass, 1998), as examples of efforts to reclaim voices that had been doubly submerged.

5. See Gay L. Byron, *Symbolic Blackness and Ethnic Difference in Early Christian Literature* (London: Routledge, 2002), for provocative critical discussion and the listing of pertinent literatures re: this figure and the employment of other signs and symbols of blackness in advancement of Christian identity formation.

6. For discussions regarding black Muslims in the African Diaspora see: Behnaz A. Mizrai, et al, *Slavery, Islam and Diaspora* (Trenton, NJ: Africa World Press, Inc., 2009); Michael A. Gomez, *Black Crescent: The Experience and Legacy of African Muslims in the Americas* (New York: Cambridge University Press, 2005); *Exchanging Our Country Marks: The Transformation of African Identities in the Colonial and Antebellum South* (Chapel Hill NC: University of North Carolina Press,1998); Muhammad A. Al-Ahari, ed., *Five Classic Muslim Slave Narratives* (Chicago: Magribine Press, 2006); Ala Alryyes, ed., trans., *A Muslim American Slave: The Life of Omar Ibn Said* (Madison: University of Wisconsin Press, 2011); and Sylviane A. Diouf, *Servants of Allah: African Muslims Enslaved in the Americas* (New York: New York University Press, 1998).

7. According to Webster's Dictionary, this word can be understood as archaic (1656) transitive verb that means "to entrap or lure." This meaning fits Equiano's narrative situation.

8. See Carretta, ed., *Olaudah Equiano,* note # 505.

9. Ecclesiastes 1:9.

10. See on this phenomenon the eye-opening books by: Susan Friend Harding, *The Book of Jerry Falwell: Fundamentalist Language and Politics* (Princeton: Princeton University Press, 2000); and Kathleen C. Boone, *The Bible Tells*

Them So: the Discourse of Protestant Fundamentalism (Albany: SUNY Press, 1989).

11. See *Asceticism*, ed. Wimbush and Valantasis, especially essays by Ware and Wyschogrod, and panel discussion re popular contemporary issues. Also see: Jill Raitt, et al, eds., *Christian Spirituality: High Middle Ages and Reformation.* World Spirituality: An Encyclopedia History of the Religious Quest. Vol 17. (New York: Crossroad, 1987); Jean Delumeau, *Sin and Fear: The Emergence of a Western Guilt Culture: Thirteenth-Eighteenth Centuries*, trans. Eric Nicholson (New York: St. Martin's Press, 1990). It remains to be determined whether and in what respects Equiano was influenced by these developments. It is not obvious that the behavior reflects traditional African practices. It should be kept in mind that Equiano the writer aims to depict his journeying into Christian existence.
12. The real issue that should be raised here has to do with how it is that critical interpretation, not the popular scripted rhetorics of the converted, ever came to assume a dimension or texture so flat that "salvation" would not be understood as encompassing all that Equiano had to negotiate.
13. "Neither is there salvation in any other, for there is no other name under heaven given among men whereby we must be saved, but only Jesus Christ."
14. This position, of course, begs several questions, including the question whether others—individuals, groups, movements, Catholics—were suggesting other ways or avenues for salvation. This could reflect a straw man argument of a sort: in play here, beyond the clamor for safe space for dissent and reform, was Protestant polemic with Catholics, including some legitimate differences and some distortions of Catholic traditions regarding salvation.
15. See *Evangelicalism: Comparative Studies of Popular Protestantism in North America, the British Isles, and Beyond, 1700–1990*, ed. Mark A. Noll et al.. (New York: Oxford University Press, 1994); Susan Friend Harding, *The Book of Jerry Falwell*, chap. 1; David W. Kling, *The Bible in History: How the Texts Have Shaped the Times*, (New York: Oxford University Press, 2004), 305–307.
16. Psalm 19:10.
17. Although I am not a fervent believer in commentaries, some iterations of the genre may sometimes prove helpful, especially for providing information on consensus = canonical views (precisely the issue I have with the genre itself). At any rate, commentaries and critical studies are voluminous. For literary-, rhetorical-, and historical-critical perspectives, including extensive reviews of literature, I recommend Hans Conzelmann, *Acts of the Apostles: A Commentary on the Acts of the Apostles*, trans. James Limburg et al. ed. Eldon Jap Epp, with Christopher R. Matthews. Hermenia Commentary Series. (Philadelphia: Augsburg Fortress, 1987); Ben Witherington, *Acts of the Apostles: A Socio-Rhetorical Commentary* (Grand Rapids, MI: W. B. Eerdmans Publishing Company, 1998); Blount et al., *True to Our Native Land;* (Minneapolis: Fortress

Press, 2007); *Africana Bible: Reading Israel's Scriptures from Africa and the African Diaspora*, ed. Hugh R. Page, Jr., et al. (Minneapolis: Fortress Press, 2009); and Cottrell R. Carson, "'Do You Understand What You Are Reading?' Reading of the Ethiopian Eunuch Story (Acts 8:29–40) from a Site of Cultural Marronage," Ph.D. diss., Union Theological Seminary in the City of New York, 1999.

18. See Byron, *Symbolic Blackness*, and follow her treatment of the literature on this issue.
19. See Ramsay MacMullen, *Enemies of the Roman Order: Treason, Unrest, and Alienation in the Empire* (London: Routledge, 1992 [1966]); Wayne A. Meeks, *First Urban Christians: The Social World of the Apostle Paul* (New Haven: Yale University Press, [1983] 2003; *Origins of Christian Morality: The First Two Centuries* (New Haven: Yale University Press, 1993); G. E. M. de Ste. Croix, *Class Struggle in the Ancient Greek World: From the Archaic Age to the Arab Conquest* (Ithaca, NY: Cornell University Press, 1981); and John H. Kautsky, *Politics of Aristocratic Empires* (Chapel Hill: University of North Carolina Press, 1982).
20. See Byron, *Symbolic Blackness*, chaps 1, 3, 5; and Robert E. Hood, *Begrimed and Black: Christian Traditions on Blacks and Blackness* (Minneapolis: Augsburg Fortress, 1994), chap 3; Vincent L. Wimbush, "Ascetic Behavior and Color-ful Language: Stories About Ethiopian Moses," *Semeia* 58 (Fall 1992): 81–91; Reading Darkness, Reading Scriptures," in *African Americans and the Bible*; "Signifying on Scriptures: An African Diaspora Proposal for Radical Readings," in *Feminist New Testament Studies: Global and Future Perspectives*, ed. Kathleen O. Wicker et al. (New York: Palgrave MacMillan, 2005), for critical treatments and information on primary and secondary literature. Frank M. Snowden, *Before Color Prejudice: The Ancient View* (Cambridge: Harvard University Press, 1983), in a stance that is different from that of most black scholars who have weighed in on these matters, has represented the benign view—that there was little or no (antiblack) color prejudice before the modern period.
21. Re: decontextualization see Bauman and Briggs, *Voices of Modernity, 312.*
22. About this Africanized scriptures, more in chapter 7.
23. See Colin Kidd, *Forging of Races: Race and Scripture in the Protestant Atlantic World, 1600–2000* (Cambridge: Cambridge University Press, 2006); David M. Goldenberg, *Curse of Ham: Race and Slavery in Early Judaism, Christianity, and Islam* (Princeton: Princeton University Press, 2003); Charles B. Copher, *Black Biblical Studies: An Anthology of Charles B. Copher: Biblical and Theological Issues on the Black Presence in the Bible* (Chicago: Black Light Fellowship, 1993); Cain Hope Felder, *Race, Racism, and the Biblical Narratives* (Minneapolis: Fortress Press, 2002).
24. Here I think I am in (ironic) agreement with Snowden (*Before Color Prejudice*, 82):

Greeks and Romans resembled people in general who, according to research on [the cultural orientations governing] color symbolism, have a basic tendency to equate blackness with evil and white with goodness... It was obviously because of a deeply rooted tradition linking blackness with death... dark-skinned peoples... into all ill-omened contexts.

Yes, I am in agreement with him that the sentiments regarding the symbolics of color reflected a "basic tendency" and was "deeply rooted" in the collective minds of nonblack ancient and modern writers. I think these ancients and their modern readers and tradents thought themselves deprovincialized, cosmopolitan thinkers; they most likely did not think themselves to be registering prejudicial statements. They seemed even oblivious to their contributing to toxic interpretive practices around color symbolizations, since these were clearly infected discourses. Such obfuscation or cluelessness on the part of the likes of Snowden, and the likes of Rodney Needham (ed., *Right and Left: Essays on Dual Symbolic Classification* [Chicago: University of Chicago Press, 1973]) makes the formulations and tropes all the more dangerous. See in general support of the way I view these matters: Joseph E. Harris, ed., *Africa and Africans as Seen by Classical Writers: The William Leo Hansberry African History Notebook*, 2 vols (Washington, DC: Howard University Press, 1977); Cheik Anta Diop, *The African Origin of Civilization: Myth or Reality*, trans. Mercer Cook (Westport, CT: Lawrence Hill, 1974); Benjamin Isaac, *The Invention of Racism in Classical Antiquity* (Princeton: Princeton University Press, 2004); *Image of the Black in Western Art*, vol 1–2, 4, (gen.) ed. Ladislas Bugner (Cambridge: Harvard University Press, 1976—); Hood, *Begrimed and Black*; and Byron, *Symbolic Blackness*.

25. See pp 189, 190, 191; and at end of hymn that follows on pp 194–97. The last stanza provides a summarizing and paraphrasing of Acts 4:12:

He dy'd for all who ever saw
No help in them, nor by the law:
I this have seen and gladly own
"Salvation is by Christ alone!"

26. A recontextualization of Isaiah 25:7: "And he will destroy in this mountain the face of the covering cast over all people, and the veil that is spread over the nations." Included in editions 8 and 9.
27. P. 182 is something of an exception, although one can see an affinity: "Notwithstanding all this, the reader may easily discern, if a believer, that I was still in nature's darkness."
28. See the debate between Srinivas Aravamudan and Adam Potkay in the special "Forum: Teaching Equiano's Interesting Narrative" in: *Eighteenth Century Studies* 34.4 (Summer 2001): Potkay, "History, Oratory, and God in Equiano's

Interesting Narrative," 601–614; Aravamudan, "Equiano Lite."*Eighteenth-Century Studies* 34, no. 4 (Summer 2001): 615–619; and Wheeler, Roxann. "Domesticating Equiano's Interesting Narrative." *Eighteenth-Century Studies* 34, no. 4 (Summer 2001):620–624. Wheeler may have positioned herself between the two. This may also have been a part of the interest of Daniel O'Quinn in his essay, "The State of Things: Olauadah Equiano and the Volatile Politics of Heteronomic Desire," in *History of Romantic Sexuality: A Praxis Volume*, ed. Richard C. Sha (Jan. 2006). Online access: www.rc.umd.edu/praxis/sexuality/oquinn/oquinn.html.

29. According to Webster's Dictionary, this spelling is earlier alternative form or spelling of "indict," meaning "accuse," "charge with a fault," and so forth. The earlier form, as transitive verb, carried the meaning "to proclaim," "to give literary or formal expression," and so forth. In Equiano's narrative the two meanings are chillingly con-fused: The "Spirit" both convicts and facilitates expression, articulation.
30. See Titus 1:11, 13, 16b. For more perspective on the ancient world dynamics, see Margaret Y. MacDonald, *The Pauline Churches: A Socio-historical Study of Institutionalization in the Pauline and Deutero-pauline Writings* (New York: Cambridge University Press, 1988).
31. Titus 1:15a.

CHAPTER 6

1. White male is what must be assumed here. Royalty aside, with British socialization, who otherwise would be considered so? Given the means to purchase a sloop and command others to follow him in support of his initiatives, who but a white man can be assumed here? What follows in this episode makes that identity all the more significant.
2. Carretta, ed., *Olaudah Equiano*, note #563 re: Musquito Indians. He quotes Thomas Jefferys (*The West India Atlas* [1794]), who indicates that the British essentially exploited the "Miskito" peoples' hatred for the Spaniards, who had conquered them and had driven their ancestors from their homeland near Lake Nicaragua. The British were opportunists, looking for ways to take advantage of this situation.
3. John Fox (1517–1587) was an English historian and martyrologist. His famous work lauds the courage and faith of martyrs from the first to sixteenth century, with particular focus on the persecutions experienced by the English Protestants of the sixteenth century and their forerunners from the fourteenth century through the reign of Mary I. In the eighteenth century there were many reprints in abridged editions, with woodcut illustrations. See Carretta, ed., *Olaudah Equiano*, note #563. Also William Haller, *Foxe's First Book of Martyrs and the Elect Nation* (London: Jonathan Cape, 1963).

4. See discussion to follow in chapter 7.
5. In what is modern-day Nicaragua and Honduras, off the Atlantic coast.
6. And, of course, its imbrication in mercantilism/emergent capitalism. See on the matter of Equiano's relationship to these phenomena, Houston Baker, *Blues, Ideology, and AfroAmerican Literature*, 31; and Joseph Fichtelberg, "World between Word: The Economy of Equiano's *Narative*," *American Literary History* 5.3 (1993): 459–480.
7. I find it startling that this term that Equiano used here is also used in one of the texts, written by Diego Mendez regarding mythic events that took place during Columbus's fourth voyage:... *e yo di el ardid y la manera con que se debia hacer*... See *The Four Voyages of Columbus: A History of Eight Documents, Including Five by Christopher Columbus, in the Original Spanish, with English Translations*, trans. and ed. Cecil Jane (New York: Dover Publications, Inc., 1988), 118–119. Diego Mendez de Segura sailed on the fourth voyage with Columbus as squire in the caravel *Santiago de Palos*, captained by Francisco de Porras. Not much more beyond his efforts to vindicate Columbus is known about him. See editor's note #2, p. 112. The use of the translated term "stratagem" is suggestive: might Equiano have taken his language directly from translation of this source? The other sources of this event do not use such language. Furthermore, *el ardid* (stratagem, artifice, cunning) is suggestive of the "magic" of the white men that Equiano aimed to surface and play with.
8. See note #7 above re: Mendez.
9. See *The Life of the Admiral Christopher Columbus by His Son Ferdinand*, trans. and annotated by Benjamin Keen (New Brunswick, NJ: Rutgers University Press, 1959).
10. See *Short Account of the Destruction of the Indies*, trans. Nigel Griffin (London: Penguin, 1999).
11. Jane, *Four Voyages*, 134.
12. Keen, *Life of the Admiral*, 272–273.
13. See pp. 52 (re: awareness of difference), 55, 57, 58, 59, 62–69, 77–78.
14. See Carla Gardina Pestana, *Protestant Empire*, chaps 5–7; Colley, *Britons*; William R. Hutchison and Hartmut Lehrmann, eds., *Many Are Chosen*, chaps. 2, 4, 5; Christopher Hill, *The English Bible and the Seventeenth Century Revolution* (New York: Allen Lane/The Penguin Press, 1993), 413–435, chaps, 10, 11, for good discussions of critical issues and of complex historical backgrounds and contexts.
15. See for comprehensive discussion re: developments in sixteenth- and seventeenth-century England, Keith Thomas, *Religion and the Decline of Magic* (New York: Scribner, 1971), chaps. 7–9, 14–17, 19–20.
16. Those preserving and advancing the myth of Columbus do not use a specific term in reference to Columbus's power. It is as though it was important to keep

secret even the concept by which what was being done was done. The Columbus myth is a fascinating example of the formation of a modern cult hero. This includes his own writings, in addition to the clearly vindicationist apologetic writings of others. Beyond that, a cult developed that still obtains throughout the North Atlantic worlds. In his mimetics in relationship to Columbus, Equiano seemed to be very much tuned in to, or an apt reader of, large dynamic trends.

17. It might be helpful to investigate the modern American fantasy Wizard of Oz, especially the depiction of the wizard, in relationship to the "magic" that Equiano encounters. The one may illuminate the other. See for critical perspectives Ranjit S. Dighe, ed., *The Historian's Wizard of Oz: Reading L. Frank Baum's Classic as a Philosophical and Monetary Allegory* (Westport, CT: Praeger, 2002); Paul Nathanson, *Over the Rainbow: The Wizard of Oz as a Secular Myth of America* (Albany: SUNY Press, 1991); and Evan I. Schwartz, *Finding Oz: How L. Frank Baum Discovered the Great American Story* (Boston: Houghton Mifflin, 2009).
18. On this point, for creative literary-critical and historical and comparative analysis, including some striking parallels having to do with strategies of dominance and of resistance, see Mary Louise Pratt, *Imperial Eyes: Travel Writing and Transculturation* (New York: Routledge, 2008 [1992]), Part III; "Scratches on the face of the country; or, what Mr. Burrow saw in the land of the Bushmen," in Gates, ed., *"Race," Writing, and Difference*; Pratt, *Apocalypse in the Andes: Contact Zones and the Struggle for Interpretive Power* (Washington, DC: IDB Cultural Center, 1996); Jean and John Comaroff, *Of Revolution and Revolution,* chaps. 3, 5, 7; Chidester, *Savage Systems,* chaps. 1–3.
19. (London: Orbis Publishing Ltd., 1979).
20. Blackburn, Julia. *The White Men: The First Response of Aboriginal Peoples to the White Man* (London: Orbis Publishing Ltd., 1979), 36. "Slightly adapted" from W. Lloyd Warner, *A Black Civilization* (New York: Harper & Row, 1937 and 1965).
21. Blackburn, *White Men,* 55.
22. So Chidester, *Savage Systems,* xv.
23. On this issue, in addition to Taussig, *Mimesis and Alterity,* and Blackburn, *White Men*; see now: for social-scientifically-informed and critical and provocative arguments and analysis, as well as striking historical examples and parallels, see Ira Bashkow, *The Meaning of White Men: Race and Modernity in the Orokaiva Cultural World* (Chicago: University of Chicago Press, 2006), chaps. 1, 2, 6.
24. See above, Prologue, 14–15.
25. Taussig, *Mimesis,* 237. See also his *The Nervous System* (New York: Routledge,1992), which elaborates on this phenomenon.
26. Blackburn, *White Men,* 12, 13; Taussig, *Mimesis,* 239 (caption), attributes the photo to Herbert M. Cole, 1967.

27. Taussig, *Mimesis*, 238, 240.
28. Even Columbus's non-Englishness was overcome by his daring and boldness, his standing as heroic figure and symbol of the prowess of white men.
29. See Michael Mann's Causal IEMP model of organized power in *Sources of Social Power*, Vol. 1, vol. 1, 29 (elaboration, 1–34). The major set of assumptions that frame his comprehensive and elaborate argument is compelling:

> Human beings are restless, purposive, and rational, striving to increase their enjoyment of the good things of life, and capable of choosing and pursuing appropriate means for doing so. Or, at least, enough of them do this to provide the dynamism that is characteristic of human life and gives it a history lacking for other species. These human characteristics are... the original source of power. (4)

30. On this matter, see John H. Kautsky, *Politics of Aristocratic Empires* (Chapel Hill: University of North Carolina Press, 1982). chaps. 15, 16.
31. Yuri M. Lotman, *Universe of the Mind*, 4 for extensive discussion and analysis of semiotics and explicit interest in how such may be applied to different types of critical projects.
33. Pierre Bourdieu, trans. Richard Nice, *Outline of a Theory of Practice* (Cambridge: Cambridge University Press, 1977), 167.
34. I am drawing here on the brilliant analysis provided by Bauman and Briggs, *Voices of Modernity*, chap. 1, esp. pp. 36–40.
35. Ed. with an Introduction by Peter H. Nidditich (Oxford: Oxford University Press, 1975), 7.
36. The term I pick up from Bauman and Briggs, *Voices of Modernity*, 18, 314, 316, 319. Interestingly, as important as it is in their argument, they do not make it clear from the beginning of their argument how they mean and draw on the term. It clearly captures their basic argument about the politics and ideologies of language. It is as if they were saving the term, building up to its use in the conclusion. I found the specific term only in the Conclusion, on pp. 312, 313, 315. See Charles L. Briggs, "Metadiscursive Practices and Scholarly Authority in Folkloristics," in *Journal of American Folklore* 106 (1993): 387–434.
37. A concept developed by Renato Rosaldo, "The Rhetoric of Control: Illongots Viewed as Natural Bandits and Wild Indians," in *The Reversible World: Symbolic Inversion in Art and Society* (Ithaca: Cornell University Press, 1978), 240–257. See Chidester's use of the concept in *Savage Systems*, 3, in which application is made to religion in the dynamics of modern world formations.
38. J. and J. Comaroff, *Revelation and Revolution*, vol. 1, 18. Quoting Stuart Hall quoting Gramsci.
39. J. and J. Comaroff, *Revelation and Revolution*, vol. 1, 22.
40. Edmund Burke, *Reflections on the French Revolution*, ed. C. W. Eliot. Harvard Classics (New York: P. F. Collier and Sons, 1909–1914), vol. 24, Pt. III, para. 133.

See also Edmund Burke, *Reflections on the French Revolution: A Critical Edition*, ed. J. C. D. Clark (Stanford: Stanford University Press, 2001). See online text at www.bartleby.com/24/3/6.html.

41. See on these matters Olivia Smith, *The Politics of Language*, 22; Bauman and Briggs, *Voices of Modernity*, 127; and François Furstenberg, *In the Name of the Father*, chaps. 3 and 4.

CHAPTER 7

1. See Toni Morrison's meditations on memory, remembrance, "re-memory," in the autobiographical narratives among ex-slave black writers, in "Site of Memory." Equiano is included among those who, according to Morrison, veil their innermost sentiments. Although most critics would agree with Morrison that these writings represent veiling, some nuance if not skeptical questioning of such analysis is in order: beyond the issue of lack of safe space for the raising of the black voice, there is, with Equiano, at any rate, the matter of strategic play and interest that must be looked at more carefully. This is the point of my arguments in this book. See Christine Levecq, *Slavery and Sentiment: The Politics of Feeling in Black Atlantic Antislavery Writing, 1770–1850* (Hanover, NH: University Press of New England, 2008). More discussion about Morrison and her engagement of this issue below.
2. The term "Africa," like the place itself, is fraught with controversy, with little or no consensus about basic matters. The origin of the term "Africa" is not clear. This situation is not altogether unique. What is clear is that the peoples to which it refers did not create and own it—until recent decades, doubtlessly after they became resigned in the face of the dominance and pressures of Europeans. The term and the ideas that have since the fifteenth century and the beginnings of the modern "contact" with Europe been associated with it are a European construct. This term came from ancient imperial Roman reference to the province it called North Africa, a latinization of the name of a Berber tribe (possibly "land of the "Afri" or "Afarika"), covering Libya and modern-day Tunisia. This designation over time among Europeans was extended southward to refer to the entire continent. See Jeffrey A. Fortin, "Idea of Africa," in *Africana: Oxford African American Studies Center Online*. (New York: Oxford University Press, 2006–). From *Encyclopedia of African American History, 1619–1895: From the Colonial Period to the Age of Frederick Douglass* (New York: Oxford University Press, 2006).
3. I am here in agreement with James Sidbury, as he develops this argument in *Becoming African in America*. See chap. 2 re: Equiano.
4. See Michael A. Gomez, *Exchanging Our Country Marks*, chaps. 6, 9 Gomez displays enormous range and creative thinking in this work. This complex

analysis of the more complex situation in the United States applies to Equiano and the British situation.

5. On this point, re: enslavement as a kind of social death, see Orlando Patterson, *Slavery and Social Death: A Comparative Study* (Cambridge: Harvard University Press, 1982).
6. Long, *Significations*, 2, 4. For the sake of maintaining dominance it, has always been better to impose a name and identity on the dominated. The imposition of names becomes an important theme throughout Equiano's narrative.
7. Long, *Significations*, 2.
8. Hurston, *Mules and Men*, 3.
9. "[O]ur Saviour speaks of" makes it clear that the source referred to here is Jesus, as remembered by the Western canonical traditions.
10. At this point in Equiano's story, there is no problem with the Bible speaking to Equiano or Equiano hearing the Bible speak. Earlier, the problem was that Equiano was outsider, unable to understand and participate in the cultural practice. This positionality also afforded him opportunity to look critically at such an odd practice. Beyond Equiano's maturation, including his learning to read and write, the reader must wonder whether Equiano is in this passage not also raising the issue about what subject the Bible speaks about (or is made to speak about). A book that is silent is a book that does not speak in fundamental terms about a person's immediate situation.
11. See discussion above names or labels in Michael T. Ryan, "Assimilating New Worlds," 519–538, esp. pp. 522–527. I react with some skepticism about the self-reflexivity and general critical positionality of scholars like Ryan when they use the terms "pagan," "heathen," "savage," and the like. To be sure, these terms are found in the primary sources, and the scholars are of course quite adept at making clear how the early modern writers used them. But their problematization of these terms does not pass the test for me. Some of the terms may be hard to retain, but the easy retention and use of "pagan," for example, is troubling. What does its unproblematizied retention suggest about critical positionality? Who identifies with whom here?
12. See reference to Burke's language above, note #13 in chapter 2. Also see Smith, *The Politics of Language*, for historical background on the politics of literature and the literature of politics.
13. See Carretta, *Equiano the African*, 20, 256–57; Sidbury, *Becoming African in America*, chap. 1.
14. See Michael Taussig, *Mimesis and Alterity*, xiii-xiv, 254–255.
15. See Sidbury, *Becoming African in America*, 55–65, re: Equiano's pluralist vision.
16. 13:23; cf. also Acts 4:12.
17. David M. Goldenberg, *Curse of Ham: Race and Slavery in Early Judaism, Christianity, and Islam* (Princeton: Princeton University Press, 2003), Parts

One, Four, Conclusion, re: Jewish interpretations; Benjamin Isaac, *The Invention of Racism in Classical Antiquity* (Princeton: Princeton University Press, 2004), re: classical-era preludes; and Colin Kidd, *The Forging of Races: Race and Scripture in the Protesant Atlantic World, 1600–2000* (Cambridge: Cambridge University Press, 2006), re: early modern and modern Protestant world.

18. See Elizabeth A. Clark, *Reading Renunciation: Asceticism and Scripture in Early Christianity* (Princeton: Princeton University Press, 1999), for a provocative discussion re: the activation/production and use of asceticized scriptures. I see this phenomenon as useful comparison to Equiano's Africanized scriptures.
19. See James C. Scott, Domination and the Arts of Resistance: *Hidden Transcripts* (New Haven: Yale University Press, 1990,) for comparative critical analysis of modes of resistance.
20. Cf. 1 Cor 1: 21–22; 2: 5–7, 15–16.
21. "Denomination" here should be understood as differentiation in terms of ethnicity, background, and status, not religious affiliation.
22. I am reminded of President Barack Obama's speech delivered (July 16, 2009) on the occasion of the 100th anniversary of the founding of the NAACP. Obama's message, with its key theme about education as the key to liberation, resonates with Equiano's depiction of himself as one almost obsessed with learning to read. The same sort of message is found in the life stories of many other well-known successful black figures—from Frederick Douglass to Sojourner Truth to Benjamin Mays. But this was also the case among many whose names we will never know. See Janet Duitsman Cornelius, *"When I Can Read My Title Clear": Literacy, Slavery, and Religion in the Antebellum South* (Charleston: University of South Carolina Press, 1991), re: the history of quest among blacks to learn to read. What Equiano's glosses suggest, however, is that at issue in such messages is very likely more than training—it is about formation of self and community.
23. Except, for the understandable agenda: the tone-setting purposes in his first two chapters. And even in these chapters the summarizing sections at the end anticipate the sentiment more clearly evident in other parts of the narrative.
24. Carretta, ed., *Olaudah Equiano, app. #E3.*
25. Carretta, ed., *Olaudah Equiano,* app. #E12.
26. Carretta, ed., *Olaudah Equiano,* app. #E13.
27. Carretta, ed., *Olaudah Equiano,* app. #E18.
28. Caretta, ed., *Olaudah Equiano,* app. #E8.
29. Notably William Hughes, 1788, and James Ramsay, 1788. See Caretta, *Equiano the African,* 253, 261. See text in *Eighteenth Century Collections Online.*
30. Harris, *Scriptural Researches,* vi, vii.
31. Harris, *Scriptural Researches,* 75, 77.

32. See Saidiya Hartman, *Lose Your Mother: A Journey Along the Atlantic Slave Trade* (New York: Farrar, Straus and Giroux, 2007), for a sensitive and wrenching contemporary meditation on what it means to be a stranger, to be severed from kin and past.
33. See Sudbury, *Becoming African*, 51–55; Carretta, *Equiano the African*, chap 10.
34. Carretta, ed., Cugoano, 113.
35. Carretta, ed., Cugoano, 145.
36. Carretta, ed., Cugoano, 38.
37. Richard Bauman, "Contextualization, Tradition, and the Dialogue of Genres: Icelandic Legends of the kraftaskald," in *Rethinking Context: Language as an Interactive Phenomenon*, ed. Alessandro Duranti and Charles Goodwin (Cambridge: Cambridge University Press, 1992), 142.
38. I agree completely with Carretta, *Equiano, the African*, 287, in his argument that Equiano shows unusual command in the frontispiece: "For the first time in a book by a writer of African descent, the author Equiano asserts the equality of his free social status with that of his viewers and readers... he looks directly at them."
39. Again, on this phenomenon, including musings on reading for pleasure and enlightenment and empowerment see Bloom, *A Map of Misreading*.
40. See Hurston, *Mules and Men*, 33, 218. See my reference to this expression in the Prologue above.
41. See the critical questions about signifying practices by Leonard Harris, "Against Signifying: Psychosocial Needs and Natural Evil," 206–13; and Ranu Smautrai, "Who Needs the Subaltern?," 278–283, in Wimbush, ed., *Theorizing Scriptures*. Obviously, this book reflects my view of the importance of signifying practices.
42. See Michael Gomez, *Exchanging our Country Marks*, 282 who, after a rather dazzling display of skills of historical interpretation in accounting for the transformation of African identities in the diaspora, raises the question about what accounted for the transformation and the cohesion that ensued. In the end, channeling theologian Howard Thurman, he points not to social programs that were reflective of uplift programs and agenda, but the perduring deep haunting questions, having to do with the vexing problem of evil and suffering in the world. So he turns to a spiritual song that is itself a compelling exegetical treatment of scriptures and as such a channeling of Equiano's interpretive work:

    We hab a jest Gawd ter plead our cause,
        —Plead our cause.
    We hab a jest Gawd ter plead our cause,
    Fur we are de chillun of Gawd.

43. See Kort, *'Take, Read'*, for engaging wide-ranging literary and cultural critical discussion about such matters.

44. Although the relationship may seem far from interpretation of the Bible and other canonical texts, I think it is worth the effort to examine literature also on blacks and minstrel traditions. See Louis Onuorah Chude-Sokei, *The last "darky": Bert Williams, black-on-black minstrelsy, and the African Diaspora/* (Durham: Duke University Press, 2006).
45. (New York: Bantam, 1989). All references and quotations are taken from this edition. The discussion that follows is a summary revision of an article I wrote: " 'Naturally Veiled and Half Articulate': Scriptures, Modernity, and the Formation of African America," in *Still at the Margins*, ed. R. S. Sugirtharajah (Maryknoll, NY: Orbis Books, 2008).
46. The term "veil" has interesting etymology: Middle English veile, taken from old North French, ultimately taken from Latin *vela*, plural of *velum*=sail, awning: used allusively in various prepositional phrases, such as behind, beyond or within the veil: Tyndale 1528; Wollaston 1722; Tennyson 1850; E Fitzgerald 1859; A.J. Ross 1877; to conceal from apprehension, knowledge or perception; to disguise: D'Israel 1841. In Du Bois's time these uses were very much in the air of popular discourse and in letters. See *The Oxford English Dictionary*, sub verbo, 3c, volXIX, 2d ed. (Oxford: Clarendon Press, 1989).
47. Du Bois, *Souls*, 2–3.
48. Du Bois, *Souls*, 55, 56.
49. Du Bois, *Souls*, 127, 142.
50. Du Bois, *Souls*, 64.
51. Du Bois, *Souls*, 147, 148, 150, 156, 159, 165.
52. Du Bois, *Souls*, 149.
53. Du Bois, *Souls*, 76, 153.
54. Du Bois, Souls, 56.
55. Du Bois, *Souls*, 151.
56. Du Bois, *Souls*, 187.
57. See literary critics Shamoon Zamir, *Dark Voices: W.E.B. Dubois and American Thought, 1888–1903* (Chicago: University of Chicago Press, 1995), Part 2; and Arnold Rampersad, *Art and Imagination of W.E.B. Dubois* (Cambridge: Harvard University Press, 1976), chap 4.
58. Hegel's concern (*Phenomenology of Mind*, trans. J. B. Baillie (New York: Harper Textbooks, 1967 [1807, trans. 1910] 211, 212–213)) had been about the "unhappy consciousnesss" as part of the dialectics of the master-slave relationship and that moment in which such consciousness is transformed, when self-consciousness discovers itself beyond the realm of appearances, that moment in which the "curtain" is drawn aside:

> Thiscurtain [ofappearance]... hanging before the inner world is withdrawn, and we have here the inner being gazing into the inner realm... What we have here is Self-consciousness. It is manifest that behind the so-called

curtain, which is to hide the inner world, there is nothing to be seen unless we ourselves go there, as much in order that we may thereby see, as that there may be something behind there which can be seen.

Quoted in Zamir, *Dark Voices*, 135.

59. In the book of Exodus (26:33) the "veil" (GK LXX: *to katapetasma*) separates the Holy of Holies, the sanctuary for the Ark of the Covenant, from everything else; in 1 Corinthians (13:12) Paul makes reference to humans, even repentant ones, being able to see only partial truths—"darkly as through a veil" (*en ainigmati*); in the letter to the Hebrews (6:19) the unknown writer refers to entering into the domain of the "veil" (*eis to esoteron tou katapetasmatos*) to mark the change in those who although having been enlightened, nevertheless in the face of persecution have "fallen away"; and, perhaps, most poignantly, the writer of the Gospel of Matthew, having depicted Jesus crying out loud and dying on the cross, indicates that "the veil" of the temple was "rent in two" from top to bottom (*to katapetasma tou vaou eschisthe eis duo apo anothen hoes kato*, 27:50–54).
60. Du Bois died the day before Martin Luther King, Jr., delivered his now famous, some think, era changing "I Have a Dream" speech in Washington, DC. There is no doubt that the legal changes that were wrought here in connection with the civil rights struggles of the 1950s, 1960s, and 1970s represented a degree of rending of the veil for which Du Bois had fought and hoped.
61. Du Bois, *Souls*, 182–85. My emphases.
62. Hurston, *Mules and Men*, 33, 218; 3.
63. Hurston, *Mules and Men*, 125 (emphasis mine). Black Fantastic.
64. See Hasan-Roken and Shulman, eds., *Untying the Knot*, for wide-ranging discussion—a comparative focus.
65. See Joseph R. Washington, *Black Religion: the Negro and Christianity in the United States* (Boston: Beacon Press, 1964). This somewhat shrill essay is dated in terms of some detail, but the sentiment it reflects—that blacks peoples are not legitimate and adequate interpreters and tradents of Christianism—is very much alive.
66. See note #1 above.
67. Morrison, "Site of Memory," 109–110.
68. Morrison, "Site of Memory," 110.
69. Morrison, "Site of Memory," 110–111. My emphasis.
70. From interview with Thomas Leclair, "'The Language Must Not Sweat': A Conversation with Toni Morrison," in *Toni Morrison: Critical Perspectives Past and Present*, ed. Henry Louis Gates, Jr., and K. A. Appiah, Amistad Literary Series (New York: Amistad, 1993), 371.
71. Leclair, "'Language Must Not Sweat,'" 370–71.
72. Actually, it is a quotation of Hosea 2:25, with actual word agreement with the LXX version of 1:9.

73. 11:25.
74. Gk. *apotrepein*: that which averts or wards off evil.
75. See Bourdieu, *Outline of a Theory of Practice*, 170.
76. Morrison, *Beloved*, 151, 153.
77. Bourdieu, *Outline of a Theory of Practice*, 168.
78. Baker, *Afro-American Poetics*, 106, 109. Susan Sontag, "Aesthetics of Silence," in *A Susan Sontag Reader* (New York: Vantage, 1983), 181–204. My next book I take as an effort to take up Baker's call for "criticism of silence."
79. Baker, *Afro-American Poetics*, 106.
80. Benston, *Performing Blackness*, 131, 133, 134.
81. Nora, "Between Memory and History, 300.
82. Morrison, "Site of Memory," 119, 120.
83. Taussig, *Mimesis*, 240.
84. See *The Fundamentalism Project*, ed. Martin E Marty and R. Scottt Appleby, 5 vols. (Chicago: University of Chicago Press, 1991–1995); Martin E Marty and R. Scott Appleby, *Glory and The Power: The Fundamentalist Challenge to the Modern World* (Boston: Beacon Press, 1992); Philip Jenkins, *Next Christendom: The Coming of Global Christianity* (New York: Oxford University Press, 2002); *New Faces of Christianity: Believing the Bible in the Global South* (New York: Oxford University Press, 2006); *Religious Fundamentalism in Developing Countries*, ed. Santosh V. Saha and Thomas K. Carr (Westport, CT: Greenwood Press, 2001); Tariq Ali, *The Clash of Fundamentalism: Crusades, Jihads and Modernity* (New York: Verso, 2002); John W. Pulis, "In the beginning": A chapter from the living testament of Rastafari; and Rosamond C. Rodman, "We Are Anglicans, They Are the Church of England": Uses of Scripture in the Anglican Crisis," in James Bielo, ed., *Social Life of Scriptures Cross-Cultural Perspectives on Biblicism* (New Brunswick: Rutgers University Press, 2009). Attention to the phenomenon among African Americans has barely begun, but see for a start the essay by Albert J. Miller, "The Construction of a Black Fundamentalist Worldview," in V. L.Wimbush, ed., *African Americans and the Bible*, 712–27.
85. See Satya P. Mohanty, *Literary Theory and the Claims of History: Postmodernism, Objectivity, Multicultural Politics* (Ithaca, NY: Cornell University Press, 1997); Dipesh Chakrabarty, *Provincializing Europe* (Princeton: Princeton University Press, 2000); and John Law, *Aircraft Stories: Decentering the Object in Technoscience*. Science and Cultural Theory (Durham, NC: Duke University Press, 2002).
86. Nora, "Between Memory and History," 300.

EPILOGUE

1. With all due regard for Harold Bloom, *Shakespeare: The Invention of the Human* (New York: Riverhead Books, 1998).

2. Here I am in agreement with Houston Baker's analysis, in his *Blues, Ideology and Afro-American Literature,* of Equiano's text as work whose protagonist "masters the rudiments of economics" (33). I add only the perspective that such mastering is based on reading the structuring of that world in terms of scripturalization.
3. See his bestseller *The Stuff of Thought: Language as a Window into Human Nature* (New York: Viking Penguin, 2007), 432–34.
4. Ibid., 439.
5. Ibid., 434.
6. Ibid., 432–33.
7. Ibid., 434
8. These remarks the "Libyan Sibyl" is reported by Stanton to have made in 1867. See Elizabeth Cady Stanton, Susan B. Anthony, and Matilda Joslyn, eds., *History of Woman Suffrage, vol 2*; e-text (#28039) prepared by Richard J. Shiffer (Project Gutenberg Online; www.gutenberg.org, release date Feb 9, 2009), 1014.
9. Part of the album (1972, Tamla) entitled *Talking Book*!

Bibliography

Acholonu, Catherine Obianju. "The Home of Olaudah Equiano—A Linguistic and Anthropological Search." *The Journal of Commonwealth Literature* 22 (1987): 5–16.

Alabi, Adetayo. *Telling Our Stories: Continuities and Divergences in Black Autobiographies*. 1st ed. New York: Palgrave MacMillan, 2005.

Ali, Tariq. *The Clash of Fundamentalisms: Crusades, Jihads and Modernity*. New York: Verso, 2002.

Aravamudan, Srinivas. *Tropicopolitans: Colonialism and Agency, 1688–1804*. Post-contemporary Interventions. Durham, NC: Duke University Press, 1999.

Aravamudan, Srinivas. "Equiano Lite." *Eighteenth-Century Studies* 34, no. 4 (Summer 2001): 615–619.

Armstrong, Karen. *The Great Transformation: The Beginning of our Religious Traditions*. New York: Alfred A. Knopf, 2006.

Arnheim, Rudolf. *The Power of the Center: A Study of Composition in the Visual Arts*. Berkeley: University of California Press, 1982.

Baker, Houston A., Jr. *Blues, Ideology, and Afro-American Literature: A Vernacular Theory*. Chicago: University of Chicago Press, 1984.

Baker, Houston A., Jr. *Modernism and the Harlem Renaisssance*. Chicago: University of Chicago Press, 1987.

Baker, Houston A., Jr. *Afro-American Poetics: Revisions of Harlem and the Black Aesthetic*. Madison: University of Wisconsin Press, 1988.

Baker, Houston A., Jr. *Workings of The Spirit: The Poetics of Afro-American Women's Writing*. Black Literature and Culture. Chicago: University of Chicago Press, 1991.

Bashkow, Ira. The Meaning of Whitemen: Race and Modernity in the Orokaiva Cultural World. Chicago: University of Chicago Press, 2006.

Bauman, Richard. "Contextualization, Tradition, and the Dialogue of Genres: Icelandic Legends of the Kraftaskald." In *Rethinking Context: language as an Interactive Phenomenon*, edited by Alessandro Duranti and Charles Goodwin, 125–145. Cambridge: Cambridge University Press, 1992.

Bauman, Richard, and Charles L. Briggs. *Voices of Modernity: Language Ideologies and the Politics of Inequality. Studies in the Social and Cultural Foundations of Language 21*. New York: Cambridge University Press, 2003.

Bennett, Tony. "Texts, Readers, Reading Formations." *MMLA* 16.1 (Spring 1983): 3–17

Bennett, Tony. "Texts in History: The Determinations of Readings and Their Texts." *MMLA* 18.1 (Fall 1985): 1–16.

Benston, Kimberly W. *Performing Blackness: Enactments of African-American Modernism*. New York: Routledge, 2000.

Bhabha, Homi K. *Location of Culture*. New York: Routledge, 1994.

Blackburn, Julia. *The White Men: The First Response of Aboriginal Peoples to the White Man*. London: Orbis Publishing Ltd., 1979.

Bland, Sterling Lacater, Jr. *Voices of the Fugitives: Runaway Slave Stories and their Fictions of Self-Creation*. Westport, CT: Praeger Publishers, 2000.

Bloom, Harold. *A Map of Misreading*. New York: Oxford University Press, [1975] 2003.

Bloom Harold. *Shakespeare: The Invention of the Human*. New York: Riverhead Books, 1998.

Blount, Brian K., et al., eds. *True to our Native Land: An African American New Testament Commentary*. Minneapolis: Fortress Press, 2007.

Boone, Kathleen C. *The Bible Tells Them So: the Discourse of Protestant Fundamentalism*. Albany, NY: SUNY Press, 1989.

Bourdieu, Pierre. *Outline of a Theory of Practice*. Translated by Richard Nice. Cambridge Studies in Social Anthropology 16. Cambridge: Cambridge University Press, 1977.

Boyarin, Jonathan, ed. *Ethnography of Reading*. Berkeley: University of California Press, 1993.

Briggs, Charles L. "Metadiscursive Practices and Scholarly Authority in Folkloristics." *Journal of American Folklore* 106 (1993): 387–434.

Bugner, Ladislas, ed. *Image of the Black in Western Art*. Vols. 1–2, 4. Cambridge: Harvard University Press, 1976.

Bunyan, John. *The Pilgrim's Progress*. London: Nathaniel Ponder, 1678.

Burke, Edmund. *Reflections on the Revolution in France*. London: J. Dodsley, 1790.

Burke, Edmund. *Reflections on the French Revolution*. Edited by C. W. Eliot. Harvard Classics. Vol. 4. New York: P. F. Collier and Sons, 1909–1914.

Burke, Edmund. *Reflections on the French Revolution: A Critical Edition*. Edited by. J. C. D. Clark. Stanford: Stanford University Press, 2001. *http://www.bartleby.com/24/3/6.html* (accessed April 29, 2011).

Byron, Gay L. *Symbolic Blackness and Ethnic Difference in Early Christian Literature*. London: Routledge, 2002.

Carretta, Vincent. *Equiano the African: Biography of a Self-Made Man*. Athens: University of Georgia Press, 2005.

Carson, Cottrell R. "'Do you Understand What You are Reading?' Reading of the Ethiopian Eunuch Story (Acts 8:29–40) from a Site of Cultural Marronage." Ph.D. diss., Union Theological Seminary, New York, 1999.

Casas, Bartolome de las. *Short Account of the Destruction of the Indies*. Translated by Nigel Griffin. London: Penguin, 1999.

Castelli, Elizabeth A. with the assistance of Rosamond C. Rodman, ed. *Women, Gender, Religion: A Reader*. 1st ed. New York: Palgrave, 2001.

Cavallo, Guglielmo, and Roger Chartier, eds. *A History of Reading in the West*. Translated by Lydia G. Cochrane. Studies in Print Culture and the History of the Book Amherst: University of Massachusetts Press, 1999 [1995].

Chakrabarty, Dipesh. *Provincializing Europe: Postcolonial Thought and Historical Difference*. Princeton: Princeton University Press, 2000.

Chidester, David. *Savage Systems: Colonialism and Comparative Religion in Southern Africa. Studies in Religion and Culture*. Charlottesville, VA: University Press of Virginia, 1996.

Chude-Sokei, Louis Onuorah. *The Last "Darky": Bert Williams, Black-on-black Minstrelsy, and the African Diaspora*. Durham, NC: Duke University Press, 2006.

Clark, Elizabeth A. *Reading Renunciation: Asceticism and Scripture in Early Christianity*. Princeton: Princeton University Press, 1999.

Cole, Alan. *Text as Father: Paternal Seductions in Early Mahayana Buddhist Literature*. Berkeley: University of California Press, 2005.

Colley, Linda. *Britons: Forging the Nation, 1707–1837*. New Haven: Yale University Press, 1992.

Collier-Thomas, Bettye. *Daughters of Thunder: Black Women preachers and their Sermons, 1850–1879*. 1st ed. San Francisco: Jossey-Bass, 1998.

Colón, Fernando. *The Life of the Admiral Christopher Columbus by His Son Ferdinand*. Translated and Annotated by Benjamin Keen. New Brunswick, NJ: Rutgers University Press, 1959.

Columbus, Christopher. The Four Voyages of Columbus: A History of Eight Documents, Including Five by Christopher Columbus, in the Original Spanish, with English Translations. Translated and Edited by Cecil Jane. Dover Books on Travel, Adventure. New York: Dover Publications, Inc., 1988.

Comaroff, Jean and John Comaroff. *Of Revolution and Revolution: Christianity, Colonialism, and Consciousness in South Africa*. Vol. 1. Chicago: University of Chicago Press, 1991.

Conzelmann, Hans. *Acts of the Apostles: A Commentary on the Acts of the Apostle*. Translated by James Limburg, A. Thomas Kraabel, and Donald H. Juel. Edited by Eldon Jay Epp with Christopher R. Matthews. Hermenia Commentary Series. Philadelphia: Augsburg Fortress, 1987.

Copher, Charles B. *Black Biblical Studies: An Anthology of Charles B. Copher: Biblical and Theological Issues on the Black Presence in the Bible*. 1st ed. Chicago: Black Light Fellowship, 1993.

Cornelius, Janet Duitsman. *"When I Can Read My Title Clear": Literacy, Slavery, and Religion in the Antebellum South*. Charleston: University of South Carolina Press, 1991.

Cugoano, Quobna Ottobah. *Thoughts and Sentiments on the Evil of Slavery*. Edited with an Introduction and Notes by Vincent Carretta. *Penguin Classics*. New York: Penguin Books, [1787] 1999.

Davidson, Cathy N. ed., *Reading in America: Literature and Social History*. Baltimore: Johns Hopkins University Press, 1989.

de la Vega, Garcilaso. *Historia General del Peru*. Cordoba: Viuda de Andres Barrera, 1617.

de la Vega, Garcilaso. *Historia General del Perú*. Part II of *Commentarios Reales del Perú*. London: Miles Flesher, 1688.

Dei, George J. Sefa, Budd L. Hall, and Dorothy Goldin Rosenberg, eds. *Indigenous Knowledges in Global Contexts: Multiple Readings of Our World*. Toronto: University of Toronto Press, 2000.

Delumeau, Jean. *Sin and Fear: The Emergence of a Western Guilt Culture: Thirteenth-Eighteenth Centuries*. Translated by Eric Nicholson. New York: St. Martin's Press, 1990.

De Ste. Croix, G. E. M. *Class Struggle in the Ancient Greek World: from the Archaic Age to the Arab Conquest*. Ithaca, NY: Cornell University Press, 1981.

Dighe, Ranjit S., ed. *The Historian's Wizard of Oz: Reading L. Frank Baum's Classic as a Philosophical and Monetary Allegory*. Westport, CT: Praeger, 2002.

Diop, Cheik Anta. *The African Origin of Civilization: Myth or Reality*. Translated by Mercer Cook. Westport, CT: Lawrence Hill, 1974.

Du Bois, W.E.B. *The Souls of Black Folk*. New York: Bantam Books, 1989.

Eaton, Isaac, ed. *Politics for the People or a Salmagundy for Swine*. London: D.I. Eaton, 1794–5.

Eisenstadt, S. N., ed. *Origins and Diversity of Axial Age Civilizations*. SUNY Series in Near Eastern Studies. Albany: SUNY Press, 1986.

Eisenstadt, S.N. "Introduction." In *The Origins and Diversity of Axial Age Civilizations*, edited by S.N. Eisenstadt, *SUNY Series in Near Eastern Studies*. Albany: State University of New York Press, 1986.

Eisenstadt, S. N. and B. Wittrock, eds. *Axial Civilizations and World History*. Jerusalem Studies in Religion and Culture. Leiden/Boston: Brill, 2005.

Elrod, Eileen Razzari. *Piety and Dissent: Race, Gender, and Biblical Rhetoric in Early American Autobiography*. Amherst, MA: University of Massachusetts Press, 2008.

Equiano, Olaudah. *Olaudah Equiano: The Interesting Narrative and Other Writings*. Edited and with an Introduction by Vincent Carretta. New York: Penguin Books, 2003.

Eze, Emmanuel Chukwudi, ed. *Race and the Enlightenment: A Reader*. Malden, MA: Blackwell Publishers, 1997.

Felder, Cain Hope. *Race, Racism, and the Biblical Narratives*. Facets. Minneapolis: Fortress Press, 2002.

Fernandez, James W., "Afterword." In *African Divination Systems: Ways of Knowing*, edited by Philip M. Peek, 213–221. Bloomington, IN: Indiana University Press, 1991.

Fichtelberg, Joseph. "Word Between Worlds: The Economy of Equiano's Narrative." *American Literary History* 5.3 (Fall 1993): 459–480.

Finkelman, Paul, ed. *Encyclopedia of African American History, 1619–1895: From the Colonial Period to the Age of Frederick Douglass*. New York: Oxford University Press, 2006.

Fiorenza, Elisabeth Schüssler. *Bread Not Stone: the Challenge of Feminist Biblical Interpretation*. Boston: Beacon Press, 1995.

Fiorenza, Elisabeth Schüssler. *In Memory of Her: a Feminist Theological Reconstruction of Christian Origins*. New York: Crossroads, 1983.

Fiorenza, Elisabeth Schüssler. *Rhetoric and Ethic: the Politics of Biblical Studies*. Minneapolis: Fortress Press, 1999.

Fortin, Jeffrey A. "Idea of Africa." In *Africana: Oxford African American Studies Center Online*. New York: Oxford University Press, 2006.

Foster, Francis Smith. *Written By Herself: Literary Production by African American Women, 1746–1892*. Blacks in the Diaspora. Bloomington: Indiana University Press, 1993.

Foucault, Michel. *Power/Knowledge: Selected Interviews and Other Writings, 1972–1977*. Edited and Translated by Colin Gordon. 1st American ed. New York: Pantheon Books, 1980.

Fryer, Peter. *Staying Power: Black People in Britain Since 1504*. Atlantic Highlands, NJ: Humanities Press, 1984.

Furstenberg, François. *In the Name of the Father: Washington's Legacy, Slavery, and the Making of a Nation*. New York: Penguin Press, 2006.

Gates, Henry Louis Jr. and William L. Andrews, eds. *Pioneers of the Black Atlantic: Five Slave Narratives from the Enlightenment, 1772–1815*. Washington, D.C.: Civitas, 1998.

Gates, Henry Louis, Jr. ed. *"Race," Writing, and Difference*. Chicago: University of Chicago Press, 1986.

Gates, Henry Louis, Jr. ed. *The Signifying Monkey: A Theory of African American Literary Criticism*. New York: Oxford University Press, 1988.

Goldenberg, David M. *Curse of Ham: Race and Slavery in Early Judaism, Christianity, and Islam*. Princeton: Princeton University Press, 2003.

Gomez, Michael A. *Exchanging Our Country Marks: the Transformation of African Identities in the Colonial and Antebellum South*. Chapel Hill: University of North Carolina Press, 1988.

Goody, Jack. *Power of the Written Tradition*. Smithsonian Series in Ethnographic Inquiry. Washington, D.C.: Smithsonian Institution Press, 2000.

Grafton, Anthony, with April Shelford and Nancy Siraisi. *New Worlds, Ancient Texts: the Power of Tradition and the Shock of Discovery*. Cambridge: Belknap Press of Harvard University Press, 1992.

Gundaker, Grey. *Signs of Diaspora, Diaspora of Signs: Literacies, Creolization, and Vernacular Practice in African America. The Commonwealth Center Studies in American Culture*. New York: Oxford University Press, 1998.

Haller, William. *Foxe's First Book of Martyrs and the Elect Nation*. London: Jonathan Cape, 1963.

Harding, Susan Friend. *The Book of Jerry Falwell: Fundamentalist Language and Politics*. Princeton: Princeton University Press, 2000.

Harris, Joseph E., ed. *Africa and Africans as Seen by Classical Writers: The William Leo Hansberry African History Notebook*. 2 vols. Washington, D.C.: Howard University Press, 1977.

Hartman, Saidiya. *Lose Your Mother: A Journey Across the Atlantic Slave Route*. New York: Farrar, Straus and Giroux, 2008.

Hasan-Rokem, Galit and David Shulman, eds. *Untying the Knot: On Riddles and Other Enigmatic Modes*. New York: Oxford University Press, 1996.

Haywood, Chanta M. *Prophesying Daughters: Black Women Preachers and the Word, 1823–1913*. Columbia and London: University of Missouri Press, 2003.

Hegel, G.W.F. *The Phenomenology of Mind*. Translated by J.B. Baillie. New York: Harper Textbooks, 1967.

Heschel, Susanna. *Aryan Jesus: Christian Theologies and the Bible in Nazi Germany*. Princeton University Press, 2008.

Hochschild, Adam. *Bury the Chains: Prophets and Rebels in the Fight to Free an Empire's Slaves*. New York: Houghton Mifflin Company/Mariner Books, 2005.

Hodge, Robert and Gunther Kress. *Social Semiotics*. Ithaca, NY: Cornell University Press, 1988.

Holden, Margaret T. *Early Anthropology in the Sixteenth and Seventeenth Centuries*. Philadelphia: University of Pennsylvania Press, 1964.

Hood, Robert E. *Begrimed and Black: Christian Traditions on Blacks and Blackness*. Minneapolis: Augsburg Fortress, 1994.

Hughes, William. "An Answer to the Rev. Mr. Harris's 'Scriptural Researches on the Licitness of the Slave-trade.'" *Eighteenth Century Collections Online*. London: Printed for T. Cadell, 1788.

Huizinga, Johan. *Homo Ludens: A Study of Play-Element in Culture*. Beacon Paperbacks PB 15. Boston: Beacon Press, 1955 [1950].

Hunter, J. Paul. *The Reluctant Pilgrim: Defoe's Emblematic Method and Quest for Form in Robinson Crusoe*. Baltimore: The Johns Hopkins University Press, 1966.

Hurston, Zora Neale. *Mules and Men*. Prefaced by Franz Boas with a New Foreword by Arnold Rampersad and Illustrations by Miguel Covarrubias. New York: Perennial Library, 1990 [1935].

Hutchison, William R. and Hartmut Lehmann, eds. *Many Are Chosen: Divine Election and Western Nationalisms*. Harvard Theological Studies. Minneapolis, MN: Fortress Press, 1994.

Isaac, Benjamin. *The Invention of Racism in Classical Antiquity*. Princeton: Princeton University Press, 2004.

Jefferson, Thomas. *Notes on the State of Virginia*. Edited with an Introduction and Notes by Frank Shuffelton. Penguin Classics. New York: Penguin Books, 1999 [1785].

Jefferys, Thomas. *The West India Atlas*. London: 1794.

Jenkins, Philip. *Next Christendom: The Coming of Global Christianity*. New York: Oxford University Press, 2002.

Jenkins, Philip. *New Faces of Christianity: Believing the Bible in the Global South*. New York: Oxford University Press, 2006.

Johnson Sylvester A. "Colonialism, Biblical World-Making and Temporalities in Olaudah Equiano's *Interesting Narrative*." *Church History* 77 (2008): 1003–1024.

Juergensmeyer, Mark, ed. *Global Religions: an Introduction*. New York: Oxford University Press, 2003.

Kautsky, John H. *Politics of Aristocratic Empires*. Chapel Hill: University of North Carolina Press, 1982.

Keane, Webb. *Christian Moderns: Freedom and Fetish in the Missionary Encounter*. Berkeley: University of California Press, 2007.

Kidd, Colin. *The Forging of Races: Race and Scripture in the Protest Atlantic World, 1600–2000*. Cambridge: Cambridge University Press, 2006.

Kling, David W. *The Bible in History: How the Texts Have Shaped the Times*. New York: Oxford University Press, 2004.

Kort, Wesley A. *"Take, Read": Scripture, Textuality, and Cultural Practice*. University Park: Pennsylvania State University Press, 1996.

Krips, Henry. *Fetish: An Erotics of Culture*. Ithaca NY: Cornell University Press, 1999.

Kristeva, Julia. *Strangers to Ourselves*. Translated by Leon S. Roudiez. New York: Columbia University Press, 1991.

Latour, Bruno. *Petite Rèflexion sur le Culte Moderne des Dieux Faitiches*. Paris: Synthelabo, 1996.

Law, John. *Aircraft Stories: Decentering the Object in Technoscience*. Science and Cultural Theory. Durham, NC: Duke University Press, 2002.

Leclair, Thomas. "'The Language Must Not Sweat': A Conversation with Toni Morrison." In *Toni Morrison: Critical Perspectives Past and Present*, edited by Henry Louis Gates, Jr. and K. A. Appiah. Amistad Literary Series. New York: Amistad, 1993.

Levecq, Christine. *Slavery and Sentiment: the Politics of Feeling in Black Atlantic Antislavery Writing, 1770–1850*. Becoming Modern. Lebanon NH: University of New Hampshire Press, 2008.

Levy, Pierre. *Collective Intelligence: Mankind's Emerging World in Cyberspace.* Translated by Robert Bonino. Cambridge MA: Perseus Books, 1997.

Linebaugh, Peter and Marcus Rediker. *The Many-Headed Hydra: Sailors, Slaves, Commoners, and the Hidden History of the Revolutionary Atlantic.* Boston: Beacon Press, 2000.

Littau, Karin. *Theories of Reading: Books, Bodies and Bibliomania.* Malden, MA: Polity Press, 2006.

Locke, John. *An Essay Concerning Human Understanding.* Edited with an Introduction, Critical apparatus, and Glossary by Peter H. Nidditich. Oxford: Clarendon Press, 1975.

Locke, John. *Some Thoughts Concerning Education.* Edited with an Introduction, Notes, and Critical Apparatus by John W. and Jean S. Yolton. Oxford: Clarendon Press, 1989.

Long, Charles H., *Significations: Signs, Symbols, and Images in the Interpretation of Religion.* Philadelphia: Fortress, 1986.

Lotman, Yuri M. *Universe of the Mind: A Semiotic Theory of Culture.* London/ New York: I. B. Taurus Publishers, 2001.

MacMullen, Ramsay. *Enemies of the Roman Order: Treason, Unrest, and Alienation in the Empire.* London: Routledge, [1966] 1992.

MacDonald, Margaret Y. *The Pauline Churches: A Socio-historical Study of Institutionalization in the Pauline and Deutero-pauline Writings.* New York: Cambridge University Press, 1988.

Mann, Michael. *Sources of Social Power.* Vol. 1. New York: Cambridge University Press, 1986.

Marrouchi, Mustapha. *Signifying with a Vengeance: Theories, Literatures, Storytellers.* Albany: State University of New York Press, 2002.

Marty, Martin E. and R. Scottt Appleby, eds. *The Fundamentalism Project.* 5 vols. Chicago: University of Chicago Press, 1991–1995.

Marty, Martin E. and R. Scott Appleby. *Glory and The Power: the Fundamentalist Challenge to the Modern World.* Boston: Beacon Press, 1992.

Matsuzawa, Tomoko. *The Invention of World Religions: Or, How European Universalism Was Preserved in the Language of Pluralism.* Chicago: University of Chicago Press, 2005.

McCalman, Iain. *Radical Underworld: Prophets, Revolutionaries and Pornographers in London, 1795–1840.* Cambridge: Cambridge University Press, 1988.

Meeks, Wayne A. *First Urban Christians: the Social World of the Apostle Paul.* New Haven: Yale University Press, [1983] 2003.

Meeks, Wayne A. *Origins of Christian Morality: the First Two Centuries.* New Haven: Yale University Press, 1993.

Mohanty, Satya P. *Literary Theory And The Claims Of History: Postmodernism, Objectivity, Multicultural Politics.* Ithaca: Cornell University Press, 1997.

Morrison, Toni. "The Site of Memory." In *Inventing the Truth: The Art and Craft of Memoir*, edited by William Zinsser, 109–110. Boston: Houghton Mifflin, 1995.

Morrison, Toni. *Beloved: A Novel*. New York: Columbia University Press, 1998.

Murphy, Geraldine. "Olaudah Equiano, Accidental Tourist." *Eighteenth-Century Studies* 27.4 (Summer 1994): 551–568.

Murphy, Jerome. *Working the Spirit: Ceremonies of the African Diaspora*. Boston: Beacon Press, 1994.

Nathanson, Paul. *Over the Rainbow: the Wizard of Oz as a Secular Myth of America*. Albany: SUNY Press, 1991.

Needham, Rodney, ed. *Right and Left: Essays on Dual Symbolic Classification*. Foreword by E. E. Evans-Pritchard. Chicago: University of Chicago Press, 1973.

Noll, Mark A., David W. Bebbington, and George A. Rawlyk, eds. *Evangelicalism: Comparative Studies of Popular Protestantism in North America, the British Isles, and Beyond, 1700–1990*. Religion in America Series. New York: Oxford University Press, 1994.

Nora, Pierre. "Between Memory and History: Les Lieux de Memoire." In *History and Memory in African-American Culture*, ed. Genevieve Fabre and Robert O,Meally, 300. New York: Oxford University Press, 1994.

O'Quinn, Daniel. "The State of Things: Olauadah Equiano and the Volatile Politics of Heterocosmic Desire." http://www.rc.umd.edu/praxis/sexuality/oquinn/oquinn.html (accessed April 29, 2011)

Olson, David R. and Nancy Torrance, eds. *Modes of Thought: Explorations in Culture and Cognition*. Cambridge: Cambridge University Press, 1996.

Olupona, Jacob, ed. *Beyond Primitivism: Indigenous Religious Tradition and Modernity*. New York: Routledge, 2004.

Ong, Walter. *Interfaces of the Word: Studies in the Evolution of Consciousness and Culture*. Ithaca, NY: Cornell University Press, 1977.

Ong, Walter. *Orality and Literacy: The Technologizing of the Word*. New York: Methuen, 1982.

Page, Hugh R., Jr., et al, eds. *Africana Bible: Reading Israel's Scriptures from Africa and the African Diaspora*. Minneapolis: Fortress Press, 2009.

Pastoureau, Michel. *Black: The History of a Color*. Princeton: Princeton University Press, 1999.

Patterson, Orlando. *Slavery and Social Death: A Comparative Study*. Cambridge: Harvard University Press, 1982.

Peek, Philip M., ed. *African Divination Systems: Ways of Knowing*. Bloomington, IN: Indiana University Press, 1991.

Pestana, Carla Gardina. *Protestant Empire: Religion and the Making of the British Atlantic World*. Philadelphia: University of Pennsylvania Press, 2009.

Pietz, William. "The Problem of the Fetish, I." *Res: Anthropology and Aesthetics* 9 (Spring 1985): 5–17.

Pietz, William. "The Problem of the Fetish, II: The Origins of the Fetish." Res: Anthropology and Aesthetics 13 (Spring 1987): 23–45.

Pietz, William. "The Problem of the Fetish, IIIa: Bosman's Guinea and the Enlightenment Theory of Fetishism." *Res: Anthropology and Aesthetics* 16 (Autumn 1988): 105–123.

Pinker, Steven. *The Stuff of Thought: Language as a Window into Human Nature.* New York: Viking Penguin, 2007.

Pietz, William. "Fetishism and Materialism: The Limits of Theory in Marx." In *Fetishism as Cultural Discourse,* ed. Emily Apter and William Pietz, 152–185. Ithaca: Cornell University Press, 1993.

Pollock, Sheldon. *The Language of the Gods in The World of Men: Sanskrit, Culture, and Power in Premodern India.* Berkeley: University of California Press, 2006.

Potkay, Adam. "History, Oratory, and God in Equiano's Interesting Narrative." *Eighteenth- Century Studies* 34, no. 4 (Summer 2001): 601–614.

Potkay, Adam, and Sandra Burr. eds., *Black Atlantic Writers of the Eighteenth Century: Living the New Exodus in England and the Americas.* New York: St. Martin's Press, 1995.

Pratt, Mary Louise. *Apocalypse in the Andes: Contact Zones and the Struggle for Interpretive Power* Washington, DC: IDB Cultural Center, 1996.

Pratt, Mary Louise. *Imperial Eyes: Travel Writing and Transculturation.* New York: Routledge, [1992] 2008.

Pulis, John W. " 'In the beginning': A Chapter from the Living Testament of Rastafari." In Social Life of Scriptures: Cross-cultural Perspectives on Biblicism, edited by James Bielo, 30–43. New Brunswick, NJ: Rutgers University Press, 2009.

Raitt, Jill, Bernard McGinn, and John Meyendorff, eds. *Christian Spirituality: High Middle Ages and Reformation.* World Spirituality: An Encyclopedia History of the Religious Quest 17. New York: Crossroad, 1987.

Rampersad, Arnold. *Art and Imagination of W.E.B. Dubois.* Cambridge: Harvard University Press, 1976.

Ramsay, James. "Examination of the Rev. Mr. Harris's Scriptural Researches on the Licitness of the Slave-trade." *Eighteenth Century Collections Online.* London: Printed by James Phillips, 1788.

Reid, Jennifer I. M., ed., *Religion and Global Culture: New Terrain in the Study of Religion and the Work of Charles H. Long.* Lanham MD: Lexington Books, 2003.

Rilke, Rainer Maria. "Solange du Selbstgeworfnes faengst." In *Uncollected Poems: Rainer Maria Rilke.* Edited and translated by Edward Snow, 138–9. New York: North Point Press; Farrar, Straus and Giroux, 1996.

Rodman, Rosamond C. " 'We are Anglicans, They are the Church of England': Uses of Scripture in the Anglican Crisis." In Bielo, *Social Life of Scriptures,* 100–113.

Rosaldo, Renato. "The Rhetoric of Control: Illongots Viewed as Natural Bandits and Wild Indians." *The Reversible World: Symbolic Inversion in Art and Society*, edited with an introduction by Barbara A. Babcock, 240–257. Ithaca: Cornell University Press, 1978.

Saha, Santosh V. and Thomas K. Carr, eds. *Religious Fundamentalism in Developing Countries*. Westport CT: Greenwood Press, 2001.

Samuels, Wilfred D. "Disguised Voice in The interesting Narrative of Olaudah Equiano, or Gustavus Vassa the African." *Black American Literature Forum* 19 (1985): 64–69.

Sandiford, Keith. *Measuring the Moment: Strategies of Protest in Eighteenth-Century Afro-English Writing*. Selinsgrove, PA: Susquehanna University Press, 1988.

Sawyer, John F. A. *Sacred Languages and Sacred Texts*. New York: Routledge, 1999.

Schama, Simon. *Rough Crossings: Britain, the Slaves, and the American Revolution*. New York: HarperCollins, 2006.

Schilling, Heinz. *Konfessionalisierung und Staatsinteressen: Internantionale Beziehungen, 1559–1660*. Paderborn: Schoeningh, 2007.

Schilling, Heinz. *Early Modern European Civilization and Its Political and Cultural Dynamism*. The Menaham Stern Jerusalem Lectures. Hanover, NH: University Press of New England, 2008.

Schwartz, Evan I. *Finding Oz: How L. Frank Baum Discovered the Great American Story*. Boston: Houghton Mifflin, 2009.

Scott, James C. *Domination and the Arts of Resistance: Hidden Transcripts*. New Haven: Yale University Press, 1990.

Sha, Richard C., ed. *Historicizing Romantic Sexuality*. http://www.rc.umd.edu/praxis/sexuality/oquinn/oquinn.html (accessed May 2, 2011).

Sharot, Stephen. *A Comparative Sociology of World Religions: Virtuosos, Priests, and Popular Religion*. New York: New York University Press, 2001.

Sidbury, James. *Becoming African in America: Race and Nation in the Early Black Atlantic*. New York: Oxford University Press, 2007.

Smith, Jonathan Z. *Drudgery Divine: On the Comparison of Early Christianities and the Religions of Late Antiquity*. *Jordan Lectures in Comparative Religion 14*. Chicago: University of Chicago Press, 1990.

Smith, Olivia. *The Politics of Language, 1791–1819*. Oxford: Clarendon Press, 1984.

Smith, Valerie. *Self-Discovery and Authority in Afro-American Literature*. Cambridge: Harvard University Press, 1987.

Snowden, Frank M. *Before Color Prejudice: the Ancient View*. Cambridge: Harvard University Press, 1983.

Sobel, Mechal. *Trabelin' On: The Slave Journey to an Afro-Baptist Faith*. Princeton, NJ: Princeton University Press, [1975]1988.

Sontag, Susan. "Aesthetics of Silence." In *A Susan Sontag Reader*, 181–204. New York: Farrar, Straus, Giroux, 1963 [1982].

Spence, Thomas, ed. *Pigs' Meat or Lessons for The Swinish Multitude*. London: T. Spence, 1795.

Stanton, Elizabeth Cady, Susan B. Anthony, and Matilds Joslyn Gage, eds. *History of Woman Suffrage. Volume 2*. Gutenberg Online. February 9, 2009.

Starr, G. A. *Defoe and Spiritual Autobiography*. Princeton: Princeton University Press, 1965.

Styers, Randall. *Making Magic: Religion, Magic, and Science in the Modern World*. New York: Oxford University Press, 2003.

Taussig, Michael. *Shamanism, Colonialism, and the Wild Man: A Study in Terror and Healing*. Chicago: University of Chicago Press, 1987.

Taussig, Michael. *The Nervous System*. New York: Routledge, 1992.

Taussig, Michael. *Mimesis; Mimesis and Alterity: A Particular History of the Senses*. New York: Routledge, 1993.

Terrill, Edward. *The Records of a Church of Christ in Bristol, 1640–1687*. Edited by Roger Hayden. 3rd ed. Bristol: Bristol Record Society, 1974.

The Oxford English Dictionary. Vol. XIX. 2nd ed. Oxford: Clarendon Press, 1989.

Thomas, Helen. *Romanticism and Slave Narratives: Transatlantic Testimonies. Cambridge Studies in Romanticism 38*. Cambridge: Cambridge University Press, 2000 [2001].

Thomas, Keith. *Religion and the Decline of Magic*. New York: Scribner, 1971.

Thomas, Paine. *Rights of Man: Being an Answer to Mr. Burke's Attack on the French Revolution*. London: J. S. Jordan, 1791.

Thornton, John K. *Africa and Africans in the Making of the Atlantic World, 1400–1800*. Cambridge: Cambridge University Press, 1996.

Viswanathan, Gauri. *Outside the Fold: Conversion, Modernity, and Belief*. Princeton: Princeton University Press, 1998.

Ware, Kallistos. "The Way of the Acestics: Negative or Affirmative?" In *Asceticism*, edited by Vincent L. Wimbush and Richard Valantasis, 3–15. New York: Oxford University Press, 1995.

Warner, W. Lloyd. *A Black Civilization: A Social Study of an Australian Tribe*. New York: Harper & Row, 1937 and 1965.

Warren, Robert Penn. "Pondy Woods." In *New and Selected Poems: 1923–1985*. 1st Random House ed., 319–321. New York: Random House, 1985.

Warren, Susan. "Between Slavery and Freedom: The Transgressive Self in Olaudah Equiano's Autobiography." *PMLA* 108.1 (January 1993): 94–105.

Washington, Joseph R. *Black Religion: the Negro and Christianity in the United States*. Boston: Beacon Press, 1964.

Wheeler, Roxann. "Domesticating Equiano's Interesting Narrative." *Eighteenth-Century Studies* 34, no. 4 (Summer 2001): 620–624.

Williams, Sherley Anne. *Dessa Rose*. New York: Harper Perennial, 1999 [1986].

Wimbush, Vincent L. "The Bible and African Americans: An Outline of an Interpretative History." In *Stony the Road We Trod: African American Biblical Interpretation*, edited by Cain H. Felder, 81–97. Minneapolis: Fortress, 1991.

Wimbush, Vincent L. "Ascetic Behavior and Color-ful Language: Stories About Ethiopian Moses." *Semeia* 58 (Fall 1992): 81–91.

Wimbush, Vincent L. "African American Traditions and the Bible." In *Oxford Companion to the Bible*, edited by Bruce M. Metzger and Michael D. Coogan, 12–15. New York: Oxford University Press, 1993.

Wimbush, Vincent L. "Reading Texts as Reading Ourselves: A Chapter in the History of African American Biblical Interpretation." In *Reading From This Place: Social Location and Biblical Interpretation*, edited by Fernando F. Segovia and Mary Ann Tolbert, 95–108. Philadelphia: Fortress Press, 1995a.

Wimbush, Vincent L. "The Bible in African American Culture." In *The Encyclopedia of African American Culture and History*, edited by Jack Salzman, David Lionel Smith, and Cornel West. Vol. 1, 315–316. New York: Macmillan Library Reference USA; Macmillan, 1995b.

Wimbush, Vincent L. "Interrupting the Spin: What Would Happen Were African Americans to Become the Starting Point for Biblical Studies." *Union Seminary Quarterly Review* 52, nos. 1–2 (1998): 61–76.

Wimbush, Vincent L. With the assistance of Rosamond C. Rodman, ed. *African Americans and the Bible: Sacred Texts and Social Textures*. New York: Continuum International, 2000, 2001.

Wimbush, Vincent L. "Introduction: Reading Darkness, Reading Scriptures." In *African Americans and the Bible: Sacred Texts and Social Textures*, edited by V. L. Wimbush, with the assistance of R. C. Rodman, 1–43. New York: Continuum International, 2000, 2001.

Wimbush, Vincent L. *The Bible and African Americans: A Brief History*. Facets. Minneapolis: Fortress, 2003.

Wimbush, Vincent L. "Signifying on Scriptures: An African Diaspora Proposal for Radical Readings." *In Feminist New Testament Studies: Global and Future Perspectives, edited by Kathleen O'Brien Wicker, Althea Spencer Miller, and Musa* W. Dube, 245–258. New York: Palgrave MacMillan, 2005.

Wimbush, Vincent L. "We Will Make Our Own Future Text: A Proposal for an Alternate Interpretive Orientation." In *True to our Native Land: African American New Testament Commentary*, edited by Brian Blount, et al., 43–53. Philadelphia: Fortress, 2007.

Wimbush, Vincent L. " 'Naturally Veiled and Half Articulate': Scriptures, Modernity, and the Formation of African America." In *Still at the Margins*, edited by R. S. Sugirtharajah, 56–68. Maryknoll, NY: Orbis Books, 2008a.

Wimbush, Vincent L. ed. *Theorizing Scriptures: New Critical Orientations to a Cultural Phenomenon*. Signifying (on) Scriptures. New Brunswick: Rutgers University Press, 2008b.

Wimbush, Vincent L. "Scriptures for Strangers: the Making of an Africanized Bible." In *Postcolonial Interventions: Essays in Honor of R. S. Sugirtharajah*, edited by Tat-siong Benny Liew, 162–177. Sheffield Phoenix Press, 2009.

Witherington, Ben. *Acts of the Apostles: A Socio-Rhetorical Commentary*. Grand Rapids, MI: W. B. Eerdmans Publishing Company, 1998.

Woodward, Helena. *African-British Writings in the Eighteenth Century: The Politics of Race and Reason*. Westport, CT: Greenwood Press, 1999.

Wyschogrod, Edith. "The Howl of Oedipus, the Cry of Heloise: From Asceticism to Postmodern Ethics." In *Asceticism*, edited by Vincent L. Wimbush and Richard Valantasis, 16–30. New York: Oxford University Press, 1995.

Zamir, Shamoon. *Dark Voices: W.E.B. Du Bois and American Thought, 1888–1903*. Chicago: University of Chicago Press, 1995.

Index

CPSIA information can be obtained at www.ICGtesting.com
Printed in the USA
BVOW04s1540280114

343105BV00003B/9/P

9 780199 344390